# The Price of Silence

# The Price of Silence

A Mom's Perspective on Mental Illness

## LIZA LONG

*Foreword by Harold S. Koplewicz, MD*

HUDSON
STREET
PRESS

HUDSON STREET PRESS
Published by the Penguin Group
Penguin Group (USA) LLC
375 Hudson Street
New York, New York 10014

USA | Canada | UK | Ireland | Australia | New Zealand | India | South Africa | China
penguin.com
A Penguin Random House Company

First published by Hudson Street Press, a member of Penguin Group (USA) LLC, 2014

REGISTERED TRADEMARK—MARCA REGISTRADA

HUDSON
STREET
PRESS

LIBRARY OF CONGRESS CATALOGING-IN-PUBLICATION DATA
Long, Liza.
    The price of silence : a mom's perspective on mental illness / Liza Long ; foreword by
Harold Koplewicz.
        pages cm
    Includes bibliographical references and index.
    ISBN 978-1-59463-257-0 (hardback)
    1. Children with mental disabilities—Psychology. 2. Violence in children. 3. Parents of
children with disabilities. I. Title.
    HV891.L5966 2014
    362.2083—dc23          2014009322

Printed in the United States of America
10  9  8  7  6  5  4  3  2  1

Set in Goudy Oldstyle Std
Designed by Eve L. Kirch

*For "Michael" and the one in five children who have mental illness*

# CONTENTS

# FOREWORD

I've admired Liza Long since she made the decision, at a very dark time for all of us, to speak up in a courageous and constructive way.

When Adam Lanza walked into Sandy Hook Elementary School and killed twenty children and six of their teachers, Liza felt anguish not only because so many were senselessly murdered, but because she identified with Nancy Lanza, Adam's mother and his first victim.

Liza identified with the story of a woman struggling to help a child with mental illness. She raised her voice in a blog post that would go viral called "I Am Adam Lanza's Mother."

In that blog post Liza shared her own experience of living with a child with mental illness—a son well loved and loving, too—who has a pattern of erupting in unpredictable bouts of violence. She'd been terrified by her son's threats of suicide, bruised by his rages, and chronically worried about the possibility that he might hurt someone else. They'd been through a range of diagnoses, from ADHD to oppositional defiant disorder to intermittent explosive disorder. She'd been as private as she could about her struggles to get care for him, to protect them both from the shame and stigma that attaches to mental illness. Like so many parents of children with psychiatric illness, she didn't want him to be marginalized, and she didn't want to admit how bad things really were.

"Like many parents, I have tried for years to 'manage' my son's condition essentially on my own," she writes in this new book. "I've thought that I could wish him into wellness. I've even denied that he had problems. The emotional anguish of my blog post came out of that space, as a national tragedy sparked a private moment of raw honesty."

What Liza found out when her raw honesty went viral was how many, many other parents there are who are struggling and worrying as she had been, but also afraid to be public about their struggles and worries. With that post Liza took the brave step of becoming an advocate for better understanding, and better resources, for families struggling with mental illness.

This book is another step in that direction: to use her painful experiences as a catalyst for change by sharing the kinds of details that are so often kept private. And her son, too—a very bright young man who, of course, doesn't want to be a child with uncontrollable rages—has come to hope that telling his story will help lead to the kind of treatment that would liberate him from these harmful episodes.

I had the opportunity to meet Liza in Washington, D.C., at a congressional hearing on how we can improve mental health care, where I was struck by the power of her testimony. It's one thing for professionals like me to advocate greater understanding and acceptance of mental illness, as I've been doing for thirty years as a child and adolescent psychiatrist. But it's only with passionate and articulate parents speaking up about what they're going through, sharing real experiences, that we will truly break down the barriers to getting quality care for more kids.

Liza has come to see the world in terms of two groups—both of whom she addresses in this book, and both of which are terribly familiar to me.

The first is families, like hers, who have a child with a developmental disorder or mental illness, for whom the difficulty and complexity and anxiety of living with it and struggling to get care are now their "normal." I know many, many of these families, and I know the remarkable lengths they will go, at great personal cost, to help their kids.

The second are families who don't have that firsthand experience. While many are understanding and supportive, among their ranks are, unfortunately, too many others who make judgments about parents who do. It pains me every time I read accusations that parents are inventing or exaggerating their kids' problems, causing their kids' problem with bad parenting, gaming the system so their kids can get ahead. This is so far from the truth of the families I see, who are in true distress. This is why speaking up for kids with mental illness is so important.

Liza uses her own story as a lens through which to examine the system that families find themselves dependent on—from the schools to the juvenile justice system. And lest you think the latter is only relevant to families where parents don't care, or don't try, or kids who are "just plain bad kids," consider Liza's account of her eleven-year-old sobbing in her arms after being arrested for assaulting his father.

One of the things we are least willing to recognize is the number of children with untreated mental illness who end up in the juvenile justice system and later the penal system. Making it easier for them to get help when they are young is not only infinitely more humane, it saves squandered resources. How can it be that we as a society can't find the funds for young children to get effective behavioral treatment, for overwhelmed parents to get respite, for enough effective residential treatment facilities for children who are a danger to themselves or others, but we can spend over $200,000 a year to incarcerate them when they are teenagers or adults? The math doesn't add up.

Liza notes, for instance, a statistic from the Boise School District that should alert us to what's happening here. She noticed at a children's mental health subcommittee meeting that when the numbers of students who were diagnosed with ADHD, emotional or mood disorders, and autism spectrum disorders were broken down by age, the numbers dropped by more than half after children turned sixteen. That clearly wasn't because they were all getting miraculously cured. "Between age fifteen and sixteen, these children drop out of school and end up in jail," she writes. "That's why moms like Nancy Lanza end up homeschooling their children: it's just too hard to deal with the frequent calls, the bullying, the frustration of . . . public school."

Liza also writes compellingly about the varieties of stigma that keep mental illness underground, and parents locked in frustrating battles, not the least of which is what she calls "toxic perfectionism," the fervent need to feel that our families are perfect. She says this defined her behavior for over a decade as she was a stay-at-home mom of four children. But divorce, debilitating problems with Michael, and the frustration of being unable to create a "perfect" childhood for any of her kids made her finally speak out.

And when she did go public, she was widely attacked for doing so, especially by other mothers. As she says in the book, "Why is a mother who speaks out about her child with mental illness any different from a mother who speaks out about her child with cancer? Should we not celebrate recoveries and mourn losses for children with mental illness in the same way that we do for children affected with physical disease?"

I applaud Liza's efforts in this book to help other families navigate the institutions and systems that parents depend on for care for their kids. She's been through a lot, and talked to other parents who have been through a lot, and there is a good deal of collective wisdom—not to mention honesty—here. But above all I appreciate Liza's willingness to put herself on the line to fight stigma. As she puts it: "There are effective interventions and treatments. Before you can find a treatment, you have to be able to talk about the problem."

—HAROLD S. KOPLEWICZ, MD
President and Founder
Child Mind Institute

# INTRODUCTION

You probably don't know me. But chances are good you've read something I wrote. On December 14, 2012, two days after my thirteen-year-old son—let's call him Michael—was placed in an acute care mental hospital, twenty-year-old Adam Lanza shot his mother, then went to Sandy Hook Elementary School and killed twenty first graders, six educators, and himself. My second thought on hearing that horrible news was probably similar to most people's first thought. I wanted to rush to my children's elementary school, to hold my second-grade daughter and fourth-grade son in my arms.

But my first thought was something else. My first thought was, "What if that's my son someday?" That night, I sat down and wrote my truth. I admitted my feelings of pain and fear and helplessness about my son's condition and my inability to help him. I wrote about the years of missed diagnoses, ineffective medications, and costly therapies. I expressed my fear at my son's unpredictable and sometimes violent rages. I shared the pain of watching my son handcuffed, in the back of a police car. Then I posted the essay, entitled "Thinking the Unthinkable," to my formerly anonymous mommy blog, *The Anarchist Soccer Mom*.

Here is some of what I wrote:

This problem is too big for me to handle on my own. Sometimes there are no good options. So you just pray for grace and trust that in hindsight, it will all make sense.

I am sharing this story because I am Adam Lanza's mother. I am Dylan Klebold's and Eric Harris's mother. I am James Holmes's mother. I am Jared Loughner's mother. I am Seung-Hui Cho's mother. And these boys—and their mothers—need help. In the wake of another horrific national tragedy, it's easy to talk about guns. But it's time to talk about mental illness.

I sent my anonymous cry for help screaming into the Internet abyss. To my surprise, I heard an echo. After I posted the anonymous essay to my Facebook page and encouraged my friends to share it, they did, and so did their friends, in record numbers. The next day, my good friend Nathaniel Hoffman, editor of Boise State University's online journal the *Blue Review* and one of the few people who knew about my blog, called me and said, "I want this piece. It's important." I readily agreed. "And I want you to put your name on it," he added. "Until people start putting their names on these stories, they aren't real."

Nate's request made me pause. I was afraid—not of what the world would think—but of what my friends, my coworkers, my community would think. Nate was one of just a handful of people who knew about my ongoing struggles with my son's mental illness, who knew why I had to miss work so often or why I sometimes cried in my cubicle or cringed when my cell phone rang.

But in the end, I agreed to publish the essay with Nate's suggested (and better) new title, "I Am Adam Lanza's Mother." I discovered that words have power. These were my words, and this is my story.

The Internet response to my cry for help was overwhelming. Before December 14, 2012, my formerly anonymous blog had about 4,000 hits total. Now *The Anarchist Soccer Mom* has had more than 3 million views and nearly 4,000 comments. The reprint on the *Huffington Post* (which picked the story up from the *Blue Review* and the *Seattle Stranger*) was one of the most popular articles for days. It received 1.2 million likes on Facebook (and 323,000 shares), more than 15,000 comments, 16,800 tweets, and 29,800 e-mails.

People are still talking about it. I clearly touched a nerve in sharing my family's painful experiences with mental illness. Journalists from Anderson Cooper to Miles O'Brien to Diane Sawyer have asked me to tell our truth. But not everybody gets it. I have learned through this experience that stigma, for children and for families who struggle with mental illness and mental disorders, is still very real.

I'm writing this book for two very different audiences. The first audience knows mental illness and lives with it every day. For this audience—the audience I know best—mental illness is a blond boy with a butterfly, a parent putting a meal on the table after a long day at the office, a patient expressing frustration over a new medication's unpleasant side effects. This first audience experiences life with mental illness as "normal." And its members—mothers, fathers, children—cried out in solidarity with me: "You shared my story! Thank you for putting into words something I did not dare to say."

But I am also writing for a second audience, an audience that is surprised to learn that one in five children in the United States will suffer from a serious and debilitating mental disorder, an audience that believes mental illness is something we still shouldn't talk about except behind closed doors in private rooms, an audience that is convinced that the sometimes maladaptive behaviors of mental illness are a "choice." The second audience knows mental illness as a series of hollow-eyed young men flashed on screens above shocking and horrific statistics, body counts in a war with no named enemy except the enemy within. This audience's primary understanding of mental illness comes from distorted and exaggerated media portrayals rather than from everyday encounters. This audience is afraid.

Make no mistake: I believe based on my own very real and often frightening experiences that people with mental illness, when not properly treated, can be dangerous to themselves and others, with potentially horrific consequences for themselves, their families, and society. When we talk about mental illness, we must also talk about violence, no matter how uncomfortable that conversation is. I shared my own story of frustration and pain in response to a horrific act of brutality that took the lives of innocent children and teachers. While it's true that people who have mental illness are more likely to suffer violence than perpetrate it, the never-ending threat of unpredictable, senseless brutal acts is what makes the stress of day-to-day life with a child who has mental illness similar to what soldiers in combat experience.

But I also love my son. And I believe that effective treatments exist, and that even more effective treatments are moving from the margins to the mainstream every day. As Michael commented after reading a 2013 article in *Smithsonian* magazine about the promise of 3-D printing, "Maybe I'll invent a teleporter that does more than just transport people to where they want to go—it also reads their DNA for mistakes, then fixes those mistakes and prints out a new, perfect copy of the person."

Maybe. Or maybe we'll find gene therapies, or medications that actually work, or new modes of therapeutic treatment. Maybe we will take the burden of care for mental illness off the already heavily laden backs of law enforcement and the criminal justice system. Maybe we'll learn how to provide appropriate educations for children with mental disorders. Maybe we'll provide meaningful support to families.

I'm writing this book to give a voice to parents of children with mental illness. But I am also writing because I believe that those of us in the first audience have an obligation to share our experiences with the second audience. We have to say, "I have mental illness. My child has mental illness. The woman who cuts my hair or researches my stock-market portfolio, the man who bags my groceries, or teaches my children, has mental illness. And all of us want what any person would want: to live healthy, happy, productive lives." By sharing our stories, by putting familiar faces to a frightening, misunderstood, complicated disease (or rather, a group of diseases, a cluster of developmental disorders), we can begin to chisel real change from the massive edifice of stigma that has stood too long in the way of effective treatments.

Every minority group in history has had to fight for rights, for recognition, for respect. Less than one hundred years ago, women could not vote. Even twenty years ago, gays were viewed with hostility and suspicion, AIDS as a "homosexual disease." And yet today, a majority of Americans support gay marriage, and just four years after Proposition 8 promulgated hate in California, the Supreme Court overturned the Defense of Marriage Act and restored equality to a class of citizens that had been denied majority rights.

But in our country, people who have mental illness are still treated like second-class citizens. We treat illness above the neck differently than from the neck down. Certainly no one advocates a return to the days of institutionalization. But when the institutions closed, where did people with mental illness go? The promise of community-based resources to provide much-needed care proved illusory. Instead, today we "treat" those with mental illness or mental disorders, including our children, in prison. And in many underprivileged areas, where the stress of poverty is a pervasive and persistent trigger for mental illness, a "school-to-prison" pipeline has denied millions of children a meaningful future. The bad institutions closed and were replaced by something much, much worse, as mental health advocate and author Pete Earley details so vividly in *Crazy: A Father's Search through America's Mental Health Madness*, which uses his son's experience with the law to examine how people with mental illness are mistreated by the criminal justice system.

Then when a tragedy like Newtown happens, former National Rifle Association president Sandy Froman (and a host of others) can say things like, "We have to keep guns out of the hands of these insane people."

Aside: This is not a book about gun rights. I live in Idaho, and we like to hunt here. But as the parent of a child with mental illness, I would never own firearms, let alone keep them in my home. In this one respect, I cannot understand Nancy Lanza, though in other ways, her experiences with her son Adam are hauntingly familiar to me.

This book is not about keeping guns out of the hands of dangerous people, though certainly that question deserves exploration. It's about making children—and people—less dangerous.

The second audience refused to believe what I wrote about my son when I put my story into the ruthless stockade of public opinion. "You're telling me that your only option for your son is jail?" one incredulous reporter asked me after my blog post went viral. "There's no way that can be true." It was, and it still is in Idaho and in other states. In fact, a 2013 study conducted by the George Washington University Center for Health and Health Care in Schools concluded, "From significant disconnects among the multiple institutions that serve children and their families to chronic financial instability, the children's mental health system is fragile and at-risk." In this book, I'll introduce psychiatrists, lawyers, law enforcement officers, educators, and disability rights advocates who can all witness to the fragility of our current patchwork and costly systems.

I'll also share stories from other parents who have endured the same societal blame and stigma for their children's behavior that I have personally experienced with my own son. When I wrote about my experiences with my child in my blog, the second audience blamed me, just as psychiatrists blamed so-called Refrigerator Mothers in the 1950s when children presented with the baffling (then and now) symptoms of autism. As a mother of four who has seen the Mommy Wars from both fronts—I was a stay-at-home mother for thirteen years and have subsequently embraced the world of work with perhaps too much enthusiasm—I actually understand this criticism well. What loving mother would not examine her own parenting, from her history of depression to her failed marriage to her decision to reenter the workforce, and not find herself somehow wanting? When our children suffer—whether it's mental illness or cancer or allergies—we want to know why, and we naturally start with ourselves as the root cause.

When my painful story went public, I thought that I was the only mother in America who felt the way I did. But I quickly realized that I was far from alone in my struggles to find care, support, and understanding for my son and for myself. This book follows my own journey through the labyrinth of impassive institutions and jargon-ridden systems that parents of children with mental illness and mental disorders must navigate, chasing false promises of hope (this elimination diet, that antipsychotic drug, another behavioral intervention) and finding real promises of treatment and quality of life.

I have divided the journey into stages, using the loosely chronological arc of my son's life to expose the endemic problems with patchwork systems that form the current pathetic state of children's mental health services. These systems include hospitals, schools, courts, and detention centers. Each institution requires parents to become versed in an alphabet soup of acronyms: in education—IEP, 504, ADA, IDEA, BIP, AT, CD, DOC, ED, FERPA, FAPE, BA, LRE, OHI, OSEP, OT, PT, SBS; in health care—SMI, ACA, PRN, HIPAA, EMR, NIMH, DD, DSM-5, EBM, EOB. That's just for starters.

I have mentioned only in passing things that did not directly affect my own family and which have been eloquently covered elsewhere— addiction and substance abuse, for example, which David Sheff writes about in his heart-rending book *Beautiful Boy*, or depression, for which I could refer the reader to a host of books, though perhaps my personal favorite is Andrew Solomon's *The Noonday Demon*.

But the journey starts with me. I did not realize it at the time, but my academic training in Classics (a little Latin, more Greek, and everything and everyone those two languages and cultures touched through the history of Western civilization) prepared me well to be the mother of a son who has both developmental disabilities and a serious mental illness. As a lifelong student of the humanities, I fear that our increasing reliance on science for answers about the brain will cause us to lose our appreciation for the soul. Indeed, the soul's condition is the traditional purview of the psychiatrist, who by definition is not a mind healer but a "soul healer."

Our apprehension of mental illness began within the context of stigma; history and religion continue to shape our understanding of mental illness and mental disorders, but they also contribute to the "otherness" of those who have mental illness, perhaps because we are afraid to look in the mirrors they carry and see ourselves. Freudian analysis, though now widely discredited, finds its roots in ancient Greek mythology, in tales of horror that rival our modern media bloodbaths. Consider Oedipus, for example, or Thyestes, who eats his own children, or Medea, the spurned consort who murders her sons when Jason leaves her for another woman.

As a mother who has faced the stigma of mental illness head-on, I believe that we have not quite left the cultural underpinnings that ascribe mental illness to "evil spirits" or witchcraft. Yet in our society's worthy quest to understand and heal the brain, it is important that we don't forget the soul—what makes each of us and our experiences unique—or relegate it to a lesser state, viewing the brain as merely another physical organ, to be treated like the liver, the pancreas, the heart.

I spend perhaps more time than the average person thinking about theodicy, the problem of evil in the world. This problem is one that religion seeks to reconcile: if God is good, and if his creations are good, then where does evil come from? Many modern-minded people face the problem of evil and decide to abandon theology altogether. But I have taken Søren Kierkegaard as my model—I have tried to make the leap of faith that Abraham made when he agreed to sacrifice his only son, the miracle child God gave him in his old age. I conceive of mental illness as an explanation for some of the evil in the world, an explanation, but not an excuse. Adam Lanza, James Holmes, Jared Loughner, Dylan Klebold, Aaron Alexis all had explanations for what they did. But explanations are not excuses.

When I poured out my fears about my own son's mental illness to the world, I wrote, "I am Adam Lanza's mother," comparing myself to a mother who knew her son was in trouble but who was unable to get him the help they both desperately needed, with devastating consequences. I wrote this book because I don't want to be Adam Lanza's mother—dead. And I don't want to be Columbine murderer Dylan Klebold's mother, alive, but haunted by a search for answers to impossible questions.

Increasingly, local governments are holding parents accountable for their children's moral behavior. But how much control do parents really have? I keep a copy of the second-century-CE Roman emperor Marcus Aurelius's *Meditations* on my nightstand. Aurelius, often called "the last good emperor," was a Stoic, always striving to be in harmony with nature.

"Accept the things to which fate binds you, and love the people with whom fate brings you together, but do so with all your heart," he wrote, words that have given me strength through my most challenging experiences with my son.

Marcus Aurelius's only surviving son, Commodus, who succeeded him as emperor, was a monster.

I don't want to wait for Rome to burn, or for another elementary school or theater or political gathering or community college to get shot up, to ask, "Why did this happen?" These horrific acts are the price of silence, the outward manifestation of inward suffering on an epic scale.

I want to ask instead, "How can we help children and families and communities to become less dangerous right now, today?" By asking those kinds of questions before another tragedy occurs, we can improve quality of life. We can decrease dependence on state and federal aid. We can provide new outlets for creativity and productivity of minds that work differently from our own and provide much-needed community support to children and families. Maybe we can even write a happy ending to the mental health crisis in America.

But first, we have to tell our stories. This is mine.

# The Price of Silence

# ONE

# A Day in My Life

The cradle rocks above an abyss.
—Vladimir Nabokov, *Speak, Memory*

I f your child does not have a mental illness or mental disorder, then my normal is not your normal. On the surface, my life may look like yours, but for the one in five American children who will experience a serious and debilitating mental disorder at some point in their lives and for their families, a "normal" day may include a three-hour tantrum, a frightening manic cleaning episode, bullying (both giving and receiving), refusal to wear any clothes with tags or eat any food that is not white (or red, or brown, depending on the child), threats of harm to self and others, visits from law enforcement, and even a trip to the hospital or juvenile detention center.

I'm a single mother with four children and a career in student services at a health sciences two-year college. A typical weekday in my house starts early: I wake Michael up at 6:00 a.m. so he can catch a bus at 6:15 to a special alternative school for children with behavioral and emotional problems—our school district has decided that these children cannot attend mainstream classrooms. The school is on the other side of the valley from my modest town home in the hundred-year-old Collister neighborhood of Boise, an area where roosters still crow and horses are pastured just minutes from State Street, one of the busiest thoroughfares in the area.

If Michael misses his bus, my entire day cascades into chaos. Michael cannot wake himself up—though he almost never loses a game of chess and he studied algebra as a sixth grader, he struggles with day-to-day activities that most of us take for granted, like waking himself up to an alarm, brushing his teeth, or even tying his shoes. Like many teens, he's not a morning person, and the early hour is difficult for him. Unlike most teens, he can become unpredictably violent at even the most mundane request, as he did one morning when I told him he was wearing the wrong color pants. That morning, he ended up at Intermountain Hospital, the only inpatient acute care mental health facility (other than the Ada County Jail) in my community. That was not a good day.

Michael's school has a strict dress code: black or khaki pants and a plain dark green, blue, or black shirt. On a good day, he dresses appropriately and takes his medications without argument (he's currently on four different ones—Trileptal and lithium at night, bupropion and Intuniv in the morning). On a good day, he eats a key lime–flavored yogurt for breakfast or grabs a bagel on the way out the door. He is not allowed to bring books or a backpack in or out of school. Every day starts and ends with a wanding to detect any weapons he might have stashed in his pockets. Because Michael so often finishes his work early, we got special permission for him to bring in outside books to read (usually Harry Potter or Percy Jackson), but that concession quickly became a point of contention with staff when he would retreat into his books rather than do his classroom work, so he lost the privilege.

On a good day, Michael leaves the house at 6:15 for the bus stop, dressed and fed and medicated. On a good day, he participates in his classes and returns home to his day care provider at 2:45. On a good day, I enjoy a pleasant and productive workday free from calls from the school or, worse, the police.

Not every day is a good day.

After Michael catches his bus, I have a few minutes to catch my breath while his older brother showers and gets ready for school. We have to leave the house to take James to his bus no later than 6:55 a.m. James attends an out-of-district charter school that focuses on the medical arts, but he can catch a public school bus just a few miles from our house. I wake up seven-year-old Anna and nine-year-old Jonathan and bundle them into the car, Anna clutching "Blue," the light blue minky blankie, trimmed in white satin, that my mother made for her when, despite three gender-revealing ultrasounds, I was convinced that I would give birth to a fourth son.

James and I listen to NPR and discuss the news as Anna and Jonathan sleep in the backseat. I drop James off at his bus stop. On a good day, Anna, Jonathan, and I stop at River City, the local café, for a much-needed cup of coffee for Mom and day-old fifty-cent baked treats for the kids. We return home to dress for school and work; when the weather is good and when I can go into work a few minutes late, we walk to school, the oldest school in Boise, a classical studies magnet program where my kids are learning to insult each other in Latin.

I miss those good days. I haven't been able to walk Anna and Jonathan to school since my blog went viral and a judge determined that their brother was a threat to their safety. On many days since that day, I have wished that I had never shared my "normal" with the world: the consequences of telling my truth were exceptionally painful for my family. In fact, I often tell Michael that I wish he would invent the time machine he is always talking about, so that I could go back in time and change my decision to attach my name to my truth. I am truly an accidental advocate.

On a good day, after I drop Anna and Jonathan off at school, I drive or bike to work, where I spend my day solving other people's problems, trying to forget that I cannot solve my own. After school, Michael heads to his day care provider, or sometimes I pick him up from school for occupational therapy or therapist or psychiatrist appointments. Anna and Jonathan walk home with their day care provider's children, who attend the same school. James walks or bikes the two miles home from his bus stop and starts the five to six hours of daily homework his accelerated, college-credit high school program requires.

I pick the children up at 5:30 p.m. Dinner is simmering in the slow cooker or waiting in the freezer for the microwave. We eat together at a crowded table in our small kitchen. Then we work on homework, play video games, practice the piano or violin, and read for a half hour before bed. After the children are down, I usually put in a few more hours of work, writing for local publications to supplement my income, since Michael's medical care eats up one-fourth to one-third of my take-home pay each month, even with good health insurance.

As I said, on good days, in many respects, my life probably looks quite a bit like yours as I juggle the demands and joys of children and work.

But not every day is a good day.

I cannot predict when a day will not be good. I cannot predict what will trigger a violent outburst.

For bad days, we have a safety plan. Families of children with mental illness know what a safety plan is. It's a written document, sometimes developed with a physician, a therapist, or their state's Department of Health and Human Services, that describes what you will do when you're not having a good day.

Every family who has a child with mental illness must have a safety plan. On my refrigerator, along with a picture of us on the logjam ride at Knott's Berry Farm from a few spring breaks ago, and the requisite crayon drawings from my daughter, we have a picture of Glassman, a cartoon figure drawn by Michael's occupational therapist. Glassman is Michael's alter ego, the Mr. Hyde to his Dr. Jekyll. We also have a list of triggers— Jonathan's teasing, James's condescension, Anna's crying—that can sometimes set Glassman off.

This is what a bad day looks like at my house: rage, police, ambulance. Threats, fear, pain. Promises of revenge. Tears. Hopelessness.

Here's what I've learned from Glassman: I've learned to patch holes in walls. I've learned to keep my knives and scissors and other sharp tools in a Tupperware container that travels with me in my car, meaning these implements are under my direct supervision at all times. I've learned not to take things personally. I've learned to maintain a serene, detached calm, though I sometimes wonder if people know just how hard it is to stay calm when your son is threatening to kill himself and you and punching holes in walls and knocking books off shelves. This is why I would never own firearms, not for any reason.

Once a month we check in with a psychiatrist, who manages and tweaks Michael's complicated cocktail of medications to reflect the diagnosis du jour. Every week, we attend either occupational therapy or therapist appointments to help Michael navigate his world, which I have come to understand is different from mine. I wish I could afford weekly occupational therapy (OT). My insurance company authorizes only twenty OT visits per year and wants Michael to be cured within two months. Unfortunately, this experience is not uncommon for parents of children with mental illness: one insurance company refused to pay for hospitalization of a fourteen-year-old with bipolar disorder, arguing that since she was not likely to get better, the treatment should not be covered.

Because Michael has been hospitalized twice this year alone, my health insurance company has assigned me to a health management and information company, to make sure I'm making "educated choices" about my child's health care. I have sent them the most current research on juvenile bipolar disorder. I know about my son's illness. I have to know. Managing his care is a full-time job, on top of my full-time job. And too often, there is no one to help. There are no good options.

## Where Can I Go for Help?

On December 12, 2012, I was filling out paperwork again. It's always the same repetitive, time-consuming, simultaneously mind numbing and guilt-ridden exercise: "When did you first observe . . . At what age did your child . . ." My vision blurred—I was probably crying. I tried not to think about it as the other people in the waiting room tried not to stare. The hospital waiting room was a soothing, neutral tan—carpet, tile, wall paint, upholstery, even the abstract paintings on the walls, as if tan is the signature color of mental health, just the way pink belongs to breast cancer.

The room was calm now that my thirteen-year-old son's rage was contained beyond the locked, soundproofed doors, where he was carried by three police officers as he kicked and screamed curses, threats, promises of revenge.

One of them, to a police officer: "I wish I had a knife so I could run at you and you'd shoot me dead."

Another one, to me: "You never loved me. If you put me in the mental hospital, you will take home a corpse in a body bag."

Every time he says words like these, I know he doesn't mean any of it. These are almost like lines in a script that we've enacted and reenacted over the past few years. But I'd be lying if I said they didn't hurt. Any parent who has a child like Michael learns early not to take these words personally, though. That day, I hurt physically, too—my body ached from the restraint I'd used to keep him from bolting into oncoming traffic, and there were fresh, purple bite marks on my arm.

"Can I see him?" I asked as I turned in my clipboard with my inadequate answers to baffling questions and, of course, my health insurance card, our ticket to services my son needs.

"Let me check," the receptionist said. She picked up the phone, pursed her lips, looked at me.

"Probably not a good idea," she said, hanging up. "He has calmed down some, but he's still blaming you. He's not really in a good space. Let's give him some time. I'll have the doctor call you later."

She went over the paperwork—patient codes, parent expectations, visiting hours on Thursdays, Saturdays, and Sundays, phone calls between 6:00 and 8:00 p.m.

I blotted my tears with a tissue, tried to clean up the mascara streaks, tugged my lanyard and badge over my head, and went to work.

I am lucky. Work is a refuge for me. My children sometimes complain I work too much, and perhaps they are right. When I'm at work, I feel like I have some measure of control. I feel safe. The only time I ever feel entirely safe at home is when my son Michael is in the hospital. Many parents of mentally ill children never get any downtime. The exhaustion level alone is something only full-time caregivers can truly understand—every day is a handcart trek across gray treeless plains with no water or shade in sight.

When I called Michael the next day, he was still in denial and threatening revenge. "I know you put me in here because you don't love me," he yelled. "You lied to them because you don't want me anymore."

His social worker called a few hours later, after interviewing Michael about the incident. "You need to call the police and press charges for battery," he said, telling me something I'd heard too many times before. "If you don't get him back in the criminal justice system, we can't do a whole lot for him once he gets out of the hospital."

That's the way Idaho and many other states have chosen to care for children who have mental illness. When your child is in juvenile detention, he or she will be screened for mental illness and disorders. The juvenile magistrate will order a slew of social services under the rubric of Idaho Code, Section 20-511A, with a diversion team to develop a comprehensive treatment plan and coordinate services and care for your child. As long as your child is on probation, you can access these services for minimal or no cost. Michael and I have already been down this road. It's a shame that the real cost of obtaining mental health care is the devastating gut check of watching a uniformed officer handcuff your child and transport him to juvenile detention facilities in the back of a police car.

Two days later, December 14, 2012, it was a lazy Friday. I got to work ready to tackle a few projects, when my phone buzzed. I smiled to see the picture of my partner, Ed Pack, a kind, bright, always-laughing man who has bravely traded a quiet life with two cats for the barely controlled chaos of four children and their perpetually triple-booked mother.

"Hey, babe," he said, his voice lacking its usual lilt. "Have you heard the news?"

I opened my Facebook page and saw nothing but sadness streaming from my East Coast friends' feeds. Twenty children dead. No one knew why. The shooter: a young man named Adam Lanza.

I knew why.

Boise is nestled in foothills that glow golden in the morning sunlight. Every Sunday afternoon, when my kids are in Mormon day care (I am raising them LDS—in the Church of Jesus Christ of Latter-day Saints—as

I was raised), I've made my own new religious practice of running in those foothills, beneath a sky as blue as true love, through sagebrush- and wildflower-dotted landscape. And every weekday morning, as I drop my kids off at their various bus stops and schools, I look to those hills and recite a psalm to myself: "I will lift up mine eyes unto the hills, from whence cometh my help." Ancient words, from an ancient prophet whose own son probably had mental illness: "Absalom, O Absalom!" How many parents, through how many thousands of years, have uttered similar cries of anguish for their own children? How many mothers since Eve have buried sons because of violence?

## What It Feels Like to Send Your Child to Jail

Two years earlier, on October 6, 2010, my then-eleven-year-old son Michael was arrested and sent to juvenile detention when his father charged him with battery during one of Michael's terrifying rages. The Department of Corrections staff let me visit my son a few hours after he was processed. My little boy was waiting in a small bare-walled room lit with harsh fluorescent light. We sat on cracked plastic chairs and looked at each other. Michael was pale and scared and looked much younger than his age, drowning in a green T-shirt and baggy pants designed to fit a much larger youth. His lower lip trembled. "Mommy," he cried, crushing his head against my chest and beginning to sob. I cried, too, silently.

This was not the first time the police had been called on my son. I was the first parent to call the police, when Michael was nine years old and pulled a knife out one summer day, threatening to stab himself in the heart after I asked him to clean his room. We were already trying to manage Michael's still unknown condition with medication. After talking with the officers, I decided not to have them file formal charges, hoping that we could explore better solutions with his therapist and psychiatrist.

I did not want to admit that my son had a mental illness. His father and schoolteachers were convinced Michael was on the autism spectrum, but I didn't want to believe it. I wanted to wish him well, to rely on my own magical thinking to "cure" my child. Though I had never heard of "it's all in your head" psychiatrist Thomas Szasz at that point, if I had read his book, I would have agreed: there's no such thing as mental illness. Everything was situational. Michael was normal; he would simply grow out of these two- to three-hour whirlwinds that terrified me and my other children.

In October 2010, staring at my son in the juvenile detention holding cell, I had to concede defeat. This was not normal.

I wiped the tears away and went back to work.

As I mentioned, work has become a source of strength, a safe space where I feel successful and in control, in ways that I can never feel at home with my son. But like many parents whose children struggle with mental illness, I have lived in fear of losing a job (and benefits) because of my child's extra needs. Every time I see the school on my phone, my heart races. And sometimes my phone blows up with Ada County numbers—police, social workers, juvenile detention.

In 2010, when Michael's always-present behavioral challenges began to escalate dramatically, I was the department chair of general education at a small private career college in Boise, Idaho. In many ways, it was my dream job—intellectually stimulating and challenging, with a flexible but demanding schedule. The for-profit college sector gave me the opportunity to enter the workforce after thirteen years as a stay-at-home mother at a level that recognized my intellectual and academic achievements in my twenties without punishing me for my decision to take ten years off and raise four children. Traditional academia, especially in my field, Classics, would have turned up its collective nose at me, but my school was happy to use my natural talents for leadership and organization, as well as my ability to teach a wide range of classes, from English literature to art history.

The week that Michael went to juvenile detention for the first time, I became obsessed with Afghanistan, with the empty niches carved into worn sandstone where the Bamiyan Buddhas once stood to welcome travelers along the ancient Silk Road. I was teaching art history that month and preparing for my first doctoral program residency in Dallas, Texas, that weekend. I called my adviser to cancel my trip, my voice strangely calm as I explained what had happened.

"Are you okay?" he asked. "Are you sure you're okay?"

Silly question.

The Bamiyan Buddhas and Bruegel's *Fall of Icarus*—that's what I most remember from the day my eleven-year-old son went to jail. I stared at this picture on my art history slide show for several minutes, thinking about children, choices, and things beyond our control. Auden was right when he wrote about that painting: "About suffering they were never wrong; / The Old Masters." A lush landscape, a farmer hard at work plowing his sun-dappled field. A ship, sails furled in the wind. And in the distance, a speck of a boy falls from the sky, wings melting, with no one to save him, an unimportant failure. In fact, it's almost funny in a dark, twisted way that if you google this image, it's likely that in the version you find, Icarus has been cropped from the painting. We do not see his suffering, or his father's.

That's what it feels like when your child is sent to jail a few weeks after his eleventh birthday. That's what it feels like when you stand in a courtroom, seeing your small boy hunched in a chair, in bright green sweats that engulf his skinny limbs, his hands in cold metal cuffs.

All around you, people are going about their lives as usual. They are shopping at supermarkets, talking on cell phones, ordering venti caramel machiattos at Starbucks. And everything in your world is falling to pieces. I'm reminded of Michel Foucault's observation in *Madness and Civilization* that madmen replaced lepers during the Middle Ages. We still prefer to keep our madmen like lepers, out of sight and out of mind. Or worse, we scapegoat them.

Even though they have special protections under federal law, children with learning disabilities and mental illness are far more likely to be pushed out of mainstream schools and into the criminal justice system than their peers: a 2001 survey found that incarcerated children were four times more likely than the general population to have a disability that affected learning. My son was one of those children, charged with a status offense: juvenile beyond control. It's an ineffective and inefficient way to address mental illness in children: for example, the cost of providing care for one minor in juvenile detention in California in 2011–12 was a staggering $179,400 per year. That number is per child, not a total. And it actually represents a significant savings when compared to 2008–09 figures: that year, the cost per minor in the Division of Juvenile Justice was $245,000, according to a state government budget analysis. By comparison, California public schools spent just over $9,000 per pupil in 2011.

The problem is huge, and children are being sent to prison at younger and younger ages. In 1996, Illinois became the first state in the nation to pass a law allowing incarceration for children as young as ten, after a horrific case where two children, age ten and eleven, dropped a five-year-old boy from a fourteenth-floor window to his death because the younger child refused to steal candy for them. Some states, including Pennsylvania, have no minimum age limit for when children can be tried as adults, which Elizabeth Scott and Laurence Steinberg argued against in their 2009 book, *Rethinking Juvenile Justice*, noting that children and young teens simply do not have adult brains and cannot be expected to comprehend the magnitude of choices like these.

That weekend, I went to the detention center during visiting hours, fidgeting in the waiting area with all the other parents. Usually I'm pretty gregarious and can make friends with any group of strangers. But no one felt like talking. None of us could even look at each other. The vestibule of the juvenile detention center was a far cry from an honors award ceremony I'd attended with my oldest son earlier that week, that's for sure.

We marched back to the gym, single file, avoiding each other's eyes. One of the guards, a pleasant-looking dark-haired woman, pulled me aside. "Your son is a really sweet kid," she told me. "I just want you to know we are all looking out for him. I'm a mom, too."

I sat at a cafeteria-style lunch table, waiting. He shuffled in, head down, those baggy pants secured around his waist with a piece of rope. We played chess for an hour. Michael beat me over and over again, his eyes sparkling when he captured a pawn en passant or castled his king. I'm an adequate chess player, but I've only stalemated Michael twice in all our games, and that was only because he wasn't paying attention.

A few days later, at his detention review hearing, the juvenile judge released Michael to my custody pending his trial. And suddenly, just like that, I was a full-time single mother of a child with mental illness. Until that day, I had shared half-time custody of Michael and his three siblings with their father. On my weeks off, I had a chance to rest, to catch up on missed work, to even enjoy life. I spent my weekends off in San Francisco or Salt Lake City or Las Vegas visiting friends, or backpacking in Idaho's wilderness. I would not enjoy that kind of rest again for quite a while.

I wasn't ready to admit the enormity of the challenge I was facing to myself, or to anyone. Not even my closest friends knew the struggles I lived with daily. There's a reason for that: being a single mother with a child who has mental illness is the hardest thing I've ever done, and I've never set the bar low. In one 2004 study, more than half of mothers of children with autism reported significant psychological stress, with single parenting and being the parent of a son marked as significant risk factors. In fact, as I mentioned earlier, the stress of parenting a child with autism has been compared to the stress that soldiers experience under fire.

## COURT-ORDERED THERAPIES

At first Michael and I went through a honeymoon period as we awaited his trial. He was arrested in October—the trial was scheduled for June, a seemingly interminable distance from crisp autumn leaves and harvest festivities. In the interim, the court ordered a 20-511A team to develop a plan for my son, with representatives from the Department of Health and Welfare and the Boise School District assembled monthly to discuss treatment options and chart his progress. We obtained diagnostic services through Children's Mental Health, something we'd previously had to pay for out of pocket. Weekly psychosocial rehabilitation (PSR) from a local service provider was also provided free of charge. On the negative side, my calendar was soon full of meetings and appointments. I had to attend them all or face the possibility of contempt of court charges.

As this book will explain in subsequent chapters, public schools and juvenile justice programs are the two main ways most parents access mental health care for their school-age children. The 20-511A team discussed the possibility of initiating an individualized education plan (IEP) with the school district. An IEP is essentially a contract that explains how a school district plans to comply with various federal legislation including Title II of the Americans with Disabilities Act of 1990 and with the Individuals with Disabilities Education Act (IDEA), which mandates a free and appropriate education (FAPE) for all children at taxpayer expense. A less restrictive Section 504 plan, named for Section 504 of the Rehabilitation Act, provides accommodations for students with disabilities but does not require specialized instruction or related services.

Michael had been on a Section 504 plan for several years to accommodate his dysgraphia, a learning disability that prevents him from writing clearly and organizing his thoughts on a page. Though Michael can perform complex mathematical calculations in his head, he can barely write his name and must use a keyboard for most classroom work. Ultimately, the team decided to keep our less restrictive Section 504 plan in place, with modifications for Michael's sensory integration and behavioral issues. Despite the array of services that would become available to him through an IEP, I did not want one for my son because I was ignorant of the benefits and sensitive to the stigma that attaches to children who receive "specialized instruction," a label that may actually limit educational opportunities for students with learning disabilities.

Now I know better. But parents of children with mental disorders should take note: it's not the school district's job to educate you about what constitutes a "free and appropriate education" for your child—and the district is not always on your (or your child's) side, as we'll see in chapter 5.

Michael continued weekly therapy visits and added occupational therapy to the mix. Occupational therapy is his favorite treatment. He spends an hour in what looks like a giant playground, with rope swings, hammocks, and giant foam blocks that can be used as obstacle courses. Sometimes he plays games; he also learns to be still and to self-regulate. His greatest challenges are moving through space and motor planning, something most of us take for granted. Motor planning is unconscious for most of us—we instinctively know how to find our keys, open the car door, adjust the mirrors, turn the key in the ignition, and put the car into reverse. Complex motor tasks are difficult for Michael; sometimes even changing course on a sidewalk to avoid collision is more than he can do. Manipulating the combination lock on his middle school locker was nearly impossible for him.

We adjusted Michael's medication, taking him off the Zyprexa that had caused him to gain nearly thirty pounds in one year without positively affecting his labile moods. His psychiatrist recommended Celexa instead, and the weight quickly came off within a few months. On the advice of his therapist, who had read an article about mood improvements in children whose tonsils were removed, I had Michael tested for sleep apnea.

The night of the sleep study did not start well. Michael is extremely sensitive to touch, and the attachment of nodes to his buzz-cut head almost triggered one of his rages. But he calmed down and was eventually able to fall asleep. The study revealed moderate apnea, and we scheduled the adenotonsillectomy. Later studies have not confirmed the assertion that adenotonsillectomy improves behavior, but in Michael's case, I saw some immediate improvements, perhaps because he was sleeping better. The role of sleep disruption in children and adults with mental illness is one area of high interest for the research community.

In June 2011, as Michael and I waited outside the juvenile courtroom with his school principal, who was there to testify on his behalf, the prosecutor struck a last-minute deal. He dropped the battery charges, and Michael pled guilty to charges of disturbing the peace and juvenile beyond control. The latter charge is what's called a status offense, meaning that Michael's behavior was only criminal because he was a child. Other examples of common status offenses include truancy and underage substance abuse. The judge accepted the plea bargain and sentenced him to a year of probation, which he completed successfully.

But everyone involved in Michael's care looked to his imminent transition to middle school with dread, and our fears were not unfounded. On the strength of his assessment test scores, Michael was admitted as a sixth grader to Treasure Valley Math and Science Center (TVMSC), a prestigious, advanced public school for gifted children. But after just a few days of class, it was clear that he couldn't navigate the baffling world of middle school as a sixth grader, so I returned him to his home elementary school, a classical studies magnet program where teachers and the school principal understood his needs and appreciated his quirky humor, blazing intelligence, and occasional inappropriate outbursts and behaviors.

Michael couldn't handle TVMSC as a seventh grader, either. Within a few weeks, he had threatened a classmate with scissors, spit on another classmate, and disrupted the environment, on average, according to one of his instructors, thirty times per hour. When placed in a "safe" room to calm down, he removed his glasses and attempted to electrocute himself by shoving them into an outlet. Once, in his English class, he stood in the middle of the room and in a sonorous voice called down death and destruction on his classmates.

The school had received numerous complaints from parents about Michael. The principal was frustrated by him and couldn't understand why he would "waste so much potential." At first we tried transferring him to a regular junior high school, but things went from bad to worse. He couldn't open his locker. He couldn't handle the disruption of class changes. Michael was increasingly depressed and despondent. Finally, we got the IEP in place to address his significant emotional and behavioral issues and transferred him to ASCENT, a grade 7–12 program for emotionally and behaviorally disturbed children, mostly boys. This program does not even begin to address my son's intellectual needs. But he can make it through a school day, most days, without having the principal call me, which means I can stay at work and support my family.

## THE PERSONAL COST

As Michael's story illustrates, in America we deal with our children who have mental illness through two institutions: schools, where in the best-case scenarios they are placed on IEPs and mainstreamed with teachers who are struggling with too-large classes in which one in five children has a diagnosable mental disorder; and juvenile detention, where up to 75 percent of the population has at least one mental disorder. And often, the failure of the first institution to manage the child's condition leads to the second institution, a place of last resort. In some states, this transition from school to prison is so regular that it's been called a "pipeline," one that disproportionately affects poor children and their families.

At a meeting of the Region IV Children's Mental Health Subcommittee in February 2013, the Boise School District presented its numbers of students on IEPs who were diagnosed with attention-deficit/hyperactivity disorder (ADHD), emotional or mood disorders, and autism spectrum disorders. The numbers dropped by more than half after children turned sixteen.

"Am I the only one seeing this?" I asked, pointing out the huge discrepancy. I looked across the room at the representative from Juvenile Corrections. He met my eyes and nodded.

"What you're thinking is probably spot-on," he said. "We would need to look at data across multiple years, but . . ." He shrugged helplessly.

I was thinking that somewhere between age fifteen and sixteen, these children drop out of school and end up in jail. That's why moms like Nancy Lanza end up homeschooling their children: it's just too hard to deal with the frequent calls, the bullying, the frustration and humiliation (for both parent and child) of dealing with public schools.

The night my blog post went viral, my partner, Ed, and I visited my son at Intermountain Hospital for the first time since his admittance. I was still bruised and hurting from the encounter that had put him in the hospital days before. On the way to school that Wednesday morning, we got in an argument about the color of pants he was allowed to wear. When I told him that he was grounded from video games for his disrespectful atti-tude, he turned cold. "Then I'm just going to kill myself," he said.

December 12, 2012, was the Rubicon for me. I had told Michael that if he ever threatened to kill himself again, I would take him straight to the hospital. And I did.

That Saturday night, Michael was apologetic and anxious.

"Your mom still has bruises," Ed told him. "You really hurt her. Do you understand how serious this is?"

Michael nodded and hugged me. "I'm really sorry, Mommy," he said. "Can you get me out of here? I just want to go home."

"Let's see what the doctor says next week," I replied. I wasn't ready to have him home. That night, I wasn't sure if I ever would be.

And later that evening my blog post went viral. On my computer screen I watched with fascination as my post multiplied and divided expo-nentially, like cells in a strange new organism.

At our next visiting hours, I had to tell my son about what I had writ-ten. His father had called him and read the blog to him. When I showed up, Michael's chin quivered; he bit his lip. "Is it true that you, um, wrote something about me? Did you write that I was going to kill people?"

I told him everything—described the school shooting (which he still didn't know about, though he had heard whispers). I told him how I wrote the blog, the agony of my life with him, the fear I lived with daily.

"So let me get this straight," he said. "You compared me to a serial killer."

"Not at all," I said. "I compared myself to a serial killer's mom. I said I was afraid that you might grow up and do something terrible, and that I didn't know how to get help. And I am. I'm afraid of you. But I love you. And I think you are a really neat kid."

He fell into my arms and I hugged him close, ran my fingers over his number 4 buzz-cut head (hair longer than a half inch is something he can't tolerate). His pupils were huge, swallowing the blue of his eyes. I'd learned that large pupils were usually a bad sign.

"Are you mad?" I asked.

"No." He looked away. "I'm sad. I don't want to be a bad kid, Mom.

But when this happens, I can't think. I can't even remember. I still don't remember what happened to put me here."

He looked up at me, his pupils waning. "You know what, Mom?" he said. "Maybe telling my story will help somebody. Maybe it will help someone to change, so they don't have to grow up and hurt other people or themselves."

That fear—that my son will harm himself or others—resonated with millions of readers. Even today, as my coworkers continue to joke about the "campus celebrity" and my students tease me about my social media lectures (let's just say that my LinkedIn page is no longer the first thing you see when you google my name), these numbers—these millions of hits—are nearly incomprehensible to me. My life changed overnight in ways I could not imagine, and yet the experience also clarified for me what mattered most and allowed me to create my own meaning and message from what was largely an inchoate, primal cry of despair and fear and shame. I left anarchy behind and began to blaze a new trail of advocacy.

In December 2012, a week after my son was released from Intermountain Hospital, a few days after what seemed like every media outlet in America tried to track me down, I noticed we were out of groceries. The grocery store cashier was in an annoyingly cheerful mood as I waited with my two oldest boys in line. We were all still reeling from the unexpected loss of their two younger siblings, a Christmas Eve ex parte order sought by their father, which granted him sole physical custody until Michael could be placed in a residential treatment facility.

Michael always asks for root beer. It's almost an obsession with him. I cannot remember a recent conversation that has not included the phrase "Mommy, will you buy me a root beer?"

"Do you want to take this with you?" the cashier asked my son, handing him the brown plastic bottle.

"Yes, please," he said politely. He made eye contact, took the bottle, thanked her.

"You're such a polite young man," she said. "You must have a good mother."

I almost wept, right there in Fred Meyer.

"That's probably the first time anyone has ever complimented you on your behavior in a grocery store," my oldest son snarked.

I don't completely understand the antipathy that exists between him and his brother, though I suspect it's rooted in the enormous amount of attention that Michael commands. My sons could not be more different in interests or in how they approach the world. Both are bright, but my oldest is ambitious, driven to excel, as so many oldest children are.

I have raised an oldest child who places in national competitions as a ninth grader, aces his PSATs, serves as class representative, plays "Clair de Lune" by ear on our Model M Steinway, plans school fund-raisers, is invited to join the senior debate team as a sophomore. You would think that clearly, all my energy and love and attention went into my oldest son.

The truth is nearly the opposite. One of the biggest challenges of parenting any special-needs child is a chronic lack of resources. When you have other children, the whole family suffers. My oldest son has the grades and brains and stamina to succeed at the best colleges in the nation. But he will have to attend a state school on scholarship, because my financial resources are exhausted by his younger brother.

## A Tale of Two Emergency Room Visits

As an example of how we treat mental illness differently from physical illness, consider the world's most expensive library fine. The events that led to my viral essay started with a library fine of epic proportions. Like a junkie who needed a fix, my son had checked out library books, DVDs, video games, and never returned them. Why they kept lending him stuff is a mystery to me. But needless to say, when I opened an e-mail with a bill totaling $162.50, I was more than a little nonplussed.

It seemed perfectly reasonable to me when I asked him to collect the items and return them to the library. Michael had a different opinion. Three hours later, we were sitting in Emergency Room 2 at Saint Alphonsus Regional Medical Center. Michael had to be transported there by ambulance when he tried to injure himself by repeatedly banging his head into the bars in the back of a police car, leaving bruises and bloodied lacerations on his forehead.

I called the police because Michael pointed a large kitchen knife at me and threatened to kill me, then himself. My younger two children, ages seven and nine, raced to the back bedroom and locked the door, then ran to the car when they had a clear, safe path, iPod and books in hand. As they had before, both in drills and in real life, they followed our safety plan.

By the time we reached the emergency room, Michael was calm, so the emergency room physician decided to let him go home, largely because there were no more beds that day in Intermountain, the only acute psychiatric care facility that serves teens in our area, but probably also because I didn't have insurance that would cover an inpatient stay—like many mental health facilities, Intermountain is a for-profit venture. So the doctor wrote us a prescription for Zyprexa pro re nata (PRN, meaning use as needed) and sent us on our way.

Since we had been transported by ambulance to the hospital, when they released us, we had no way to get home, and Michael didn't even have both his shoes—he had lost one in his scuffle with the police. In desperation I called Ed, who was tutoring at Boise State University that day. He left his last appointment early and picked us up at the convenience store next to the hospital. Michael and I were sitting on the curb inhaling greasy taquitos, our first meal of the day.

That morning, I had taken the day off work to spend with my children, who were out of school on a Friday holiday. Instead, I spent the day at the emergency room. The total tab for those library books: $84 library fine, $665 ambulance ride, $1,139 emergency room cost, $384 physician charge.

In contrast, three weeks later, I dropped James and his friend Weston off at the Eighth Street parking garage in downtown Boise so they could finish filming some stunts for their health occupations class video assignment. I took Michael to WinCo to do our grocery shopping for the week. I had just finished bagging our groceries—a few cents under budget at $74.32 for the week—when my son called. He had fallen and hurt himself.

"I'll be right there," I said. "Can you guys make it to the Eighth Street entrance?"

James was more lucid when we picked him up than he had been a few minutes before, but he was sporting a large laceration above his right ear that was oozing blood. He held his arms close to his body as if he were cold.

He never did remember what happened. But I found myself once again in Emergency Room 2 at Saint Alphonsus Regional Trauma Center. "They should give us a plaque or something," I joked. I certainly felt like I'd paid enough for one!

My son was more and more himself with each passing minute. X-rays determined the extent of the damage—three fractures, the most severe on his right arm, with two minor fractures on the left wrist and lower arm. He had probably also suffered from a minor concussion, but he was recovering quickly.

The prognosis was clear. X-rays diagnosed the fractures. The physician splinted my son's arms in an upright position.

When Michael was in crisis, there were no solutions. When James broke both his arms, the path to treatment was clear. Six weeks later, when casts and splints were removed, his arms had healed.

This is the point: we treat mental illness differently from the way we treat physical illness. And we're facing an ever more apparent crisis with mental health care: one in five children suffers from a diagnosable and debilitating mental disorder, according to National Institute of Mental Health data. If one in five children suffered from leukemia or juvenile diabetes, we would see an outpouring of resources, fund-raisers, telethons, tearful parents, and brave children. Instead, we mourn at innocent victims' funerals, wring our hands, talk about passing gun laws, and do nothing about mental illness.

When I lost my health insurance, I couldn't get a policy that covered Michael's mental health. And even when mental illness is covered, it's often at different rates than so-called physical illness. The Affordable Care Act of 2010 addresses ongoing issues of parity and promises to bring mental health costs in line with physical care. But too often, we continue to think that people with mental illness can just "snap out of it," or alternatively, that if we just give them a pill, they'll be fine.

In fact, mental illness is a complex condition that weaves genetics with environmental and social stimuli in ways we still do not completely understand. Just as a patient with type 2 diabetes cannot expect a complete cure with insulin replacement alone, people with mental illness require lifestyle changes, including diet, exercise, and cognitive behavior therapy, to manage their condition. A pill alone does not "fix" mental illness; many people do not respond to existing medications at all.

But we can't even talk about the problem, let alone act, leading to a national crisis that is illuminated by outlier events like Adam Lanza's tragic act of murder-suicide at Sandy Hook Elementary School in Newtown, Connecticut. Though most rampage killers fit a profile—white, male, and a "loner"—experts tell us there's no way to predict who will become a rampage killer.

In fact, mass shootings are rare events, "black swans." Most people who suffer from mental illness are not violent, and they are far more likely to be the victims of violence. According to the final report on the Sandy Hook shootings released in November 2013, there were no signs that Adam Lanza would be violent, though his mental health problems were well known. When people with mental illness do harm someone, those victims are most likely to be themselves. Suicide is a common factor in mass shootings and is the third most common cause of death for young people aged ten to twenty-four; it's the second most common cause between the ages of twenty-four and thirty-five. For me, the death of Internet whiz kid Aaron Swartz and rampage killer Adam Lanza are inextricably intertwined—both bright young men, both suicides.

Children with mental disorders often suffer from bullying. They have trouble making friends or going to college. My greatest fear for my own son is that in a moment of irrationality, he will make good on his frequent threats to end his own life, destroying a sweet, bright, sensitive soul who can contribute to this world, if only he can find a way to navigate the sensory swamp that overwhelms him. This problem of self-regulation and sensory integration is increasingly common in children; a 2009 study of sensory processing problems in elementary school children reported a prevalence of 16.5 percent of the total population. The cause of this increase in sensory processing problems is not completely understood, though it may be linked to poverty and single-parent homes. Psychologist Stuart Shanker, who has explored self-regulation for years, believes that the modern environment itself, with all its distractions and appeals to the senses, is in part responsible for the dramatic rise in emotional and behavioral disorders.

What can we do? What must we do? The solution, I believe, starts with meaningful efforts to reduce stigma, the same way we effectively combated stigma and misinformation for physical conditions like breast cancer, colon cancer, and HIV/AIDS. We have poster children for all kinds of horrible diseases—cancer, muscular dystrophy, cystic fibrosis. Maybe what mental illness needs is a poster child, a beautiful blond boy holding a butterfly. My son Michael.

Another essential part of the solution is learning more about the causes, so that we can develop more effective early diagnoses, interventions, and treatments. At a March 5, 2013, congressional forum in which I was a participant, Dr. Harold Koplewicz, director of the Child Mind Institute, said, "If anyone in this room started complaining of chest pain right now, immediately EMS would come here. On the other hand, if any of us started acting like we were psychiatrically disturbed, and jumped on the table and started yelling and cursing, we'd call the police. There is something very wrong with that system. The EMS isn't trained to deal with diseases above the neck. We have parents who are forced to get their children into the largest mental health system, which is the juvenile justice system."

After more than seven years of doctors, therapists, hospitals, education specialists, and police officers, we are finally narrowing in on a diagnosis for my son, which I'll explain in chapter 4. When I wrote my blog post in December 2012, Michael was in the hospital, and we still had no concrete idea why. A few months later, in May, as I was preparing for Children's Mental Health Week in Idaho, Michael experienced his first clearly manic episode and landed back in Intermountain Hospital. This time, the psychiatrist diagnosed him with juvenile bipolar disorder and added lithium to his complicated medication cocktail. At this writing, we are still in the process of completing a comprehensive neuropsychiatric evaluation that has leaned toward a diagnosis of PDD-NOS, a catchall that will also qualify him for disability. Pervasive developmental disorder, not otherwise specified. In other words, "We don't know what the hell is wrong with your kid, but he's clearly on the autism spectrum."

How many parents can relate to my tortured journey? Far too many.

One mother of a mentally ill son wrote to me, "My son has been evaluated by top psychiatrists and psychologists from Harvard, Cornell, Columbia, and Yale at a cost of $80,000 (borrowed) out of pocket. The diagnosis of Bipolar II, severe ADHD, immaturity. We are fortunate to be able to get the care he needs, but seriously, who can really afford this in the era of HUGE deductibles and decreased coverage? Instead, families interface with the judicial system—aka the modern era mental health system. Which leads to poor mental health care, incarceration, can't get a job, welfare, anxiety, depression, rage . . . back to jail . . . and so on."

As this mother's story illustrates, we must address the problem of access to resources. As long as we continue to "treat" mental illness through the criminal justice system, we will never end the vicious cycle that destroys individuals, families, and communities. And until we can talk about mental illness without shame and without fear, the stigma that our society attaches to criminals will continue to haunt families and children. The stigma starts with fear: the very fear that madness will lead to violent, unpredictable acts, like what happened at Columbine, in Aurora, in Tucson, and in Newtown.

## IMAGES AND REALITY

October 20, 2010. Sitting in a psychiatrist's waiting room with my son, I find myself transfixed by a magazine reprint of the classic black-and-white JFK and Jackie photo taken in Hyannis Port, 1960. They are both looking to the right—his iconic boyish smile is as bright as his crisp white linen button-down. Jackie's half smile, elegant like her perfectly pressed floral print dress, is softer, contented. They are comfortable together, two beautiful people at peace with each other and the world. It is a hauntingly intimate photo, a perfect moment that belies the storms that would rage through their loves and lives.

No one is beautiful or brave or brilliant enough to live a life free from pain.

Still, sometimes I wish that life could be distilled to the simplicity of photographs.

When I was married, I was obsessed with the perfection of my family photos. I learned Photoshop and would spend hours planning photo shoots for my children, in their matching outfits, with their beautiful blond hair—my brilliant, beautiful, perfect children. Of course, with four, I could never get them all to smile at once. So I used a digital guillotine to refashion reality. I took the best image from each shot and merged them to create a masterpiece that never existed.

Now, thinking about this, about the time I spent digitally massaging photos to create a reality that did not exist, creeps me out. Why did I care about something so artificial?

Laster, I sat in a drab doctor's office on the floor next to my son, watching him connect and disconnect little plastic bricks. He wouldn't look at his father in the corner, seated beside a stranger, his stepmother.

I closed my eyes and thought about the photographs. We had our own Hyannis Port, our own moments of grace reduced now to photographic stills, evidence of a life that no longer exists, that probably never existed.

But I wanted that life!

If you knew his real name, you could look up court documents to see that Michael's father filed for divorce in 2008, that he remarried a few weeks later, that I petitioned the court for a custody modification to seek sole physical custody of my two older sons in 2011 after they had already been living exclusively with me for several months, and that custody was formally modified in May 2012. You could also see that he petitioned the court for a custody modification granting him sole physical custody of our younger two children in June 2012, and that he successfully argued an ex parte motion to remove the younger two children from my care on December 24, 2012, a week after my blog post went viral. He did not notify me until two days after the order was issued, when I e-mailed to ask what time he was dropping off Anna and Jonathan, and he replied, "I'm not."

The judge in that case left me with a Hobson's choice: I could keep my younger two children half-time, but only if I committed Michael to long-term residential care. Two well children or one sick child. No mother should ever be faced with that kind of choice, just because one of her children is ill. But that is the choice facing me today, as I write these words. It is a choice that too many parents face.

I will say this, though: no parent should ever have to do what I am doing alone. When I wrote my blog post, I had been solely responsible for Michael's care for more than two years, except for three hours per week that he spent with his father (and he now has not seen his dad in several months outside of social settings). In all that time, a persistent, low-level anxiety has run constantly through my brain, like the three-kelvin microwave background that permeates the known universe. I am never worry free, not for one minute. When the school calls, my heart skips. When I see police officers in my neighborhood on the way home from work, I instinctively check the backseat to see if my son is behind bars again.

Like many parents, I have tried for years to "manage" my son's condition essentially on my own. I've thought that I could wish him into wellness. I've even denied that he had problems. The emotional anguish of my blog post came out of that space, as a national tragedy sparked a private moment of raw honesty.

And yet when we speak, we may subject ourselves and our families to even worse punishments. I believe that this is why the stigma associated with mental disorders has not decreased in recent years. Families are afraid to speak up about or ask for help for their sick children, for the very real fear that they will lose their healthy ones, either to another parent (as in my case) or to the state. There are other, more mundane reasons, too— that ache we feel as we long for Hyannis Port. The shame of having a child who isn't perfect—at least, by society's impossible standards.

It's easy to blame parents. When Adam Lanza shot up an elementary school, we wanted answers. So many small coffins, grieving parents, presents under Christmas trees that would never be opened. But as we always do when these outlier events occur, we inevitably looked to easy answers—guns, and parenting. In the immediate aftermath, the pundits were certain: clearly it was Nancy Lanza's fault. She should not have had guns in her home. She should have recognized how potentially violent her son was. He should not have had access to guns.

As a mother of a child with a mental disorder, I know one thing for sure: she tried to help her son. No mother wants her child to suffer like Adam Lanza did. No mother wants her son to murder first graders. Without in any way condoning what Adam Lanza did, I am still troubled by the media's reporting of twenty-six victims in that Newtown tragedy. There were twenty-eight victims. Adam Lanza and his mother were victims that day. Like too many people who suffer from mental disorders, Adam Lanza completed suicide. I say "completed" suicide because the normal phrase, "commit suicide," suggests that this ultimate act of self-harm is criminal in nature, contributing to the stigma of mental illness. When Lanza completed suicide, he committed a criminal act, taking twenty-seven other people with him. We can talk all day about gun control. But what is our obligation as a society to care for people like Adam Lanza? What should we have done for his mother?

Like Nancy Lanza, I'm a highly educated white woman with resources, with connections, with health insurance. Think how bad it is to have a child with a mental disorder if you don't have any of those things.

And so my 750 words became an accidental but powerful manifesto for children's mental health. In retrospect, I think that one of the things that resonated most strongly with parents in similar situations was the raw emotion in the piece. That's because I, as the writer, was revealing truths to myself that I had been unwilling or unable to face. My first audience was myself.

So for me, and for many other parents, this is what "normal" looks like. People said that I was brave for telling my story. I did not feel brave; I felt helpless.

This is how ordinary people become heroes. When bravery finds you, you don't have time to think. You've been preparing for this accidental moment your entire life. If you are brave, when that moment finds you, you embrace the consequences, no matter how terrible. The naïve part of me actually believed that my cry for help would reveal some meaningful answers. That's the way it works in fiction, right? You have a mystery, you follow the clues, and you solve it.

It proved to be a bit more complicated. But I have hope that the conversation I sparked might translate into something meaningful. The ancient Greeks defined their heroes on two axes: *praxis* (deeds) and *logos* (words). We've had enough of logos in this epic battle against mental illness. It's time to take action. Like so many who take a first step into the darkness, I did not mean to be brave—I was an accidental advocate. But I will accept the consequences. This is a battle waged, in the words of one of my favorite poets, Robert Frost, "for Heaven and the future's sakes."

My son Michael is a hero, too, in his own way. He spends a lot more time than most people thinking about the Greek heroes, the gods and goddesses. He is working on a novel about Greek demigods in outer space—one passage reimagines the ancient city of Pompeii in the shadow of an ice volcano, with clear glass-like crystals instead of molten lava.

My son is most at home in a world of his own imagining. I cannot understand that world—with him, I sometimes feel like a visitor to a secret laboratory, watching through a thick plate-glass window as he scurries below, performing inscrutable tasks of great consequence.

This morning, as I am folding laundry, one of Anna's brightly colored fuzzy socks stares at me. My jaw tightens; my stomach turns. "At least I'll see her for a few hours on Wednesday," I think. That's more than Ana Grace's mother can say, when she finds a hair barrette, a sock, a favorite toy. Her daughter is now enshrined in memories, those precious everyday items now holy relics. I think of Nelba Marquez-Greene's words at the Sandy Hook parents' first news conference after the shootings: "We choose love. Love wins in Newtown, and may love win in America."

That's brave.

# TWO

# STIGMA

## WHY DO WE BLAME CHILDREN AND FAMILIES FOR MENTAL ILLNESS?

Parents wonder why the streams are bitter, when they themselves have poisoned the fountain.

—John Locke

Pam Kazmaier is one of the bravest, most compassionate mothers I know. She is also a convicted child abuser finishing ten years' probation for a suicide pact she made and almost kept with her younger son, Zack, then thirteen years old. Pam and Zack both have bipolar disorder. After she joined the Church of Jesus Christ of Latter-day Saints, Pam put all her energies into creating a perfect life for herself and her family. But her son never fit in. As he became increasingly ill, her bishop suggested that she just teach Zack the gospel at home. Her son's psychiatrist disparaged her increasingly desperate pleas for help and told her to just "get used to it." She could not find a hospital that would take her son. Finally, one September Sunday afternoon, Pam and Zack came home from church and decided to die. She felt as if there were no other options.

*Stigma* is one of those tricky words that can mean different things to different people. The Google dictionary definition is "a mark of disgrace associated with a particular circumstance, quality, or person, e.g., the stigma of mental disorder." The ancient Greeks, from whom the word is borrowed, did not attach a negative connotation to the word itself—for them, it merely signified a mark, like a tattoo that could distinguish a slave. But like most world cultures throughout history, the Greeks viewed mental illness with a sense of shame, isolating afflicted people and even occasionally killing them. Ironically, children and adults who have mental illness do not always have visible signs of their disability—they look just like other people. For children with mental illness and their families, stigma means silence, shame, and isolation.

## WHAT STIGMA LOOKS LIKE

With mental illness, stigma comes in many forms, all of them pernicious and destructive. There's self-stigma: you blame yourself for your child's illness. Then there's social stigma: your culture's norms disapprove of your child's illness. Mental health providers and special education teachers are often both sources of and victims of stigma. Stigma is a mother and son with bipolar disorder who are "politely" told by their church leader that they should "study the gospel at home." Stigma is a young man with autism who is relentlessly teased by his high school peers. Stigma is a young mother who doesn't take her little girl to the playground anymore because she knows the other moms don't like her daughter. Stigma is a psychiatrist who incorrectly diagnoses ADHD instead of juvenile bipolar disorder because she doesn't want a child to "carry the burden of a serious mental illness." Stigma is the special education aide who says to a colleague in the hallway, "These kids just don't know how to behave because their parents give them anything they want."

Stigma condemns children to inferior education at best and incarceration at worst. Stigma keeps children from becoming happy, healthy, productive adults. The costs to life, liberty, and the pursuit of happiness—the very foundations of American society—are truly staggering.

The media play a tremendously important role in perpetuating our collective disapproval of people with mental illness: when I asked a group of friends to name the first movie relating to mental illness that came to mind, I got the following list: *One Flew over the Cuckoo's Nest*; *Rain Man*;

*A Beautiful Mind; Girl, Interrupted; The Three Faces of Eve; The Exorcist; Fatal Attraction;* and *Psycho.* This by no means exhaustive list contains examples of the three biggest misconceptions about mental illness: first, that people with mental illness are responsible for their illness; second, that people with mental illness have childlike, magical experiences of the world; and finally, that people with mental illness should be feared.

The popularity of movies like *Psycho* and *Fatal Attraction* illustrates why stigma is still so prevalent in our society, despite the brave and diligent efforts of advocacy groups like the National Alliance on Mental Illness (NAMI) and others. In our mass media–shaped minds, mental illness is the "crazy" knife-wielding man in the shower who seemed like such a nice boy; the poised, attractive woman who can't take no for an answer— then a young man dresses up like the Joker, opens fire at a *Batman* premiere, and the national conversation turns briefly and almost hysterically to mental illness. Fear is the heart of stigma.

Before any change is possible, we have to overcome stigma. Self-stigma is often the biggest barrier: parents have a hard time talking about their children in part because they fall victim to self-stigmatization. They are more than willing to blame themselves, and society at large is happy to reinforce that message. And yet we would never think of blaming a child with Down syndrome for her condition, nor would we blame her parents. Harold Koplewicz summed up the problem in his March 5, 2013, comments to a congressional forum on mental illness: "This country has tackled things like cancer, AIDS, and yet people are so ashamed, feeling it's either their fault or their child's fault or somebody's fault. It's time this nation really speaks up for kids, says this is real, it's common, it's treatable."

Instead, too often, we blame the children and their caregivers. If you want to know what stigma at its worst looks like, consider the chilling anonymous letter delivered to the doorstep of Brenda Millson, a Toronto grandmother of a boy with autism:

> Personally, they should take whatever non retarded body parts
> he possesses and donate it to science. What the hell else good
> is he to anyone!!!

What right do you have to do this to hard working people!!!!!!! I HATE people like you who believe, just because
you have a special needs kid, you are entitled to special treatment!!!

When this horrific missive showed up on the feed of a secret Facebook
autism mom support group to which I belong, I reposted the letter to my
personal page, adding my own observation that every mother of a child
with mental illness or a mental disorder has at some time been the victim
of intentional cruelty. My friends were outraged by this letter, yet I received a similar comment on my own blog about Michael's rages: "I would
suggest you take your child to Russia or India and have him lobotomized
before he kills one of your children, or yourself."

And the mental illness stigma needle has scarcely budged since the
"stay calm and take a Miltown" era of the 1950s and '60s. There's a real
perception gap between those who have mental illness and those who
don't: while 57 percent of healthy adults believe that people are caring
and sympathetic toward those with mental illness, only 25 percent of
adults who actually have a mental illness believe that people are caring
and sympathetic toward those with mental illness. It's no better for children and their parents. One mother expressed her sympathy with my futile
attempts to get help for my son: "I have been where you are now. I was the
single mother of an autistic child and a bipolar child. My experiences were
nearly identical to yours. In the end, I was able to save one child but not
the other, and that loss haunts me. What I find saddest, however, is that
the responses you are receiving are identical to those I got twenty to
twenty-five years ago."

The resentment expressed by the anonymous Canadian author of the
"euthanize him" letter rang true to me: as I mentioned in chapter 1, my
own son was the target of a parent campaign to have him removed from
an exclusive academic program. The fact is that every parent who has a
child with mental illness lives with stigma—self-stigma and social stigma.

But stigma has a second meaning within the Christian faith. For

Christians, stigmata are marks that correspond to Jesus's wounds sustained on the cross, and they are a sign of divine favor. I thought of this meaning while attending the vigil of a good friend and former colleague. I chose the pseudonym Michael when I wrote about my son's struggles with mental illness for two reasons. The first was the Catholic Prayer to Saint Michael. The second reason was Mike N.

## STIGMA IS PERSONAL

Mike N. and I were both departmental chairs at a small technical college when my then-eleven-year-old son was sent by his father to juvenile detention for the second time. Mike happened to be passing my cubicle and saw my tears one afternoon as I got off the phone with my son's public defender. Mike sat down across from me, his keenly intelligent, clear blue eyes worried, his normally jovial visage grim. "Tell me," he said quietly.

"The public defender says I need to try to get full custody of my boys," I told him. "I have no idea how to do that, or how to pay for it, or what that will even mean."

Mike was an experienced law enforcement planner, a former Idaho Air National Guard chief master sergeant who'd served in Iraq, Turkey, and Afghanistan. He was also a real softie, one of the most compassionate people I have ever known. He listened, then he went to work. He helped me to find the custody modification forms on the county website. He offered to serve the papers to my ex-husband personally.

When I asked him how I could repay him, he grinned and responded, "Get me a king-sized Snickers bar." I did, and a few months later, my sons were living with me full-time. Michael has not been back to juvenile detention since.

But things were not well with Mike N. We all knew Mike was in trouble, toward the end. But no one knew what to do or how to save him. He showed up to work red faced, slurring his words, and smelling like Listerine. Later, after he lost his job, he started to commit burglaries. Many of the police in the valley knew him and loved him, and at first they tried to protect him. This wasn't the Mike any of us knew. At the age of fifty-two, he took his own life after a long battle with post-traumatic stress disorder, depression, and addiction.

In his online memorial book, the word "mentor" came up over and over, from former law enforcement officers, soldiers, students, friends; from me. I miss him. His obituary read simply, "He died at home." So did Nancy Lanza. We don't mention suicide. It's too hard for any of us to talk about. My friend was instrumental in saving my sons. And now he is gone, victim to the same demons that Saint Michael promises to vanquish for the faithful.

In a small percentage of people who have mental illness, like Adam Lanza and other so-called rampage killers, those demons create a wide swath of destruction. The unpredictable and violent behavior of a small percentage of people with mental illness—Foucault's violent and unpredictable madman—has historically contributed to stigma and society's almost compulsive need to assign blame. This is why mental illness has always been hard to talk about, especially for the mothers.

Several years after the tragedy, Susan Klebold, mother of Dylan Klebold, who with classmate Eric Harris shot and killed thirteen fellow students at Columbine High School, confessed to writer Andrew Solomon that after hearing about the tragedy and her son's role in it, "I wished for my son to kill himself, and he did. . . . I think the other parents believed they had experienced loss, and I had not, because their children were of value, and mine was not. My child died, too."

## WHY IS MENTAL ILLNESS STIGMATIZED?

What do Dylan Klebold and Adam Lanza and Mike N. and my son and as many as one in four people in our population at any given time have in common? "Mental illness" is the blanket term for all diagnosable mental disorders, which the U.S. Department of Health and Human Services defines as "health conditions that are characterized by alterations in think-ing, mood, or behavior (or some combination thereof) associated with distress and/or impaired functioning." Mental disorders are the diagnos-able conditions themselves. There have been attempts to change the con-versation by creating new, less stigmatized terminology: in 1988, NAMI tried to rebrand mental disorders as neurobiological disorders, or NBDs, leading prominent psychologist John Grohol to comment, "Changing the name of mental disorders to something else (no matter what that some-thing else is) is not the answer."

One obvious reason that talking about mental illness is so difficult is that the disorders themselves, as well as their intensity, vary widely, from the most common mood disorders (e.g., depression) to environmental disorders (post-traumatic stress disorder) to developmental disabilities (autism and ADHD) to Alzheimer's disease and dementia. Substance abuse is also classified as a mental illness. As my son Michael puts it, "Mental illness is different for every person because every person's brain and experiences and environment are different. It's not like the heart, which just pumps your blood. My brain is who I am, and there's no one like me."

The main tool used to diagnose mental illness is the American Psy-chiatric Association's *Diagnostic and Statistical Manual of Mental Disorders* (*DSM*), now in its fifth and most controversial edition (referred to as *DSM-5*). The *DSM*'s reliance on symptoms rather than biomarkers con-tributes to the confusion—as a diagnostic tool, it's the equivalent of a crude hand ax trying to do a laser cutter's precision work. Consider this absurd example: a woman who has had trouble sleeping for two weeks can be diagnosed with the same disorder—depression—that applies to a man who has just tried to kill himself.

And then there's autism. Many parents of children diagnosed with developmental disabilities wriggle uncomfortably under the "mental ill-ness" patchwork quilt, for obvious reasons. In a recent conversation with a friend, she made a point of telling me that her son who has autism did not have a mental illness like my son does, but "merely a developmental disorder." This kind of stigma within the community that experiences mental illness demonstrates just how real the problem is—we can't even support each other.

When the media first suggested that Adam Lanza had been diagnosed with autism, parental advocacy groups responded with indignation and even outrage at the suggested link between this increasingly common disorder and violent behavior. Some autism advocates even argue that the disorder is not a disability at all, but rather a difference, one that can even provide advantages in certain fields, including science, technology, engineering, and math.

But we as parents cannot ignore the fact that many children with autism also have other comorbid psychiatric disorders. And children with developmental disorders including autism interact with their environment and with other people in unpredictable ways. Unfortunately, beyond anecdotal playground evidence, little is actually known about potential links between autism and violent behavior. One Swedish study found that 7 percent of patients hospitalized with autistic disorder or Asperger's syndrome had committed violent crimes. Yet mental health advocacy groups are quick—and correct—to point out that statistically, those with mental illness and mental disorders are more likely to be the victims of violence than the perpetrators. It's the fear-stigma feedback loop again: the perception of unpredictable violence creates fear, and fear perpetuates stigma.

## STIGMA AND SUICIDE

Everyone who knew my friend Mike N. knew he was in trouble. But none of us could talk about it, least of all Mike or his family. With mental illness, silence and shame can be fatal. Someone might argue that not all people who kill themselves are mentally ill. But more than 90 percent of people who complete suicide have been diagnosed with a mental illness. For many of these people, a fleeting impulse to escape becomes a permanent exit: three out of four people who survived a suicide attempt report that the length of time between deciding to end their lives and attempting to do so was less than one hour.

The threat of self-violence is the greatest risk for children and adults who have mental illness. According to the U.S. Centers for Disease Control and Prevention, suicide is the third most common cause of death for young people. As I mentioned in chapter 1, each year, about 4,600 young people between the ages of ten and twenty-four take their own lives, and the numbers soar even higher between the ages of twenty-five and thirty-four, where suicide is the second leading cause of death (it's the tenth leading cause overall). These numbers coincide with the first incidence of many mental illnesses—one in three people diagnosed with schizophrenia attempt suicide, and one in ten succeed. Typically, first incidence and diagnosis of schizophrenia occur between the ages of twenty and thirty. While these young people are typically thought of as adults, more than one-third of adult children with serious mental illness continue to reside with their parents. As we learn more about schizophrenia, we may see earlier signs: author Michael Schofield's daughter, Jani, was diagnosed with schizophrenia at the age of three.

But that's not the whole story: 157,000 emergency room visits result from self-harm attempts by young people aged ten to twenty-four every year. Boys are much more successful suicide completers—81 percent of the deaths are males—but girls are more likely to attempt suicide. Guns are used in 45 percent of the fatalities. Indeed, states with the highest percentage of gun owners—including Idaho—also have the highest suicide rates. Gun owners and their families have a risk of suicide that is two to five times higher than non-gun-owning households. Guns allow people to kill themselves with astonishing success. And yet the gun lobby continues to make statements in line with the oft-quoted assertion attributed to rocker and National Rifle Association board member Ted Nugent: "The only misuse of guns comes in environments where there are drugs, alcohol, bad parents, and undisciplined children. Period."

To put things into perspective, the leading cause of cancer death in children is childhood leukemia. In 2013, according to the Leukemia and

Lymphoma Society, 437 children died from this disease. As I said earlier, nearly ten times as many children and young people will die from suicide, and 90 percent of those children and young people have a mental disorder. Yet we don't see fund-raisers and telethons and community fun runs for children with mental illness. It remains a largely invisible disease, "treated" in special education resource rooms and later in criminal detention centers. For the one in five children with a diagnosable mental illness, stigma ensures the prognosis is grim.

## STIGMA AND RELIGION

Michael is my son. As his mother, I cannot talk about his own struggles with mental illness without examining my own attitudes, without acknowledging the self-stigma, for both mothers and children, that lies at the root of all stigma. For too many years, I wanted a perfect family, just like Pam Kazmaier did. I thought I could wish my child well, that if I prayed hard enough, God would make it all better.

Religion has traditionally helped us to make sense of our world, to provide answers to tough questions. Why do some people suffer from mental illness? Why do some people attempt or complete suicide? In the Bible, Jesus casts out demons, but even in antiquity, people understood that God alone was not the reason for mental illness. Mother-blame, however, is as old as Eve.

Today, we tend to think that the equation of sin with mental illness in the West developed during the Middle Ages. But in a survey of fifty-seven primary source descriptions of mental illness from that period, one study found that only nine accounts attributed mental illness to sin; authors seemed to understand grief, stress, "humoral imbalances," and substance abuse or intemperance as the root causes.

It seems more likely that the conflation of sin with mental illness reflects a Puritan and Protestant interpretation of sin rather than a Catholic one. The Puritan work ethic is ingrained in the foundation of our nation, along with the idea that every person can pull him- or herself up by the proverbial bootstraps, leaving the coal mines or the factories or farm fields to achieve great wealth and success. This quicksand beneath our cherished idea of the American Dream is perhaps one of the most powerful and dangerous myths that belie the reality of mental illness.

In its worst incarnations, fear and stigmatization of people with mental illness led to witch hunts and exorcisms, then to institutions and neglect. In 1522, Sir Thomas More, who became one of my childhood heroes after I read Robert Bolt's biographical play *A Man for All Seasons*, mentioned the eponymous asylum: "Think not that everything is pleasant that men for madness laugh at. For thou shalt in Bedlam see one laugh at the knocking of his own head against a post, and yet there is little pleasure therein." More then compares the relatively minor laughter of the patient who knocks himself on the head with the wicked laughter of the sinner who deliberately deceives his neighbor, drawing a clear distinction between mental illness and sin.

Yet eighteenth- and nineteenth-century mental hospitals focused on Bible reading and moral instruction as a means to restore mental health: "Emphasis was placed on patients attending religious services because such worship was believed to inspire self-control and rational behavior." This conflation of sin with suffering has dangerous implications and consequences.

I've struggled to return to church since Mike's funeral. I know the church will be waiting for me when I'm ready. And I know that the old doctrines and dogmas that barred suicides from eating at the feast in Heaven or drinking from the "great lake of beer" promised by Saint Brigit, the fifth-century mystic who built the first Irish convent, at Kildare, are no longer taught. While suicides were once denied Christian funeral rites and burials, the catechism of the Roman Catholic Church now states: "Grave psychological disturbances, anguish, or grave fear of hardship, suffering, or torture can diminish the responsibility of the one committing suicide."

The Catholic who commits suicide no longer need fear consignment to the Seventh Circle of Hell, transformed into a thorny twisted bush which Dante must have thought represented the suicide's anguished, tortured state of mind just prior to the ultimate act of self-immolation. Mike will get to imbibe heavenly nectar from that lake of beer, and I'm sure he'll enjoy every drop.

Nonbelievers find it easy to criticize religion's often judgmental view of people with mental illness. In *The Future of an Illusion*, an exegesis of religion's origins and purpose, the founder of modern psychology, Sigmund Freud, wrote tongue-in-cheek that "devout believers are safeguarded in a high degree against the risk of certain neurotic illnesses; their acceptance of the universal neurosis spares them the task of constructing a personal one." The science of psychiatry sought early on to distance itself from the mysticism of religion, with considerable success. In 2013, Oxford neuroscientist Kathleen Taylor made news when she opined that religious fundamentalism of any flavor may one day be understood as a mental illness that can be treated and cured.

Yet other research suggests that in at least one sense Freud was right about the comfort of mass delusion, and that the familiar context of religious practice may actually provide a powerful coping mechanism for people with mental illness: "Religion is an important psychological and social factor that may serve either as a powerful resource for healing or be intricately intertwined with psychopathology." Harold Koenig, MD, the director of Duke University's Center for Spirituality, Theology and Health, recommends integrating patients' religious beliefs into psychological treatment and taking a "spiritual history" that accounts for patients' experiences—both positive and negative—with organized religion.

But while religious communities can provide support to struggling families, they can also be a source of shame and stigma, especially for mothers, as Pam Kazmaier's story demonstrates. At the extreme are those who believe that mental illness is merely a manifestation of sin. Take this statement from one fundamentalist Christian website (grammatical errors left intact):

All mental illness is a behaviour choice not a bodily disease.
All the behaviours associated with mental illness are without

exception, sins listed in the Bible. Sinful living choices can lead to further sinful emotional choices like depression and anxiety, which then become the basis of a mental illness label (diagnosis) by atheistic chemical psychiatrists. Jesus commanded us not to be anxious and a "depressed Christian" is an oxymoron, considering the great joy of possessing the reward and blessing of eternal life in heaven.

"A 'depressed Christian' is an oxymoron." That's what many evangelicals think. And yet there are so many of us. And it's not just those of us who prefer the Christian flavor of religion: mental illness is stigmatized by religions and cultures around the world, though less so in some Asian societies for reasons that are not yet completely understood. Japan's high suicide rates suggest that mental illness cannot even be talked about, let alone treated—in recent years, Japanese women have become especially vulnerable to suicide. But religion can be correlated with stigma across the globe. In one study of Nigerian attitudes toward those with mental illness, for example, researchers found that "a biopsychosocial view of the causation of mental illness is associated with a more tolerant and less stigmatizing attitude than is a view that is informed by supernatural beliefs."

Is mental illness a sin? Religious experience itself often shares the language of mental illness. How do we explain Socrates's *daemon* then, or Joseph Smith, or Joan of Arc? Saint Teresa of Avila and Joan of Arc both experienced ecstatic visions that may have had their roots in epileptic seizures (which the ancient Greek physician Hippocrates termed "the sacred disease"). What the Mormon prophet Joseph Smith called a vision—God and Jesus appearing as shining men in a grove of trees to a fourteen-year-old boy in upstate New York—a modern psychiatrist might characterize as a hallucination, prescribing an antipsychotic.

Mormon and evangelical Christian women seem especially vulnerable to unrelenting pressure and unrealistic perfectionism that permeates their churches' doctrine. The self-reliant Latter-day Saint culture, with its relentless emphasis on "perfecting the Saints," perhaps unintentionally perpetuates one of the challenges to promoting awareness of mental illness and ending stigma for children and families. Mormon women bear the brunt of this perfectionism, often being expected to give up work outside the home; devote themselves to lay church service; raise perfect, polite, academically gifted children; grow a garden; preserve what they grow in their garden for their two-year food storage; and of course, stay thin, fit, and smiling in their "modest is hottest" outfits, standing beside their equally perfect, priesthood-holding husbands.

With this impossible image in mind, no one should be startled by the results of a 2001 headline-making pharmaceutical study: Utah's antidepressant per capita usage rate was much higher than other states, especially among women. A 2008 study showed higher rates of depression in Utah as well. Brigham Young University religious studies professor Daniel Judd and other Mormon apologists have framed these types of results in a positive light, arguing that the correlation actually shows a greater awareness of mental illness among the Latter-day Saint community and also reflects the fact that most Latter-day Saints do not self-medicate with illegal drugs or alcohol, turning to medical professionals for help instead. They also argue that perhaps the higher rates suggest that Utah's non–Latter-day Saint population is more depressed than in other states: "Maybe the other 25% of Utah's population, the non-LDS group, have higher level of depression levels [sic], thus boosting Utah's percentages up a few points. Unfortunately, our data are not able to test these questions."

Utah Valley University professor Kristine Doty thinks she has another explanation for why so many Latter-day Saint women are depressed: "toxic perfectionism." In a one-year qualitative study of twenty Latter-day Saint women diagnosed with depression, Doty found that unrealistic expectations and high levels of guilt characterized these women's lives. The link between sin and depression is implicitly understood by her subjects. As one thirty-two-year-old woman Doty interviewed said, "In the LDS church it's like, 'I feel depressed' and it's like, 'Oh, you must not be righteous. Maybe you should go serve somebody, and then you would be.'"

Doty's findings echo earlier narratives of unattainable perfection and psychic pain. In 1979, Jan Barker, a mother of four and a devout Mormon, shared the story of her nervous breakdown in a KSL Television documentary about Mormon women and depression:

> I found myself totally responsible for the ward Christmas party by default, several other people having fallen through. And I was Junior Sunday School coordinator. And I was saying, "I can do that. I can do that. I can do that." The day they took me into the hospital for the first time, everybody was amazed. . . .
>
> Other Mormon women make it very difficult, too. You would hear constantly: You have a wonderful husband. You have beautiful children. Your husband's active in the church. You have everything you need to be happy and you're not happy.

And toxic perfectionism certainly describes my own experiences with the LDS church, right down to being totally responsible for the ward Christmas party. I don't do anything halfway, and being Mormon was no exception. I took the church's Proclamation on the Family seriously: "By divine design, fathers are to preside over their families in love and righteousness and are responsible to provide the necessities of life and protection for their families. Mothers are primarily responsible for the nurture of their children." So I tended to my own and others' children, I baked and canned, read the Old Testament daily (yes, even the Book of Numbers), refinished furniture, laid tile, went visiting teaching to ward members, played the organ at the temple once a week, and taught the adult Sunday school class.

I told myself that it didn't matter that I had given up a promising academic career to scrub windows sparkling clean, reminded by the clear blue cleaning liquid that Vindex (pronounced "Windex") was one of the Gallic leaders whom Caesar came to, saw, and conquered.

Like many mothers of children with mental illness, my experience with stigma starts with myself. I blamed myself for my son's problems, for the fact that my family wasn't perfect, for the perhaps inevitable dissolution of my once longed-for Mormon temple eternal marriage. Accepting the breakdown of the most primary role of my life has not been easy for me. Mormonism shaped my view of myself as a mother, reinforcing the idea that if I could not raise happy, productive, and just plain nice children, I was a failure.

One Latter-day Saint prophet, David O. McKay, famously said, "No success can compensate for failure in the home." If it's unacceptable to talk about mental illness in the community at large, it's especially anathema in the Mormon community, which values hard work, a positive attitude, and self-reliance. To be fair, recent attempts by the patriarchy to separate culture from theology have emphasized that those who suffer from mental illness are not sinners; in the Saturday afternoon session of the church's October 2013 General Conference, Elder Jeffrey R. Holland, a Mormon apostle, declared: "there should be no more shame in acknowledging them [mental disorders] than in acknowledging a battle with high blood pressure or the sudden appearance of a malignant tumor." Still, for the rank-and-file members, depression is viewed as a physical manifestation of sin—why would anyone who is living the principles of the gospel of Jesus Christ be unhappy?

That's why I was so obsessed with creating the perfect pictures I described in chapter 1, unreal pictures created from composites, the physical, tangible proof that "all is well" (a line from "Come, Come Ye Saints," a famous Mormon hymn about pioneer courage). Unlike many LDS women of my generation, I came to marriage and motherhood reluctantly, a view that was not acceptable among my "sisters" in the Mormon church. The pictures were tangible reminders that "all was well." Even though it wasn't. We were far from well.

## SINS OF THE MOTHER

Mother-love is a terrible and terrifying emotion—savage, pure, inchoate. You can fall in and out of love with boyfriends, girlfriends, husbands, wives. Those loves are often conditional, no matter what the movies and e-cards say. Loving your partner is at its heart transactional, a coupling rooted in sexual attraction and sustained by compassion, cooperation, and sheer determination.

But loving your children is something else entirely—an act as close to true selflessness as any our species can contemplate (Richard Dawkins's selfish gene notwithstanding). The literary critic Alfred Kazin wrote, "If love has ever really meant anything, it has meant the largest possible risk." I have certainly found that sentiment to be true in my own experience— and the act of procreating is perhaps the riskiest manifestation of love that two humans can share.

Do the risks outweigh the benefits? Obviously, most parents decide in favor of offspring, to the benefit of the species. But most biological and adoptive parents of children at least occasionally wonder what their lives might have been like if they had chosen not to have children. I am no exception. And when your child has a mental disorder, it's only natural to feel resentment sometimes, or to feel like you've given up far more than you bargained for. The "angels of our better nature" struggle with demons of doubt and recrimination and guilt as we watch our own children suffer. And yet perhaps because we have to work so hard at loving, we get good at it: a population-based survey of mothers of autistic children concluded that "mothers of children with autism showed remarkable strengths in the parent–child relationship, social support, and stability of the household in the context of high stress and poorer mental health."

I'm reflexively resistant to the all-too-common censure that a child's behavior is entirely the mother's fault, the result of my neglect or indifference or narcissism or whatever convenient label you want to attach to it. But at the same time, I am seduced by this repugnant idea, because, frankly, we mothers are such easy targets. And to a large extent, we've made ourselves that way. I was raised and educated in the ugly trenches of the Mommy Wars, and I often think that by abandoning my academic passions, by choosing to stay home and raise four children, I chose the wrong side. A woman can take no greater financial risk for herself and her offspring than to choose to leave the labor force. I thank whatever gods may be for second chances.

Punishing the mother for the sins of her son has long-standing roots in literary tradition—the old Greek plays gave us Jocasta, the mother of Oedipus, who killed his own father and married his mother. It's no accident that Freud turned to the language of Greek mythology when he sought to describe a new science of the soul, the motivations behind desire. Through the conduit of Freud, Greece's mad matriarchs became the West's "Refrigerator Mothers." Before my blog post about my struggles in raising Michael went viral, I was completely unfamiliar with that term. This 1950s catchphrase blamed emotionally frigid mothers for children suffering from a strange and as-yet unidentified set of behavioral abnormalities that came to be understood as autism spectrum disorders. Perhaps because so many psychiatrists of that generation had cut their teeth on Freud, the largely male cadre of physicians jumped straight to the biological mother as the cause for these children's mysterious inability to interact with others. Leo Kanner, who first identified autism as a discrete disorder in 1949, mistook cause for effect when he attributed antisocial behaviors to a "genuine lack of maternal warmth"—never mind the fact that the children he treated had neurotypical, well-adjusted siblings!

While the "Refrigerator Mother" hypothesis has long been discredited in the scientific community, reactions both to Nancy Lanza and to my blog post show that mother-blame is alive and well in the noisy realm of popular opinion. *Slate*'s Hanna Rosin joined forces with blogger Sarah Kendzior in an all-too-common attack on mothers who talk about their children's mental illness: "In this era, when we worry about whether we need to keep a closer eye on the dangerous and mentally ill, 'Michael' is not the one in that family we should be monitoring."

I have nothing against Hanna Rosin—she is a smart and intelligent writer. But I would like to take her out for coffee and attempt to educate her about what it's like to live my life. In her response to my blog, Rosin extols the virtues of parents who keep their mentally ill children's identities anonymous out of concern for their children's futures, suggesting that my "tragic cadences" expose me as just another narcissistic mommy in the middle of a bad divorce who wants to call attention to myself. I would argue that it is precisely this demand for anonymity that continues to isolate parents and children in their communities. I couldn't even tell my close friends about my son's violent rages.

Is this the newest incarnation of the Mommy Wars—mothers whose children have mental disorders versus mothers whose children are "normal"? With one in five children suffering from a debilitating mental disorder, and with autism rates dramatically on the rise, this question is a legitimate one, and the war's first skirmishes are being fought every day on playgrounds and in elementary school classrooms across America.

Why are mothers the loudest critics of other mothers? Our culture, obsessed with books like Facebook COO and überwoman Sheryl Sandberg's *Lean In* and Hanna Rosin's *The End of Men*, might provide some answers. In his book on stigma and mental illness, sociologist and historian Gerhard Falk observes that "because deinstitutionalization places the burden of care on the family, this is really a feminist issue since in our culture women are the prime caregivers for ill people who remain at home. . . . Generally, outsiders, including professionals, let it be known that the family is responsible for the mental illness of the patient and that parents in particular are responsible for the condition of their children."

I now have another word for Rosin's cherished privacy: stigma. Why is a mother who speaks out about her child with mental illness any different from a mother who speaks out about her child with cancer? Should we not celebrate recoveries and mourn losses for children with mental illness in the same way that we do for children affected with physical disease?

## FIGHTING STIGMA

The more I think about the many-headed hydra of children's mental health, the more convinced I become that the only way to slay the monster is to attack stigma head-on. I came to that conclusion after I realized that I had been self-stigmatizing for several years, hiding my struggles from all but my closest friends and family. Like most people who write about mental illness, I blogged anonymously. I only found the courage to write about my son after discovering the advocacy group Bring Change 2 Mind, founded by the actress Glenn Close, whose sister Jessie has bipolar disorder. Bring Change 2 Mind's chief mission is to eliminate stigma by sharing stories of real people, people who are our neighbors, our coworkers, our friends, our parents, and our children.

This story-centered approach was pioneered by Ann Kirkwood, one of the foremost national experts on stigma and someone who happens to live in my community. Ann, a senior researcher with Idaho State University, won a 2000 Peabody Award with Idaho Public Television producer Marcia Franklin for their antistigma documentary "Hearts and Minds," part of an Idaho Department of Health and Welfare campaign designed to educate teens about mental illness. Ann has also been recognized by NAMI, the most prominent mental illness advocacy group in the United States. She "came out" about her own illness in a very public way when she testified to the Idaho state legislature about her personal experiences living with bipolar disorder.

I interviewed Ann about her experiences with stigma, mental illness, and advocacy in her office at the Meridian campus of Idaho State University. Ann grew up in Olympia, Washington. She remembers experiencing anxiety as early as age twelve, when her father was diagnosed with cancer. "Back then, cancer was something you didn't talk about," she said. "It was as stigmatized as mental illness is today."

Ann was also suffering from depression but she lacked the language to describe her experience. Her "stiff upper lip" German and Scottish parents discouraged emotional conversations. "I was very confused about what was going on. I thought everyone looked at the world that way—it was my normal," Ann explained.

She was nineteen when her father finally passed away, and like many young people—I can relate, since I lost my own father to cancer at age twenty-two—she felt robbed. "My father never got to meet my daughters," Ann said. "When you lose a parent as a child, you are never done with them. You don't have that space where you are friends as adults."

Ann's mania began to manifest in college. She didn't sleep; she did "wild things." She viewed psychology as a "pseudoscience," so she never took a psychology class. The wonderful highs lasted until her daughter was born. Then things took a turn for the worse. "I had dark winters," Ann said. "We moved to Alaska—it is quite literally dark there. I didn't know what was happening to me. In the summers, I was up. My husband and I just normalized this behavior—winters were bad, summers were good."

In her late thirties, after years of sunny summers and dark, depressing winters, Ann was finally diagnosed with depression. But the medication didn't seem to work. Some pills made her manic, and some could not touch the depths of her sadness. When she was forty-three, she was finally diagnosed with bipolar disorder. "That was a lot of years of ignorance and suffering not knowing what was going on with me," she said. "I went through multiple medications, including seven antidepressants. I was suicidal many times. When I think about teenagers and how long even six months is to them—what would it be like for a child and their parents to go through medications that don't work again and again and again? So I asked myself, what can I do to help?"

Ann was in a unique position to help people with mental illness in Idaho. She was working at Idaho's Department of Health and Welfare in 1997, when she was finally diagnosed with bipolar disorder. Coincidentally, at that time the state was looking at ways to redesign the entire mental health care delivery system. Ann visited one of the state mental hospitals, in Orofino, where she had a life-changing conversation. "A gentleman in my group was a patient who came to the information-gathering meeting and said that something needed to be done about stigma because it was worse than the actual disease," she recalled.

Ann had already tested the waters with her own illness, telling her close friends about her diagnosis; to her surprise, reactions were mixed, but she found absolutely no support. "I had normalized the stigma from my peer group," she said. "And then I drove home from that meeting and thought, that man was so compelling. To think that stigma was worse than the disease—I thought, I care about this. I have a personal stake in it. What can I do?"

She did what she had always done: she decided to take action. In the late 1990s, Ann identified funding sources and produced one of the first mental illness antistigma campaigns in the United States, deciding to target middle-school-age children. As mentioned, *Hearts and Minds* won a George Foster Peabody Award, and Ann was also recognized with a NAMI Voice Award for her community leadership. "I decided to do all this because of that single interaction with one patient—a victim of stigma who was struggling to communicate and recover," Ann said. "I thought we needed to involve consumers and families in designing our campaign. I wanted consumers and family members at the table. We pulled together a group of people and based the campaign on the lived experiences of people with mental illness and their families. Their families suffer deeply and acutely."

Ann and her team again decided to look at middle school as a good place to begin an antistigma education campaign. The Red Flags program (now called Better Todays) was designed to train adult gatekeepers and caregivers about the signs of mental illness in children so that they could provide appropriate early interventions. This one-day training seminar also received national recognition. Idaho State University has trained twelve thousand Idahoans to date. "I think we have made a real difference," Ann said. "People—especially young people—are on the cusp of change. If you try to change the minds of people with entrenched stigma and prejudice, it's so much harder. The premise of my program has been that regardless of the public mental health system, we can all make a difference one-on-one with a child. That one child you have a relationship with may be the kid you save."

Ann sees the stigma that people with mental illness face daily as nothing less than a civil rights issue. "People with physical disabilities know that," she said. "They have used the civil rights model since the seventies." She also thinks the current emphasis on recovery within a medical model is a good direction for patients and their families.

"Mental illness is something you live with every day," Ann said. "They call me high functioning. But it's not a competition. Every person has his or her own challenges."

Ann's personal experience with stigma began in earnest when she very publicly announced her illness to her community. "I came out at the legislature, where I testified on behalf of parity for state employee health insurance. I was trembling, my voice was cracking, but I did it. I was working in the director's office at Health and Welfare at that time, so all these legislators knew me personally."

After testifying, Ann walked back from the capitol building to her office. The news of her illness made it back to her department before she did. "Someone was going around asking my staff what it was like to work for me" she said with a laugh. "That was my first 'hit you in the face' encounter with stigma. I kept thinking of that gentleman in Orofino and how he couldn't speak for himself. I can speak. I have a duty to speak out for those who can't. With that baptism, I decided to tell everyone and let them make their own judgments. What I want people to know about me is that I have a meaningful career. I am involved in my community. I have been married thirty-eight years and have two wonderful self-sufficient daughters and a little wire-haired fox terrier. That's me. The mental illness is not me. What do people with mental illness look like? They look like me."

Ann works tirelessly in her community to combat stigma, especially for mothers of children with mental illness, who, she says, too often engage in self-stigma. "It's moms who really take the hit," she said. "I know too many mothers who have been fired from their jobs because they have to run to school two or three times a day, and they have other children to care for as well. It's no wonder they are on edge! Moms are reacting as best they can. I have great admiration for parents, and I know the stress on marriages. Blame gets us nowhere."

Ann researches mental illness in rural populations and knows the special challenges those communities face. "One of the things we know is that stigma is worse in rural areas. Part of that is a lack of access to care. People get really sick. Mental health problems are visible through behavior which we label as bad and label as a choice, so it becomes visible, people judge it, and stigma is worse because people can't get care. In most rural areas, people pride themselves on being self-reliant and are reluctant to ask for help."

She is also frustrated by the stigma associated with the criminalization of mental illness, even in children. "Right now, it's the only way to get help with your child. You don't want to see your child driven away in a cop car. We need an alternative. We need it all across the country. One mom from a small town told me that her daughter who has mental illness broke her arm. The local hospital refused to treat the girl's broken arm because they said they couldn't handle mental health issues. These are real stories and real parents," she said.

"We can't stop working on the problem of stigma. As parents, we have to work every day to counter the cultural images so our children learn the truth. We have to inform ourselves, and we have to educate our children. It is going to take hard work for those of us who have mental illness in our families."

## WHAT IS NORMAL?

At the root of stigma is that existential problem of self and other. In the brain-versus-soul debate that never seems to go out of style, right now the Thomas Insels of the world, with their search for biomarkers and blood tests, seem to be dominating the narrative, and maybe that's a good thing. If the brain is just another organ (so goes the thinking), then there is really no distinction between "mental" and "physical" other than the stigma we attach to the former.

As a single mother of four children, my greatest regret is that I cannot give my children what my own parents gave me: a happy childhood. Here's one of the hard truths about mental illness that Michael and I often discuss: by accepting treatment, you lose more than a bit of self. Some people don't want to become "other" to themselves: I'll freely admit that as a writer, I like to wallow occasionally in existential angst or to entertain monsters. I don't want to end up like David Foster Wallace, but I sure as hell want to write like him. There are trade-offs, sacrifices.

The question of what is "normal," with the infinite variety of genetic expression and personality shaped by experience, is a complicated one. The fear behind taking self-altering medication is also its siren lure; we don't want to lose ourselves, but we paradoxically want to live life without psychic pain. I think of *soma* and Huxley's Brave New World—take a pill and stop feeling. This is the kind of "there's a pill for that" mentality that psychiatrist Allen Frances attacks in *Saving Normal: An Insider's Revolt against Out-of-Control Psychiatric Diagnosis, DSM-5, Big Pharma, and the Medicalization of Ordinary Life*. "We should not be making patients of people who are basically normal and ignoring those who are really sick," he writes. "As we drift ever more toward the wholesale medicalization of normality, we lose touch with our strong self-healing capacities—forgetting that most problems are not sickness and that only rarely is popping a pill the best solution."

I asked Ann Kirkwood what it felt like to give up her mania, to manage her chronic bipolar disorder on medication. What she told me gave me some insight into what's "normal" for people with a mental illness, and what they lose—and gain—through medication:

> I really struggle with how to describe what psychotropic medications do to you. Your whole world-vision changes. You are a different person, and you miss the old you. As dysfunctional as it was, you were used to it. You had found some comfortable place with it. When you start on psychotropic medications,

you've lost something. There is a period of mourning. It was hard enough for me as an adult—what about children? When people wonder why people with mental illness aren't adherent [to their medication], I understand. Maybe I was tempted to be the "Ann who was Ann" all those years. Sometimes I would say to myself, when the kids are out of the home, I will go off all my meds. But I'm still on my meds.

It took me a while. But I realized I was still me. I was a happier me. People around me were happier with me. And life was good.

When you have bipolar disorder, you are in your head all the time, ruminating on what's going on inside you, so you don't experience the beauty of the world around you. I looked up, and it was like I had seen a sunset for the first time in my life. That was the moment I realized treatment works.

I asked Michael the same question in my June 2013 StoryCorps interview with him. "Would you want to be cured, or would you feel like you were a different person?" I said. His response was emphatically positive: "If I'm different and don't have to deal with these stupid rages, then I'd rather be cured, because I'm done."

"I feel powerful, like I have control, and yet I don't," he said, describing the episodes of rage. He does not like to feel that way; it frightens him. Still, I think that Allen Frances and others who decry the increased use of psychotropic medications have a valid point in many cases, perhaps because mental illness is not one monolithic disease with a simple one-size-fits-all treatment. Many emotional disturbances are temporary or situational. How do I stay "normal"? The way Frances wants me—and all the people who are diagnosed with everything from anxiety to depression to attention deficit disorder—to stay normal. I take long walks and practice yoga. I read Marcus Aurelius and work out my fears in flash fiction. And these things work for me (most of the time).

But these things do not work for my son. They do not work for millions of other children and families. My fear about Allen Frances's view (and before him Thomas Szasz, who denied the existence of mental illness altogether) is the same fear I have about religion: that we tell people it's their duty to be well, to be sane, to be normal. If they aren't, if they can't be, then it's some personal failing on their part, something within their locus of control—they are in effect "choosing" to have mental illness.

Where does that line of reasoning end? It ends with cognitive dissonance and self-stigmatization. It ends with alcoholism and addiction. It ends, too often, with suicide.

## THE PERFECT STIGMA STORM

Sometimes the relentless pressures of religion and motherhood coalesce in a perfect storm. When I first encountered the story that starts this chapter, Pam Kazmaier's 2005 essay "Losing My Mind, Bit by Bit," which describes her suicide pact with her then-thirteen-year-old son, I could not believe what I was reading. At the same time, it made more sense to me than it should have. Pam joined the Mormon church in 1985, a few years after relocating to Mesa, Arizona, a community with a large population of Latter-day Saints. Driven by relentless pressure to be perfect, she threw herself into every church calling, quit her job as a nurse to have babies and do church work, and became obsessed with genealogy—as a convert, she had plenty of ancestors to save through baptisms for the dead.

Pam's younger son, Zack, had troubles from birth. He was developmentally delayed and had juvenile bipolar disorder. Pam also had bipolar disorder, which was exacerbated by the stresses of family and church life. "I was enduring to the end. I was hoping the end was soon because this pace was killing me," she wrote. Zack also wanted to die, telling his doctor, "I want to hang myself." Despite his obvious slide, Pam couldn't find a hospital that would take her son.

One Sunday after sacrament meeting, Zack said, "Mom, let's kill ourselves!" Pam wrote about what happened next:

I felt it was my duty as a mother, since I had failed every which way here on earth to help Zack, to go with him to the other side. Neither Zack nor I would ever get better. If Zack was finally going to kill himself, I must somehow get over there, too. A few years earlier, my brother's son, Charlie, had killed himself with a gun. I always felt so badly that he died alone. His death was something our family still hadn't come to grips with. I didn't want to kill Zack, or myself, but I wanted Zack to feel relief. I didn't have the hand-eye coordination and thinking ability to effectively see my way to accomplish it. I didn't have the ability, at the time, to get us to the other side. Maybe we could just sleep. I told him we could take our meds. We could take a little extra.

Pam and Zack survived their suicide attempt. But Pam was discharged from her two-week stay in a psychiatric hospital to the custody of the Arizona police, charged with second-degree child abuse, a felony with a mandatory fifteen-year prison sentence that would keep her from ever seeing her children again. She pled guilty to a lesser charge and served ten years' probation. Pam's own struggles with mental illness have improved since this horrific experience. She left the Mormon church, found meaningful work, and has learned to set better boundaries and take better care of herself. Today her son is an adult who still lives at home.

Every time there's a mass shooting, the experts wring their hands and ask why. More often than not, the easy answer is to blame the mother. But when there are no community resources, when every institution throws up barricades to care, when every message you hear is one of stigma and shame, what can a mother do? The rest of this book will explore the institutions and systems that parents of one in five American children must navigate. There are effective interventions and treatments. But before you can find a treatment, you have to be able to talk about the problem.

# THREE

# SCIENCE

## WHAT CAUSES MENTAL ILLNESS IN CHILDREN, AND WHY ARE THE RATES INCREASING?

> For thousands of generations people lived and repro-
> duced with no need to know how the machinery of the
> brain works. . . . That is why even today people know
> more about their automobiles than they do about their
> own minds.
>
> —Edward O. Wilson, *Consilience*

In July 2013, Amy G. (not her real name) a slender, lovely mother of seven children, traveled almost three thousand miles from her home in rural Idaho to New York City. Unable to get the health care she needed in her home community, she was seeking a definitive diagnosis for her seven-year-old daughter Emma (not her real name) at Child Mind Institute. "When the doctor told me that Emma had conduct disorder (CD), and that there was no cure, it was like a death sentence," Amy told me. "I know it's awful to think this, let alone to say it out loud, but I actually wished for a minute that he had told me my daughter had cancer instead. At least if it's cancer, you can talk about it. People feel sorry for you. My daughter may never have feelings. For her, it's all about things. I'll proba-bly never have a warm fuzzy parenting experience with her. It's a huge sense of loss."

While most parents' goals for their children include college, career, and family, Amy and her husband, Robert, a family practice physician in the close-knit small town where they have chosen to raise their seven children, just hope they can keep Emma out of jail and protect their family and community from harm. Conduct disorder is the most serious behavioral and emotional diagnosis a child can have, and for that reason, psychiatrists don't assign it lightly. Since all children and adolescents act out from time to time, the diagnosis of conduct disorder depends on persistent and unemotional callous disregard for others, including multiple acts of aggression, property destruction, lying and stealing, and serious, repetitive rule breaking.

In many ways, conduct disorder is the perfect storm of mental illness in children. Risk factors include genetic predisposition, parental substance abuse, childhood trauma, and the existence of other mental disorders. Poverty is also a risk factor, with as many as 35 percent of preschool children from low-income homes exhibiting symptoms of oppositional defiant disorder (ODD) or conduct disorder (CD), compared to just 4–6 percent of young children in the general population. Children with a CD diagnosis who continue their antisocial behavior into adulthood are diagnosed with antisocial personality disorder, though the more popular term is "psychopath," a word that conjures up images of Ted Bundy rather than Amy's daughter, a beautiful, dark-haired little girl with bright eyes and a quick smile. As with any disorder, the sooner it is diagnosed, the greater the chance the condition can be managed. But there is no medication to treat conduct disorder, and there are no guarantees that therapy will be effective.

Children with conduct disorder are not just "bad kids"; evidence suggests that their brains actually function differently than those of healthy children. In a 2004 study, brain scans of children diagnosed with CD revealed that right temporal lobe and right temporal gray matter was "significantly reduced" in the brains of children with early-onset CD when compared to healthy children. The amygdalae (named for their almond shape) of both children and adults with CD are also smaller in overall size. Since the amygdala plays a role in the "fight-or-flight" response in normal brains, it makes sense that children with CD, who generally lack fear, would have abnormal amygdalae. This lack of fear and a corresponding lack of empathy in children with CD can be very dangerous to others, as Amy and her family know firsthand.

In a private blog, Amy described the events that led to their painful decision to send Emma to residential treatment:

> Despite everything we were doing, her behavior continued to escalate. Emma began talking regularly about wanting to kill our entire family and even tried to choke [infant] Mary. She had an appointment with a psychologist last Monday to begin outpatient therapy. After visiting with her for about forty-five minutes he called us into the office while she waited outside. She had told him all about her plans and what she had done to Mary without a single bit of remorse. He told us that he was very concerned about not only her behaviors, but her lack of conscience and the ease with which she shared everything with him. He did not feel that outpatient therapy was going to be beneficial . . . he recommended residential care in order to get her the immediate and consistent help that she needed and to protect the rest of our children.

That very night, Emma attacked Mary again while the baby slept in her crib. Amy and Robert made the gut-wrenching decision to send their daughter away for therapeutic residential care. After several months apart, Amy was able to take her daughter to New York to see a specialist, something beyond the reach of most rural families. In many ways, the CD diagnosis confirmed what Amy and her husband already suspected. "We live in a small town," she said. "We developed a safety plan with the local police. It wasn't like this was something we could hide." The stigma that attaches to mental illness can be especially pernicious in small, rural communities, where both knowledge about and access to quality mental health care are limited. Amy and Robert's seven children range in age from eighteen months to ten years. Their oldest son, Tyler, was diagnosed with Asperger's syndrome a few years ago; another daughter has a learning disability and sensory integration issues. Emma and her older sister were adopted when Emma was just two years old; the girls share a biological mother.

At this writing, Emma continues to live in a residential treatment facility; ODD and CD are the most common disorders for children referred to both outpatient and residential mental health care. Amy wants to bring her daughter home—but she worries about the potentially devastating consequences. "I'm afraid that if I bring her back to live with us, Child Protective Services will launch an investigation," she says. "There's always the fear in the back of our minds that they might take our other children."

Though accepting her daughter's diagnosis is difficult, for Amy, visiting Child Mind Institute put her own mind at rest. "Ever since this started, I've been asking why. Why, God? Why me? Why is my daughter like this? They told me I was a good mother, that I had done everything right," she said. "This wasn't my fault. I'm not the reason this happened."

## No Easy Answers

Whenever mothers of children with mental disorders get together, whether it's in the waiting room of the occupational therapist's office, on a Facebook support group, or at a playground date, the conversation inevitably turns to a single question: why. "Have you tried eliminating gluten from her diet?" "Did you see the article about air pollution and autism?" "I heard that terbutaline causes developmental disabilities." "Did the biological mother abuse alcohol during pregnancy?"

Amy's situation illustrates just how difficult medical care is for parents of children with mental illness. Both the causes and the diagnoses are elusive, and for families in rural communities, even obtaining access to mental health treatment is nearly impossible, in part because of the problem of stigma. Amy believes that her adopted daughter's conduct disorder is caused by genetics, something completely beyond her control. But she worries about how her own mothering might have affected her biological son Tyler. "I read a study a few days ago linking a higher incidence of autism to mothers who had their labor induced, especially with boys," she said. "I induced labor with all three of my boys. You know how it is." She shrugged. "It's so easy to blame ourselves."

Blame is sometimes the easiest answer when we ask ourselves for the causes of things we don't understand. The search for answers to the etiology of mental illness has a long history. In antiquity, mental illness was not segregated from physical illness as it is today. Fourth-century-BCE physician Hippocrates was perhaps the earliest proponent of the "chemical imbalance" theory of mental illness that has achieved widespread popular support today, perhaps still too simplistically, to explain what causes schizophrenia or bipolar disorder or depression. Hippocrates described mental disorders in simple terms of an imbalance of humors—if a person felt sad, or "melancholy," for example, that person had an excess of black bile (*melancholos*). Bringing the humors back into balance would "cure" the condition.

Galen, the second-century-CE physician, also stressed equilibrium of the four humors, but he added the insight that emotion can play a role in mental conditions, as when he described a young woman with insomnia whose pulse only raced when he mentioned a certain dancer's name (psychiatrists would probably diagnose her with depression today): "I came to the conclusion that she was suffering from a melancholy dependent on black bile, or else trouble about something she was unwilling to confess." Both Galen and Hippocrates influenced medical thinking about mental illness during the Middle Ages. Though our understanding of medical science has greatly advanced, their insights remain relevant to our modern understanding of mental disorders; the terminology is different, but we're still looking for "out-of-balance" humors.

## THE QUEST FOR BIOMARKERS

By now, most people are familiar with the "chemical imbalance" model advocated by NAMI and others, where mental illness is seen as a simple lack of the right chemicals (e.g., serotonin or dopamine) in the brain, just as diabetes is a simple chemical deficiency (insulin) of the pancreas. Using reasoning that would not feel unfamiliar to medieval physicians, pharmaceutical companies design drugs to correct this supposed imbalance, which is clinically diagnosed by patient-reported symptoms that define the disorder. But any mother of a child with mental illness knows it's not that simple—you can't just take a pill and fix everything. Science is now shifting from this "chemical imbalance" model to one that focuses on the complex interplay between genetics, parenting, and environment.

In the new biopsychosocial model, mental illness is a hardware problem, or more correctly, a hardwiring problem. In 2013, just prior to the much-anticipated release of the *DSM-5*, the National Institute of Mental Health very publically parted ways with the American Psychiatric Association and declared a new emphasis on biomarkers as a means of positively identifying mental illness. In his blog post explaining this decision, NIMH director Thomas Insel wrote: "NIMH will be re-orienting its research away from DSM categories. Going forward, we will be supporting research projects that look across current categories—or sub-divide current categories—to begin to develop a better system."

This is what Insel means by biomarkers—simple, quantitative tests for mental illness, similar to those we have for physical illness. For Amy's daughter Emma and other children, diagnosis would be confirmed not by symptoms alone, but by hard, measurable physiological proof. Early research suggests that for some conditions, such biomarker tests are already possible: a 2009 study on schizophrenia showed that children who have blood relatives with the disease exhibit differences on MRI scans during cognitive tasks. And a 2013 *Scientific American* article introduced a computer program that can reliably distinguish between two conditions when reading brain scans, which would be hugely beneficial if mental illness were not full of complex comorbidities. For example, 70 percent of children diagnosed with autism also have another mental disorder, and 50 percent of people with schizophrenia also suffer from depression. Many children with CD also have ADHD or another mental disorder. In fact, the *Scientific American* study may actually reveal the inadequacies of our current diagnostic system, as Insel argues when he advocates for NIMH's new Research Domain Criteria (RDoC).

Dr. Michael Milham works on the furthest edges of neuroimaging to identify mental disorders. He has pulled together thousands of brain scans to try to map what ADHD looks like in the brain. Milham balances his research with clinical work, because working with patients enables him to put into practice the insights he observes in the lab. "With neuroimaging, the goal is to understand what is going on—to see what's behind brain disorders like ADHD so that we can remediate or even reverse those conditions," he told me in a telephone interview. "Another goal is to try to come up with clinically relevant tools to improve diagnosis."

Although doctors don't need a brain scan to diagnose garden-variety ADHD, Milham believes that imaging will play a role in increasing the accuracy of diagnosis, especially when there are comorbid conditions, and helping doctors to select appropriate treatments. "This could make psychiatry like any other part of the medical profession," he said. "Right now, we're the only one without objective tools to guide us."

What do the brain scans reveal? Originally, scientists were looking for one brain region that could be implicated in ADHD or other disorders. Instead, as they sifted through thousands of brain scans, they found the same problems with neural networks occurring over and over. "That's why it's so complex," he said. "You aren't going to find that 'aha!' region. You need to think about networks and interactions."

Milham envisions a future in which a child who visits a psychiatrist will have an experience similar to a patient who visits a primary care provider complaining of a common cold. "If it's just a cold, you won't need specialized tests," he said. "But when there is a lack of clarity to help guide the treatment, a brain image might be ordered." He believes that today's pricey and complicated MRIs will lead to cheaper and simpler EEG (electroen-cephalograph) tests, which can be administered and read right in the clinician's office. "When you have an infection, we check blood cell counts," he noted. "It can be the same thing in psychiatry. We won't have to rely solely on the patient's symptom reports. We can follow objective data."

Objective data will prove especially useful when communication is compromised, as it often is in patients with developmental disorders like autism. But Milham cautions that brain scans are still in their infancy as a diagnostic tool. "The knowledge will build over the next few decades, but some people are prematurely using tools and claiming to already be there," he said.

## In Search of a Diagnosis

Milham's quest for reliable physiological diagnostic tests does not seem unreasonable. If your child had a persistent stomachache, you would expect your doctor to be able to diagnose the condition with a high degree of certainty in a fairly short period of time. It could be something simple, like gastroenteritis or gluten intolerance. Or it could be something much more serious, like appendicitis or a tumor. Either way, your physician would order blood tests or urine tests, measure heart rate and temperature, and perhaps require some more expensive procedures. Within the space of hours, days, or, worst-case scenario, weeks, you would know what you and your child were facing. You'd have a treatment plan that would lead to a cure, or at least a predictable outcome.

Right now, it's not like that when your child has a mental disorder. Your first point of contact—your child's pediatrician—may not know how to recognize early signs, which is especially problematic because early intervention is critical to successful outcomes. In Michael's case, I noticed something was different fairly early on. "Why does he always bang his head against the wall?" I asked. "Why does he make noises to himself? Why does he scream when I run the vacuum cleaner? Why does he crawl funny?"

I got a response that I would come to expect over the next few years. "Oh, that's normal," my pediatrician said, looking at his chart to note that Michael had hit all his milestones on time. "He'll grow out of it. He's just a boy. That's what they do."

When as a preschooler, his rages would last for several hours, she recommended that I clear his room of all sharp-cornered furniture and install a lock on the outside of the door. "You can just lock him in his room until he calms down," she said. I was by no means an expert—what new mother is? —but this did not seem like particularly sound medical advice to me.

Once the signs that something is not normal become unmistakable (usually during the early school years), parents are referred to a bevy of specialists who use a seemingly infinite variety of qualitative instruments to measure things like functioning and behavior and mood. In the course of my son's treatment, we have completed the Autism Diagnostic Observation Schedule (ADOS), the Child and Adolescent Functional Assessment Scale (CAFAS), the Sensory Integration and Praxis Test (SIPT), the Yale-Brown Obsessive Compulsive Disorder Scale (Y-BOCS), the Overt Aggression Scale (OAS), and many more instruments designed to diagnose his condition based on symptom and behavior reports from the child, parents, teachers, and health care providers. Often these experts and their tests disagree or provide conflicting information. Often the medications and therapies the experts prescribe do not work. Your child is suffering, and you can't do anything about it. There are few worse experiences in life than that.

What we do know is this: mental illness manifests from a complex cocktail of genetic predisposition, environmental factors, and family dynamics. Twins studies and multigenerational studies have unequivocally demonstrated genetic connections; recent research has also focused on de novo (spontaneous, not inherited) mutations on certain genes which may indicate a genetic predisposition for autism, schizophrenia, or bipolar disorder. Suicide, depression, and substance abuse also tend to run in families—though how much is attributable to nature and how much to nurture is still a hotly debated topic.

Not surprisingly, maternal depression is a significant risk factor for mental illness in children, as are poor parenting skills. The stress and stigma of poverty may also trigger the expression of children's mental illness in a population most at risk for stigma and least able to access care.

In their book on the sociology of mental illness, Anne Rogers and David Pilgrim note that "a fundamental problem with the illness framework in psychiatry is that it deals, in the main, with symptoms, not signs." Diagnosis depends on the patient's communication, which, as we noted above, presents special challenges for children with autism spectrum disorders for whom communication is likely compromised. And yet, many physical ailments are also etiologically confusing: why do people have lupus or multiple sclerosis? Or, to draw a closer analogy, because both conditions attach to significant stigma, what causes obesity?

## IT'S IN OUR GENES

"The fault, dear Brutus, is not in our stars, / But in ourselves, that we are underlings." For mental illness (and for obesity, and a whole host of other biological complaints), Cassius's assignment of blame in Shakespeare's *Julius Caesar* holds true at the genetic level. The connection between heredity and mental disorders is well established and better understood every day. More than half of all identical twins share autism, while less than 10 percent of fraternal twins do, strongly suggesting a genetic causation. Similarly, science has shown that schizophrenia and bipolar disorder may actually be different manifestations of illness with a single genetic coding locus of error. As one 2009 study noted, "Heritability for schizophrenia and bipolar disorder was 64% and 59%, respectively. . . . [S]chizophrenia and bipolar disorder partly share a common genetic cause. These results challenge the current nosological dichotomy between schizophrenia and bipolar disorder, and are consistent with a reappraisal of these disorders as distinct diagnostic entities." Nosology is simply the study of disease—in this case, our reliance on symptoms rather than biomarkers in the diagnosis of schizophrenia and bipolar disorder may have caused us to create a false distinction for what is actually a single illness.

With dramatic and frightening increases in autism rates since its first identification as a discrete disorder in 1949, and with males affected at four times the rate of females, it seems natural for anyone who had a high school biology class to wonder whether the problem is linked to the X chromosome. Girls inherit two X chromosomes from their parents, meaning that X-linked recessive chromosomal disorders are less likely to affect them because they have a healthy copy of the gene that can express. Boys, on the other hand, get only one shot at a healthy X chromosome. Although researchers who looked at the X chromosome failed to find anything that could be implicated in autism, one study noted that imprinted X-linked genes, which are only expressed on the X chromosome inherited from the father, are in fact correlated with autism. The paternal X-chromosome genetic connection was further strengthened by a much-publicized 2010 study reported in *Nature* linking older fathers to higher rates of autism in offspring—children of fathers older than fifty were more than two times as likely to have autism spectrum disorders compared to children of fathers under age thirty. Yet fathers have escaped the "Refrigerator Father" assignment of blame that mothers continue to experience.

Though boys are disproportionately affected by autism, girls have it, too: Kim Stagliano, an intrepid mother of *three* daughters diagnosed with autism, shares her adventures as an autism mom in a memoir that is equal parts comedy, epic, and tragedy. Describing how one of her daughters nearly flooded the entire house one afternoon, she notes that "an autism mom has more badges than an Eagle Scout, and more household hints than Heloise herself."

In 2013, diagnostic tools are already able to discover the root genetic cause of autism in as many as 30–40 percent of affected children. The most common test is chromosomal microarray (CMA), which scans for copy number variant—what we would think of as a genetic mutation—in the child's DNA. Autism spectrum disorder "hot spots" have been identified for these variants; patients with schizophrenia and bipolar disorder, which overlap in many respects when the implicated genes are examined, also show distinct differences in key areas of the human genome.

An entire chromosome may also be to blame: for example, as many as 20 percent of males with fragile X syndrome, a chromosomal abnormality, meet the diagnostic criteria for autism. Interestingly, unlike autism, schizophrenia affects men and women equally, and bipolar I disorder (characterized by at least one manic episode) seems slightly more prevalent in women, though with later onset of first symptoms in women than in men.

How are these genes expressed in the first place? Our DNA has an elegant "on/off" switch mechanism called methylation, a biochemical process that determines whether or not a gene is expressed. In healthy people, methylation works to suppress "bad" genes and express "good" ones. When something goes wrong with the methylation process, cancer or other diseases including neurological disorders may result. For this reason, methylation shows promise as a possible biomarker for disorders like autism—irregularities in DNA methylation can be observed and might help to confirm the presence of the disorder. Exactly how methylation works—and why it sometimes doesn't—is still not completely understood, though diet and environment, including the prenatal environment in the mother's womb, seem to play a role in healthy gene expression.

In 2010, researchers exploring genetic mutations on the human genome concluded that "individually rare mutations, many de novo and others a few generations old, may be collectively responsible for a substantial portion of mental illness." This study noted similar classes of genetic mutations for individuals suffering not only from schizophrenia but also from autism and developmental disorders, suggesting that these disorders may all be related to problems in the same area of the human genome. But these mutations, though grouped on the same genes, are often de novo, or new, mutations, not inherited traits, meaning that though the disorders have a tendency to run in families and can be inherited, the genetic problem may also be new and unique to the child—there might be no family history of mental illness.

Researchers' focus on the genome yields the promise that we may be able to develop epigenetic, or gene-specific, individually targeted treatments for mental illness. And yet, despite remarkable advances in genetics, it seems clear to most of us that we are more than just a twisted helix of nucleotides. We see people overcome their physical limitations all the time and rejoice in their triumph over the apparent limits of disability. The very same twins studies that demonstrate the heritable nature of mental illnesses also show that our outcomes are not predetermined by our genes, any more than our salvation is predetermined by God—the presence of a gene alone does not always mean a child will develop mental illness, even when an identical twin with the same gene does. We cannot choose the genes we are given, but we can choose within the constraints of that code that creates us to live the best life possible. Consider the lives of autism advocates like the remarkable "animal whisperer" Temple Grandin or mathematician and essayist Daniel Tammet, whose synesthesia enables him to experience numbers as colors and shapes. I hope for the same future for my own son, a future determined not by genes but by his rich imagination.

If, along with Amy G., I can keep my child out of jail.

## ENVIRONMENTAL FACTORS

Before we talk about the environment and its role in causing mental illness, we should address an ancient (in Moore's Law time) Internet myth of truly epic proportions: the purported link between autism and childhood vaccinations. The most vocal proponent of this causal theory is television personality, movie star, and parent Jenny McCarthy, and it's a classic case of mistaking correlation for causality at best—and a blatant misuse of the scientific method at worst.

In her defense, however, though the link between autism and vaccinations has not been substantiated by further studies, Jenny McCarthy may be on to something. It seems increasingly likely that environmental factors, including mercury emissions in air pollution, are playing a role in the rapid increase of autism. Chemicals in foods and household products are also likely culprits.

In 2008, one in eighty-eight children was diagnosed with an autism spectrum disorder. As of this writing, it's closer to one in fifty, though that number is still not accepted by the entire scientific community because it relies largely on parent reports. Also, it should be noted that it is difficult to compare current autism rates with historic rates, since the disorder was not historically measured consistently and with the same diagnostic criteria: before 2000, speech delays and mental retardation were often the markers used to track prevalence in a population, which would eliminate entire groups of children now understood to be on the autism spectrum.

When we consider environmental factors, the links between air pollution and autism are increasingly suggestive. A 2006 study in Texas correlated a 61 percent increase in autism rates and a 43 percent increase in special education student rates for each one thousand pounds of mercury-tainted emissions in a community. Another study of 383 children with autism spectrum disorders correlated the presence of the disorder at age eight with lifelong environmental exposure to methylene chloride, a ubiquitous clear liquid used in industrial manufacturing.

In fact, linking environmental pollution to mental illness is as old as Western civilization itself. Some scholars have posited that lead used in water pipes or as a food sweetener may have caused the ancient Romans to experience an outbreak of neurological symptoms. Now this neurotoxin, once a common ingredient in paint until it was banned in 1978, is associated with neurological disorders that disproportionately affect children in low-income homes where lead-based paint may still coat walls. For years the paint industry actually tried to blame uneducated parents for the health problems caused by lead paint. The well-established relationship between poor school performance and poverty may even have neurological underpinnings in high blood lead levels for lower-income students.

## PRENATAL AND PERINATAL CONDITIONS

External environmental factors aren't the whole story. Environmental effects on the developing brain actually begin while the fetus is in its mother's womb. For over forty years, researchers have examined the connections between neonatal care and autism. A meta-analysis found no single common cause, but noted that fetal or neonatal hypoxia (lack of oxygen) seemed to be a risk factor for the disorder. Maternal drug and alcohol use during pregnancy is irrefutably linked to developmental disabilities in offspring. Prenatal exposure to selective serotonin reuptake inhibitors (SSRIs), such as Zoloft, used to treat maternal depression, was correlated with an increased risk of autism in a 2011 study of twenty case children and fifty control children. One widely reported 2013 study suggests that inducing labor may increase a woman's risk of having a child with autism. And in a study of special interest to me personally, terbutaline (Brethine), an asthma medication used off-label to treat preterm labor contractions, may be associated with autism and other developmental disorders when administered in the third trimester.

Here's my own Jenny McCarthy moment: On a sunny Sunday morning in the spring of 2013, as I tried to ignore the sad news of the latest mass shooting—in Santa Monica, near my former home—I tunneled through the perpendicular worlds of Scholar.google.com (peer reviewed, fact based) and Google.com (popular, fear based). I was researching terbutaline, because nearly every mother of a child with developmental disabilities I talked with told me the same story: preterm labor in the third trimester, treated with a little white pill.

In 1999, I was one of those women. My contractions started after a long summer hike in my twenty-ninth week of Michael's pregnancy. At first I thought they were just strong Braxton Hicks, but when they wouldn't stop, I ended up in the emergency room. I was given an injection, hospitalized for a few days, and sent home on bed rest with a bottle of terbutaline.

What I remember most about the pills was the breathtakingly awful headaches and painful tremors they caused. I also remember feeling resentment toward the baby in my body, for making me endure so much pain. In the end, he was born on his due date—and he was the happiest, sweetest baby a mother could ask for.

And now, thirteen years later, Michael is still happy and sweet—except when he isn't. He can't tie his shoes or remember to brush his teeth. He walks with an awkward gait and has serious sensory integration issues. As I explained in chapter 1, he is almost certainly a spectrum child, and he has juvenile bipolar disorder—when confronted with this latest diagnosis, he rolled his eyes and said, "I'm bipolar until they decide I'm something else."

Which is where Ms. McCarthy comes in. I have a great deal of sympathy for Jenny McCarthy. As I said at the beginning of this chapter, any parent whose child is diagnosed with a life-changing condition, whether it's cancer or juvenile diabetes or conduct disorder or autism, wants to know why. What happened to cause this? Why did this happen to my child?

After her son was diagnosed with autism in 2005, McCarthy famously (or infamously) latched on to a 1998 *Lancet* study that incorrectly linked autism to vaccinations. That controversial study, which followed twelve children diagnosed with developmental disabilities, has now been retracted; there is no sound scientific evidence linking vaccinations, even those containing thimerosal, to autism. The repercussions in my own state, Idaho, have been severe, however, to the point where you routinely hear about whooping cough outbreaks because fewer children receive regular vaccinations, and our herd immunity is disappearing. A 2013 study of children in the United States found a dramatic increase in measles, another potentially deadly childhood disease that we thought we had eradicated. Let's hope polio isn't next.

Even though I have sympathy for McCarthy, I routinely assign the autism/vaccination controversy to my students as a critical thinking exercise in learning how easy it is to latch on to an "easy" but often wrong answer. As that wit H. L. Mencken famously said, "There is always a well-known solution to every human problem—neat, plausible, and wrong."

Mistaking correlation for causality is a symptom of the human condition, and I am not immune. So as I scoured Google Scholar for recent articles about terbutaline and autism, I had to ask myself: Was I pulling a Jenny McCarthy? Did I want this one thing to be the answer, to the exclusion of all other possible things? Did I need an easy answer, when none of the answers so far had been easy?

To be fair, the Food and Drug Administration (FDA) has taken recent studies linking terbutaline to possible developmental delays seriously, issuing a black box warning for the drug in 2011: "Terbutaline should not be used to stop or prevent premature labor in pregnant women, especially in women who are not in a hospital. Terbutaline has caused serious side effects . . . in newborns whose mothers took the medication to stop or prevent labor." And medical malpractice attorneys, already busy with Zoloft and birth defects, have begun to circle warily around terbutaline as well.

I find myself inevitably drawn to comparisons with thalidomide, the infamous 1960s drug prescribed off-label for morning sickness that caused thousands of teratogenic birth defects worldwide. Thalidomide was one of the first drugs to provide solid, irrefutable evidence that substances ingested by the mother can cross the placenta and cause harm to the developing fetus. If the link between terbutaline and autism is substantiated, then the comparison to thalidomide is an apt one; though the disabilities are less visible, they can be nearly as debilitating.

## DIET AND "GUT FEELINGS"

What if it's not prenatal exposure or environment? Maybe what we feed our children is making them—and us—unwell. I met Aspen Morrow at a community mental health resource fair hosted by my college for Children's Mental Health Week in May 2013. Morrow was accompanied by the youngest of her daughters, a bright-eyed, smiling, slightly shy four-year-old. As parents at mental health resource fairs are wont to do, Morrow and

I struck up a conversation about our children. Morrow is attractive, poised, and confident, a successful small business owner and mother who has written two books on medication-free management of chronic mental illness. Morrow suspects one or more of her children might meet the qualifications for a diagnosable mental disorder, but her children's teachers, friends, and physicians will never know it. "I finally looked up the diagnostic criteria on one of my children," Morrow told me. "I checked off fifty percent of them. My child was only four. I cried, and we immediately started on a stricter diet and micronutrients. Now my child is in normal classes with no behavior issues."

Morrow herself lives with bipolar disorder. She experienced her first psychotic break in 1998 when she was in college. "I was living in Japan, and I would have three months of mania followed by three months of intense, soul-crushing depression," she said. "I almost died. I couldn't leave my apartment." She was hospitalized when she returned to the States, diagnosed with bipolar I, and began treatment with Depakote. "Basically, my doctor told me that I had this chronic condition, that I could never live a normal life," she said.

A year later, the slender, energetic, high-achieving college student had gained sixty pounds, a common side effect of anticonvulsant medications like Depakote. Morrow fished out a colored photograph from her purse, showing an obese woman with a sad smile leaning away from an unsmiling man—her husband. "This is what medication did to me," she said. "Between bipolar and what the meds did to me, I nearly lost my marriage."

Ten years later, Morrow is still happily married—and medication free. She owns her own identity theft company, has three children, and is writing a self-help manual for people with bipolar disorder who want to live a med-free life. Like many people whose mental illness fails to respond to conventional treatments, or who experience side effects from medication that are almost worse than the illness itself, Morrow decided to search for alternative ways to manage her condition. A booming and unregulated industry now caters to patients who are seeking outside-the-box solutions for themselves and their children. Morrow started to question her doctors and conventional wisdom about bipolar disorder treatments when she stumbled on the work of Dr. Natasha Campbell-McBride, best known for the theory that most mental illness is caused by problems in the gut.

Campbell-McBride's GAPS (Gut and Psychology Syndrome) diet is typical of so-called elimination diets that offer hope to parents whose children have resisted diagnosis and do not respond well to medication. (Another popular elimination diet not yet conclusively supported by research is the gluten-free, casein-free [GFCF] diet.) Campbell-McBride developed her GAPS diet after working with Elaine Gottschall, the mother of a daughter with autism. Gotttschall claimed she had cured her own child using diet alone and described the diet in her book, *Breaking the Vicious Cycle*. Campbell-McBride's son was diagnosed with autism at age three. He followed the GAPS diet religiously and now is able to attend a mainstream school, according to Campbell-McBride's website.

But as Morrow is the first to admit, GAPS is incredibly hard to follow for children, especially for kids who are already finicky about the foods they eat. GAPS looks like a modified paleo diet, allowing eggs, fresh meat, fish, fruit, and vegetables, but restricting processed foods and refined sugars. A child on a GAPS diet will not be able to enjoy cake and ice cream at friends' birthday parties or hot dogs and s'mores on a camping trip. On Halloween she will only be able to treat herself to nuts, fruit, and yogurt.

Rather than following these stringent dietary restrictions to the letter, Morrow prefers to rely on nutritional supplements for her daughter, which she claims help her to manage her own condition as well. Morrow and her daughter also follow a modified GAPS diet in short spells, "when we need a gut reset." She now works as a distributor for one nutritional supplement company that targets mental health patients. "The only problems I have now are occasional racing thoughts and insomnia," she says. "But if I take away my therapy, I can be sick again in two weeks."

"Our understanding of mental illness is like what medicine's understanding of scurvy was two hundred fifty years ago," Morrow says. "I want people to understand that they can fully recover through natural means."

Morrow is far from alone in placing her hope for a cure on so-called natural supplements or special diets. But she admits that diet might not be the solution for everyone. And this is where I struggle with wholehearted acceptance of the views of Morrow and others like her. Their "evidence" feels largely anecdotal, in the "it worked for my kid; it should work for yours" spirit that often characterizes the med-free movement. And when I can't replicate their miraculous cures with my own child, I feel that uncomfortable emotion that too often plagues mothers of children with mental disorders: guilt. A 2013 viral blog post in which a mother "confessed" that she had caused her child's autism through vaccinations, antibiotics, and drinking Coca-Cola while pregnant is typical of the kinds of self-blame mothers experience. Describing her decision to give her son antibiotics, Mountain Mama wrote, "He had three different types of antibiotics in his system within eight days. This episode was the biggie. His gut was never the same after that. Nothing was."

The truth is that diet hasn't worked for Michael. To be fair, I haven't kept him on a strict GAPS or GFCF diet for two whole years, as Campbell-McBride recommends. But we generally avoid processed foods, aside from the occasional package of Red Vines to accompany a trip to the dollar theater. I buy and grow organic (Ed and I have our own compost pile), and I make my children's meals from fresh, natural ingredients. Like many children with mental illness, Michael exhibits preferences for bland, sugary carbohydrates, possibly because of sensitivity to environmental stimuli. As I mentioned before, his favorite ingestible—an often used behavioral carrot—is root beer. Who wants to deny their child an occasional soda?

I wonder sometimes if the diet solution isn't just another attempt at a "magic bullet," when the reality is that treating mental illness and mental disorders is a complex Rube Goldberg machine, involving not just the body but also the soul. And there are so many ways to make mothers feel guilty, just like thousands of parents who felt guilty when Jenny McCarthy pinpointed thimerosal in childhood vaccinations as the "cause" of her child's—and all children's—autism.

But scientific studies are increasingly providing support for the efficacy of special diets. For example, patients with bipolar disorder often have elevated levels of antibodies to casein, or cow milk protein, and may benefit from a lactose-free diet. Additionally, some studies suggest that omega-3 fatty acids found in fish oil and flaxseed oil could reduce severity of symptoms for children and adolescents with pediatric bipolar disorder. In any case, as more than one researcher has pointed out, eating a healthy diet may not help, but it certainly can't hurt children, which is more than can be said for some medications.

A recent UCLA study suggests that "gut feelings" may be exactly that—although the study's sample size was small, brain scans revealed clear differences in brain scans of women who consumed probiotic yogurt and women who did not, or who consumed a placebo: "the women consuming probiotics showed greater connectivity between a key brainstem region known as the periaqueductal grey and cognition-associated areas of the prefrontal cortex"—areas that affect positive mood. Though the connection is still not clearly understood, it seems that diet does indeed play a role in mental health.

## The Immune System: Our Own Worst Enemy?

It might be more than just what we eat—it might actually be who we are. We tend to think of the body's white blood cells as proverbial white knights, our valiant protectors in the face of invisible foreign invaders like viruses and bacteria. But a growing body of evidence suggests that the immune system itself may be partially to blame for a host of physical and mental ailments. Researchers are focusing on protein molecules called cytokines, named from the Greek words for "cell" and "movement." These molecules act as cell regulators or modulators—they're the equivalent of e-mails in the workplace, keeping the body humming along through a productive and efficient day. These essential proteins also appear to play a role in a variety of physical and mental disorders. When something goes wrong, cytokines contribute to inflammation and disease—think of people using the "reply all" feature to a mass e-mail.

Mental illness may actually be a manifestation of a nervous system under attack by our own immune systems, as antibodies attack the brain and interfere with development in children, or cause destruction in adult cells. Children with autism show an abnormal number of cytokines in the brain and cerebral spinal fluid, a "permanent state of brain immune disregulation" that may begin while the fetus is developing in the mother's womb. Cytokines also appear to play a role in bipolar disorder and schizophrenia. Because so many physical ailments affect people diagnosed with bipolar disorder, one researcher has suggested that bipolar disorder may actually be an inflammatory disease that affects the heart and other organs as well as the brain: "Comorbid medical illnesses in bipolar disorder might be viewed not only as the consequence of health behaviors and of psychotropic medications, but rather as an early manifestation of a multi-systemic disorder."

If you're the parent of a child with mental illness, google "PANDAS" and the first thing you'll probably see is not a cuddly black and white animal from China but the Wikipedia article on PANDAS: "Pediatric Autoimmune Neuropsychiatric Disorders Associated with Streptococcal Infections." This still controversial diagnosis posits that many children with sudden-onset obsessive-compulsive disorders (OCDs) and other tics like Tourette's syndrome are actually experiencing an autoimmune response related to a streptococcal infection—known to most mothers as the dreaded strep throat. A PANDAS diagnosis is especially controversial because of its timing: overprescribing of antibiotics to treat viral infections in children has led to the swift evolution of drug-resistant superbugs. But in 2013, a Google search on the terms "PANDAS" and "strep" yielded nearly one hundred thousand hits. The National Institute of Mental Health is actively pursuing research that explores the close correlation of sudden-onset OCDs and strep infections.

The focus on genes has come to include the almost romantic view that we are more than the sum of our parts. When I was a child, I completely immersed myself in the fantasy world of Newbery Medal–winning author Madeleine L'Engle, whose *Wrinkle in Time* trilogy provided a concrete framework for difficult intangible problems. The second book took its pro-tagonists to the microscopic cellular world to encounter sick and dying mitochondria, the energy factories that power our cells. L'Engle's image—that the microscopic bacterium and macroscopic host are linked together in a cosmic dance—is now playing out in research laboratories across the globe, as scientists discover the intricate chain of interdependence. There's a growing belief that people like Campbell-McBride with her GAPS diet may be on to something beyond diet alone: problems in the microbiome may result in allergies, gluten intolerance, autoimmune disorders, and even autism.

One of the most promising areas of research for physical health, the microbiome is the "undiscovered country" of microorganisms whose exis-tence is inextricably tied to our own. When scientists first started mapping the human genome, they expected to find more than one hundred thou-sand genes. To their surprise, the actual number was only twenty thousand or so, and humans share 60 percent of their genes with fruit flies. But sci-entists' experience with the microbiome has been exactly the opposite. In fact, there are ten times as many microbial cells as human cells in a typical human, meaning that 99 percent of the genes that form our bodies are actually microbial. Lita Proctor of the Human Microbiome Project told NPR in a 2013 interview that the microbiome could almost be understood as the eleventh organ system: "You have your lungs, you have your heart . . . you have your microbiome."

## Psychotropic Medications: A Cure Worse Than the Disease?

Medications aren't always a good thing. As we learn more about the mi-crobiome, we are realizing that broad-spectrum antibiotics often kill good gut bacteria along with bad ones, leading to a rapid increase in antibiotic-resistant bacteria. Similarly, one significant hurdle in the effective treat-ment of mental illness is the lack of effective medications. Journalist

Robert Whitaker has made the provocative argument in his book *Anatomy of an Epidemic* that psychotropic medications, especially atypical antipsychotics, are iatrogenic—that is, they actually *cause* the mental illness they are supposed to cure. For children, the "official" diagnosis itself is often dependent on finding a medication that actually works—a sort of "will it stick?" approach to treatment. It's a badly kept secret (and arguably, bad medicine) that your child's diagnosis may well depend on whether or not a medication alleviates symptoms.

When parents are unable to find answers, and when medications don't help children to manage their conditions, it's no wonder that mothers search for solutions outside of mainstream medicine, as Aspen Morrow did. Though I am not anti-med, I can understand where people like Morrow and *Anatomy of an Epidemic*'s Robert Whitaker are coming from. The medications prescribed for my son in the past five years could constitute their own pharmacopoeia—and all of them have serious side effects, as noted below:

**1. Abilify** (aripiprazole), the most popular atypical antipsychotic in 2013, is used for children with bipolar I disorder or schizophrenia, and with autism to manage irritability. As reported by the manufacturer, Otsuka Pharmaceuticals, most common side effects in children include "sleepiness, headache, vomiting, extrapyramidal disorder (for example, uncontrolled movement disorders or muscle disturbances such as restlessness, tremors and muscle stiffness), fatigue, increased appetite, insomnia, nausea, stuffy nose, and weight gain." In my son, the medication had to be discontinued rather quickly because he developed blurry vision, a reported and unpleasant side effect.

**2. Zyprexa** (olanzapine) is prescribed for adolescents with schizophrenia or bipolar I disorder. Side effects, as reported by Eli Lilly, include "sedation, weight increased, headache, increased appetite, dizziness, abdominal pain, pain in extremity, fatigue, dry mouth." My son was prescribed Zyprexa to manage oppositional defiant disorder when he was just ten years old. In one year, the medication caused severe weight gain (nearly thirty pounds) but produced no noticeable improvement in behavior or moods.

**3. Risperdal** (risperidone) is used to treat children aged five to sixteen for aggression and mood changes associated with autism; it is also prescribed for children ten and over with bipolar disorder. Side effects include anxiety, weight gain, dreaming more than usual, and sleep disruption. In boys, this drug can cause a condition called gyne-comastia, which causes them to grow breasts (as if adolescents with mental disorders aren't already subject to enough bullying!).

**4. Clonidine** is a medication used to treat high blood pressure. Like many medications, it is prescribed "off-label" for a variety of other conditions, including menstrual cramps, Tourette's syndrome, alcohol and opiate addictions, and, in children, ADHD. Side effects include headache, tiredness, nausea, and constipation—serious side effects include hives, swelling, and difficulty breathing.

**5. Celexa** (citalopram) is a selective serotonin reuptake inhibitor (SSRI) designed to alleviate depression, anxiety, and mood disorders. In 2007, the FDA requested that all SSRIs include the increased risk of suicidality for young people in a black box warning. In addition to increased suicidal thoughts, other side effects include diarrhea, weight loss, excessive tiredness, and dry mouth. It's not recommended that this drug be prescribed to children. Of all the drugs on this list, Celexa is the only one I've personally taken. I used it for a few months after my divorce, to enable me to function without feeling, a common complaint of people who take SSRIs. Sure, you don't feel sad anymore. You don't feel anything.

**6. Ritalin and Concerta** (methylphenidate) are prescribed for children and adults with ADHD/ADD. These medications are stimulants and can lead to dependence. They also lead to abuse: in his book on Ritalin as a reflection of our modern culture, physician Lawrence Diller notes that since 1990, there has been a 700 percent increase in Ritalin prescriptions. High-achieving moms, myself included, sometimes joke about stealing their kids' ADHD medication so that we can just get through a typically hectic day of proverbial juggled and dropped balls; for some moms (not me, of course), the joke may actually have some truth to it. Side effects of ADHD medications include sleep disruption, nervousness, loss of appetite, numbness or tingling in the extremities, and headaches.

7. **Trazodone** is used to treat depression and also may cause an increase in suicidal thoughts in children. Its nonserious side effects include headaches, confusion, decreased ability to concentrate, and nausea. Chest pain, shortness of breath, swelling of hands and feet, and a painful erection may all be signs of something seriously wrong.

8. **Intuniv** (guanfacine) is used to treat high blood pressure. In its slow-release form, it is also used for ADHD in children. Side effects include vomiting, nausea, constipation, tiredness, and stomach pain. Serious side effects include fainting, bradycardia (slow heart rate), blurred vision, and rash.

9. **Trileptal** (oxcarbazepine) is an anticonvulsant antiseizure medication used to treat epilepsy and other seizures. It is also used as a mood stabilizer for people with bipolar disorder. The list of side effects for this medication is too long and frightening to enumerate, affecting every major body system: the heart, the liver, the muscles, etc.

10. **Wellbutrin** (bupropion) is used for smoking cessation and to treat depression and the aptly named SAD (seasonal affective disorder). It can also be prescribed to treat the depressive episodes of bipolar disorder and is sometimes prescribed for ADHD. Like other antidepressants, it is linked to an increased suicide risk in children,

especially if doses are missed or if the medication is discontinued abruptly. Drowsiness, uncontrollable shaking, nausea, and excessive sweating are more benign side effects; seizures, hives, chest pain, difficulty breathing, and hallucinations are more serious.

**11. Lithium** is a chemical element used as an antimanic medication to control the manic episodes associated with bipolar disorder. In its ionic form, the salt from this silver-white alkali metal has become the gold standard by which all other bipolar medications are judged. The drug has been in use for more than fifty years now—one meta-study noted that "it remains the best studied drug for the prevention of relapse in bipolar patients." Lithium also has its place in popular culture—bands from Nirvana to Evanescence have used the drug to explore depression. Recent MRI scan studies have shown that lithium actually significantly increases gray matter volume in the brain for patients with bipolar disorder. Serious side effects can include kidney failure and even death.

But lithium is the first drug my son Michael has ever tried that has actually seemed to work for him. We saw no improvements at all with the so-called atypical or second-generation antipsychotics so frequently prescribed for children with behavioral and emotional disorders. Though his mood didn't improve, as noted above, Michael definitely gained weight. A 2011 study in JAMA: *The Journal of the American Medical Association* reported significant weight gain for children prescribed atypical antipsychotics such as Zyprexa, Risperdal, and Abilify. In this study, 10–36 percent of patients were overweight or obese after just eleven weeks of treatment. The authors concluded that "the benefits of second-generation antipsychotic medications must be balanced against their cardiometabolic risks through a careful assessment of the indications for their use, consideration of lower-risk alternatives, and proactive adverse effect monitoring and management."

Antipsychotics like Zyprexa, Risperdone, and Abilify are also the mainstays of treatment for schizophrenia. Though the drugs are effective in treating this condition when compared with placebos, as noted, they have severe side effects and have also been linked to brain tissue loss in animals and humans: "It is possible that, although antipsychotics relieve psychosis and its attendant suffering, these drugs may not arrest the pathophysiologic processes underlying schizophrenia and may even aggravate progressive brain tissue volume reductions." Scary stuff, especially when it's your child, and you don't know what the long-term side effects might be because the medications are not tested in children. Still, for many people suffering from serious mental illness, medication has provided a lifeline, saving them from the never-ending nightmare of psychosis. As one mother of a son with schizophrenia wrote to me, "Yoga and mindfulness have not stopped the course of this illness for even five minutes. Medical intervention has."

## POVERTY

When she was a teenager, my friend Mary E. (not her real name) trained to be a concert pianist—and she certainly had the talent to succeed. But her life took a different path: twenty years later, she subsists on welfare and disability checks, the single mother of three young boys whose father abandoned the family when she was pregnant with her youngest son. One hard day, Mary called me in tears. "I'm being evicted," she said. "The property managers got a report that Isaiah was selling his Ritalin pills to some teenagers."

At just eleven years old, her son Isaiah (not his real name) is already a drug dealer. His current diagnoses include oppositional defiant disorder and ADHD. He lies, he steals, he lights fires, he destroys property, and he flies into rages of truly epic proportions. When things came to a head in the summer of 2013, like many mothers, Mary had nowhere to turn. She called the police, but they refused to take Isaiah into custody because he was so young. "Call Health and Welfare," they said. She called Health and Welfare, where Isaiah already goes for Medicaid-supported mental health counseling. The wait list for additional services was prohibitively long. "Call Child Protection Services," Health and Welfare said, when Mary expressed fears for Isaiah's younger brother, who is sometimes the focal point of Isaiah's anger. Child Protection Services said, "Call us when he hurts someone."

Mary loves her boys. But now she faces the very real and frightening prospect of homelessness because of her son's behavioral problems. Holding down a job is difficult because she has to go to Isaiah's school so often. She cannot leave him alone with his younger brother. She feels trapped by a system with no solutions. Although he has not yet been diagnosed with conduct disorder, it is likely—and Mary knows it—that Isaiah will spend his life in prison. As I noted at the beginning of this chapter, as many as 35 percent of children from low-income homes are affected by conduct disorder or oppositional defiant disorder. In children, it seems heartbreakingly clear that the stress of poverty may actually trigger mental illness.

The emerging field of behavioral economics, or the science of happiness, has countered the proverbial wisdom that money cannot buy happiness. In fact, money can buy happiness, up to a point.

It's a chicken-and-egg question: mental illness is undeniably linked to poverty, but is it the cause or the effect? For children, the answer seems to be that in many cases, alleviating the stresses of living in poverty significantly reduces behavioral and emotional problems. In one innovative study, researchers compared Native American children before and after the opening of a casino on their reservation. For children whose families moved out of poverty, there was a significant decrease in psychiatric symptoms: "After the casino opened, the mean level of behavioral symptoms in children from ex-poor families was almost identical to that of never-poor children, and significantly lower than the mean for persistently poor children."

This means that curing many children's mental illness might be as simple as helping their families to escape poverty. As noted above, childhood poverty is correlated with an increased risk of mental illness. Learning how family poverty affects children's mental health is an essential piece of the mental illness puzzle and may help therapists to design more effective and earlier interventions for children and families.

Right now, though, poor children are usually "managed" by medication. It's not a secret at all that those nasty atypical antipsychotics, the descriptive term for second-generation antipsychotic medications like Abilify and Zyprexa, are disproportionately prescribed for children on Medicaid. A 2013 study put the number of Medicaid children on atypical antipsychotics at one in four. Some of these children are as young as two years old. Another study noted, "The expansion of antipsychotic use was most prominent among youths who were Medicaid eligible because of low family income (SCHIP) and reflects increased medication use for behavioral problems."

Socioeconomic status (SES) is a key indicator for mental health. In fact, neuroscientists have observed a cause-and-effect relationship—in both animals and humans—between socioeconomic status and neural development. The bad news is that lower SES negatively affects brain development. The good news is that at least some of these negative effects are reversible. Small changes in family income can have positive outcomes on children's mental health.

The research on neural development and poverty should play a key role in public health policy discussions at the state and national level. Our society loves to blame so-called welfare moms like Mary for their children's behavior. But Mary is doing the best she can with no resources and no support. When it all seems to be too much for her, she retreats to the only solace she has left: her piano. In a few months, she may not even have that modest comfort.

## PARENTING

As I noted in chapter 1, responses to my blog post revived a term that should have been left to languish in the 1950s: "Refrigerator Mother." The term references early expert opinions that autism reflected frigid or inattentive parenting. This view has since been widely refuted, and yet the role of parenting in children's mental illness cannot be dismissed, even though it is often inextricably knitted with genetics as a causal factor. As a young mother, I read Judith Rich Harris's controversial book, *The Nurture Assumption: Why Children Turn Out the Way They Do*, which challenged my cherished notions of parenting. As a Mormon, I had instinctively accepted the idea that "mothers are primarily responsible for the nurture of their children in the home," as the church's Proclamation on the Family states. Harris argues that in fact nurture is not the same thing as environment, and that peers are more likely to influence a child than parents: "The nurture assumption is not a truism; it is not even a universally acknowledged truth. It is a product of our culture—a cherished cultural myth."

There is also the luck factor. In a *Salon.com* essay exploring parents' moral responsibility for their children's actions, written six months after Newtown, philosopher Claire Creffield notes that "a host of chance events come together to make one imperfectly-parented child a killer and another imperfectly-parented child a well-adjusted adult." Nancy Lanza likely had the best of intentions in raising Adam. She certainly did not want him to kill a classroom full of first graders. Aspen Morrow, Mary E., Amy G., and I all want our children to grow up to become productive and happy members of society.

And yet, parents cannot be completely exonerated for their children's behavior. Numerous studies demonstrate that inconsistent or harsh discipline, as well as lack of parental involvement, has a negative impact on a child's emotional and behavioral development.

In rats, increased maternal licking of pups corresponds to improved ability to manage stress in adulthood. The rat mother-baby engagement may correspond to human maternal depression and its well-established link to emotional and behavioral problems in children; one 2013 study observed that "of the children of the chronically depressed mothers, 61 percent displayed axis I disorders, mainly anxiety and oppositional defiant disorder, compared with 15 percent of the children of nondepressed mothers." This study linked lower oxytocin levels in mothers, fathers, and children to the children's mental disorders. While a single gene in a depressed mother could predict whether her child develops a mental disorder, a simple treatment regimen of oxytocin could mitigate the gene's potential negative effects.

In the Sunday paper, the front-page story (right below the Santa Monica shooting) featured a local Boise boy headed off to UCLA at the age of fourteen—a bright, promising chess player with true gifts in math and science. The article credited the young man's parents—his father is a nationally ranked chess champion—with their son's extraordinary successes. My son Michael attended the same exclusive magnet school as this boy until he was asked to leave because his behavioral problems were too distracting to the other students.

I can't help but wonder: could that story have been about my son, if only I had refused to take terbutaline while pregnant? Or could that story have been about my son, if only I wasn't a single mother? And then I feel guilty for wondering—yet another example of self-stigma, just as Amy G. feels guilty for wishing her daughter had cancer instead of conduct disorder.

Simple answers are usually wrong. Genes, environment, nutrition, medication—all these must certainly play a role in developmental and mental disorders. But they don't determine the outcome of our lives. Michael still has choices and good options, which will only improve with ongoing research and changes in society's current understanding of mental illness and mental disorders.

Thalidomide babies were often born without limbs, or with phocomelia ("seal limbs"). But that very visible disability didn't stop Mat Fraser from becoming a drummer or Tony Melendez from playing the guitar (with his feet) or Thomas Quasthoff from singing his heart out. Michael's disability is less visible but no more deterministic. He, too, can be what he wants to be. The path just might be longer and more roundabout than I expected that summer morning, when my early-third-trimester hike triggered contractions that set my son's life—and my life—on this path.

# FOUR

# MENTAL HEALTH CARE

## HOW DO WE TREAT—AND MISTREAT—
## MENTAL ILLNESS IN CHILDREN?

> I wanted to tell her that if only something were wrong
> with my body it would be fine, I would rather have
> anything wrong with my body than something wrong
> with my head.
>
> —Sylvia Plath, *The Bell Jar*

On a sunny Tuesday morning in July 2013, I sat across from Michael on a commuter train bound from New York's Grand Central Station to Westport, Connecticut. We were about to experience what too few families of children with mental illness can afford: an appointment with one of the foremost experts in juvenile bipolar disorder. After my blog post went viral, Dr. Demitri Papolos, whose book *The Bipolar Child* sold more than two hundred thousand copies, reached out to me through his research assistant. "I think I know what's wrong with your son," he said in a January 2013 telephone conversation. "And I think I may be able to help."

Out of the many thousands of comments on my blog post, one common theme emerged: frustration with lack of access to high-quality—or even low-quality—mental health care. Parents everywhere identified with my experience: the multiple and incorrect diagnoses, the long waits for treatment, the lack of access to specialists, the encounters with police officers as first responders and juvenile detention centers as treatment facilities, and the untested medications with strange and worrisome side effects. "I live this," one mother wrote in response to my blog post. "THIS is what S is like. We restrained him 5 times today in less than 3 hours. He threatened to kill his 5-year-old brother. Right now we can manage it at home because he is only 8 . . . he is only 8 and has broken my nose, my hand twice and injured my sternum. It's so hard to get him the help he needs. Too many professionals are willing to write us off. Sometimes there isn't anywhere to turn."

And a father: "I felt I needed to write because my greatest fear is the 'alleged suspect' will one day be my daughter. They are really tough kids to raise. They test your every strength and push to the point of, 'I don't know how to do this!' What if someday it all blows up? I've asked psychologists how do I raise her and they can't even tell me."

Speaking to the chronic lack of information that frustrates struggling parents, one mother shared this tragic story:

> I have two mentally ill children. My oldest was bipolar and constantly on and off her medication. She threatened to kill herself regularly and could be aggressive toward others as well. She took her life five years ago. My oldest son is a paranoid schizophrenic, the kind of schizophrenic most likely to hurt themselves or others. He is stable and has been now for many years. But during his teens and early adult years it was a nightmare. Between the two I spent many nights awake out of fear that not only one of them could hurt me, but I would be afraid that they might hurt one of the other children and I would not know it. Getting help for them as children and as adults was next to impossible. The little help I did get was ineffective and often misguided.

My experience and the experiences of so many other desperate, tired, hopeless parents are borne out by the numbers: on average, it takes two years from onset of symptoms to treatment for children with mental disorders—and that's one in five children in any given year, according to Centers for Disease Control statistics. Parents have to navigate a baffling, jargon-ridden, often contradictory world, with insurance companies refusing to pay for necessary treatments—if you can even get insurance coverage for mental health, an inequity that the Affordable Care Act of 2010 promises to correct where the Mental Health Parity and Addiction Equity Act of 2008 failed.

The interface between parents of children with mental disorders and the medical community is a costly and incomprehensible machine, cogs whirring and gears grinding, often to no apparent purpose. "It's not that we don't know how to treat mental illness," Michael Fitzpatrick, director of NAMI, has said. "But on any given day 40 percent of the people in this country who have mental illness have no access to treatment. That's stunning. That's appalling. We need a better, tighter, and more coordinated mental health care system."

I'd heard about parents who spent the equivalent of four years' Harvard tuition and expenses on their children with mental illness—around $225,000 for a student starting in 2013. Marcie Lipsitt, a mother and advocate from Michigan and a member of Massachusetts General Hospital Pediatric Psychopharmacology Advisory Council, has flown with her son to Boston to see Dr. Janet Wozniak every month for the past fourteen years. As I mentioned before, for solidly middle-class parents like me, a consultation with this caliber of psychiatrist is usually out of reach, and most of these doctors are understandably private pay, with extensive waiting lists. Still, after speaking with Demitri Papolos, reading his research, and talking to a parent whose child had been in his care, I felt strongly that he was on to something. So I wrote a check for more than half my monthly take-home pay and booked our tickets to New York.

## WHEN DID YOU FIRST OBSERVE . . . ?

My journey with my son to see an East Coast juvenile bipolar disorder expert began many years ago, in a pediatrician's office in Southern California. We lived in Irvine at the time, our home identical to a hundred others in a tightly controlled planned community, a sunny, seventy-two-degree paradise of identical red-tiled roofs and white stucco houses, neatly trimmed Bermuda grass, immaculately groomed palm trees, and vigilant homeowners' associations. Michael was my second child, and I sensed something was wrong early, as any mother would. He crawled on time, but it was a strange army-type crawl, one side at a time instead of the cross-pattern crawling I saw with his older brother. Then there was the acute sensitivity to sound, which he has to this day. As a baby, he would begin to scream inconsolably when the vacuum cleaner was turned on. He disliked loud music or television.

When Michael first walked, close to his first birthday, his gait was awkward, unbalanced, stiff. He still walks with a strange gait and has proprioceptive deficits, meaning he can't really judge how far away he is from objects and other people. And then there was the repetitive head banging. As I mentioned previously, my pediatrician told me my concerns were unfounded, that my child was "totally normal." How many times have parents expressed similar concerns and heard those words?

Michael's tantrums started early. Temper tantrums are indeed a normal part of a toddler's development, as any parent knows. But these were not normal temper tantrums. Michael had high-end Italian sports car–style meltdowns—zero to sixty in two seconds flat. And once he was going, he kept going until he collapsed from sheer exhaustion. These tantrums would last two to three hours. I noticed after a while that he had triggers—an unexpected change in routine, for example, or too much external stimulation. I cut back our trips to the mall.

Michael has always had trouble sleeping. He tosses and turns, and wakes often with vivid nightmares. One night I sat straight up at 3:00 a.m., sensing something was very wrong. I hurried toward the boys' room and found the front door open. My three-year-old son was standing in the front yard, bathed in moonlight and fast asleep. I scooped him up in my arms, pressed my lips to his duck-fuzz downy white hair, and carried him back to his bed. The next day, I got a hotel-style chain lock for the door and installed it out of his reach.

As he grew older, things got worse. We started looking for real answers.

## FINALLY, A DIAGNOSIS

In chapter 3, I outlined the difficulties many parents face in getting a real diagnosis for their children. After my blog went viral, many people tried to reach me to share their ideas for how to cure my son. I heard everything from exorcisms to special diets to behavioral boot camps. In all that overwhelming noise, one woman, Alissa Bronsteen, senior researcher for the Juvenile Bipolar Research Foundation, stood out. She e-mailed to tell me about Demitri Papolos and his Fear of Harm phenotype. As I skimmed his research, I was amazed at how closely my son's symptoms matched the description of this subset of juvenile bipolar disorder. Sleep problems and vivid nightmares? Check. Complaining of being too hot on a cold day? Check. Sudden uncontrolled and unexplained rages? Check.

Through my connection with Alissa, I had an unexpected opportunity to obtain world-class, innovative treatment for my son. A few weeks after I made the appointment, Michael was back in the hospital, following three days of the first clearly identifiable manic episode I had observed. On Sunday night, he talked at breakneck speed for hours, solving all of the world's problems, from government (like Plato, Michael believes in a philosopher-king) to cancer (the teleporter that would screen for DNA mistakes) to our education system (three hours of recess per day—and there actually might be something to that idea, especially for children with ADHD). On Tuesday night, he cleaned his room.

On Wednesday morning, I was at work when Michael's school counselor called. "Hi," she drawled. "How's your day going?"

In the background, I heard yelling. It was unmistakably Michael.

"Sounds like it's about to get worse," I said. "Do you need me to come down?"

"As soon as possible," she replied. "Look, I had to call the school resource officer, because this is a pretty serious meltdown. He has been threatening himself and everyone. We had to put the school on lockdown." She drew a deep breath. "But I really think this is a medical issue. I'm hoping you can beat the officer here and take him to the emergency room. He's been doing so well—has there been a medication change lately?"

"No, but it sounds like there needs to be one," I said, gathering my things and writing a too-familiar note on my door: "Out of the office."

When I got to his school, Michael was curled up alone on the floor in the office sobbing. "Now I'm not going to get to see Jonathan and Anna," he said, referring to our severely limited visitation schedule with his younger brother and sister, which he knew was dependent on his good behavior. "I hate myself. I tried. I really tried. I want to be good! I hate myself. I just want to die. I don't want to exist anymore."

I've heard those heart-wrenching words so many times in my son's young life. At the age of five, after waking up from nightmares, he told me, "I just want to be a zero. I don't want to be me anymore."

I hugged him, helped him to stand, collected his things. "I think we'll take a break from school today," I told him. As we drove, he continued to cry, so he didn't notice we weren't going home until we were almost to the hospital. When he realized where we were, he became instantly defiant. "I'm not going there," he yelled.

"What if we just go in and do an assessment?" I asked. "You don't have to stay unless the nurse decides it's necessary."

This time, he agreed and came in with me. Once inside the triage room, it was clear that Michael was still experiencing mania. His speech was rapid; his eyes were wild. The nurse explained to him that he would need to stay for a few days. He bolted for the door, but the nurse planted her solid, impassive form in front of him, blocking his path.

He turned to me and began shouting, "You lied to me! You told me I didn't have to stay here."

"Mom, why don't you step outside?" the nurse said firmly, and I wedged myself out the door as two aides came in to help transport my son. I started filling out paperwork again.

This time, Michael's stay was uneventful. He quickly understood that he was in the hospital for a medication change, not for "being bad." This time, he was finally diagnosed with juvenile bipolar disorder, something I had suspected since Alissa Bronsteen had contacted me to discuss my son's symptoms and Dr. Papolos's unique approach. My son started taking a low dose of lithium and was released six days later. Two months after this hospital visit, we confirmed the diagnosis with Dr. Papolos in Westport.

After so many years and so many diagnoses and medications, Michael and I both tend to add the phrase "knock on wood" to every new diagnosis. But I felt good about this one, and—knock on wood—at the time of this writing, six months after starting lithium, he has experienced no major rages or outbursts, nor has he exhibited signs of extreme mania or depression. He's still a quirky kid with some annoying habits. But he's quirky more in the "Sheldon from *Big Bang Theory*" sense than in the "David Banner from *The Incredible Hulk*" sense. For the first time in years, we have all started to relax and think about managing his life with a chronic but treatable condition. We are even talking about which colleges he might like to attend. As I told a friend recently, if you have to have a serious mental illness, bipolar is a good one to have. It's treatable, and the medications have more than fifty years of research behind them. But why was it so hard, and why did it take so many years, so many doctors, for us to get a diagnosis for my son?

## PEDIATRICIANS

As we saw in the last chapter, in part because we still don't know what causes mental illness, for many parents of children with mental disorders, even obtaining a clear, consistent diagnosis is a Sisyphean effort. Since kindergarten, Michael has been variously diagnosed with intermittent explosive disorder; oppositional defiant disorder; pervasive developmental disorder, not otherwise specified (many teachers, aides, and PSR workers have felt that he should have been diagnosed with Asperger's syndrome); attention-deficit/hyperactivity disorder; depression; and now juvenile bipolar disorder and post-traumatic stress disorder. Unfortunately, his circuitous journey through the Wonderful World of the *Diagnostic and Statistical Manual of Mental Disorders*, the so-called bible of psychiatry, is pretty typical for children with mental disorders—and it makes treatment difficult.

One promising area is early intervention, and in this realm, pediatricians are on the front lines. While current diagnostic tools focus on perceptions and self- or parent-disclosed observation of symptoms, a biomarker diagnosis would help parents and caregivers to provide early support and direction. But early intervention depends on the child's first point of contact with the medical system: his or her pediatrician's ability to recognize symptoms. In fact, studies suggest that between 43 and 60 percent of all mental illness is treated solely by patients' primary care providers. Of people diagnosed with a disorder in one study, only 41 percent received any treatment during a twelve-month period—of these, only 12 percent were seen by a psychiatrist, while nearly 23 percent were treated by a general practitioner. But too often, pediatricians lack the level of education about mental illness to be able to diagnose those symptoms and refer the child to the right resources.

Dr. Harold Koplewicz and others have proposed that one simple solution to the children's mental health crisis is better mental health training for pediatricians—and the timing is perfect as the Affordable Care Act of 2010 comes into play. Dr. Koplewicz noted in his testimony to Congress in March 2013 that 75 percent of mental illness has its first onset before age twenty-four, reinforcing the need for early diagnosis and intervention. With the prevalence of mental illness in children, pediatricians are often called on to manage children's disorders. The primary care medical home (PCMH; also called patient-centered medical home) could serve as a coordinator for the many facets of care these children often require, managing everything from medications to occupational and speech therapy to psychosocial rehabilitation and even special-needs educational planning. That central point of contact—think health management instead of wealth management—could save money, time, and untold amounts of parental stress. With the Affordable Care Act, we may stand on the edge of a new world. Or we may not. Only time will tell.

## PSYCHIATRISTS

Another challenge facing parents who seek a reliable diagnosis is a critical nationwide shortage of child psychiatrists. According to the American Academy of Child and Adolescent Psychiatry, in 2012, there were just 8,300 practicing child and adolescent psychiatrists in the entire United States, even though the projected need for these experts was 30,000 by the year 2000. In 2001, there were only seventeen child psychiatrists in the entire state of Idaho, with a youth population of nearly four hundred thousand. Many other states experienced (and continue to experience) similar shortages.

These low numbers reflect the fact that psychiatry is not highly regarded as a career choice by future doctors. Many studies, as well as anecdotal evidence, suggest that the stigma attached to mental illness extends to its providers and caregivers: psychiatry is somehow seen as a lesser science. As one 1999 inquiry into the decline of American psychiatry noted, "Medical students enter medical school with distinctly negative attitudes toward a career in psychiatry compared with other specialties." Even now, a hundred years beyond Freud, the word still conjures up images of a white-haired old man with thick glasses, fingers steepled as he stares benignly at the patient lying on his couch and says, "Tell me about your mother."

One of my son's former psychiatrists, a brilliant, compassionate woman who really connected with Michael, confided in me that she had been advised not to pursue psychiatry as a specialty because it would be a "waste of her talent." Doctors who choose to specialize in this field often have a personal connection: In a 2007 survey of British doctors who chose to specialize in psychiatry, 36 percent identified empathy with the patient group as their primary reason.

One promising remedy to the shortage of psychiatrists is remote consultation through telemedicine. This delivery model, which uses existing technologies like videoconferencing, enables delivery of high-quality mental health care to remote and rural areas. A North Carolina study noted, "Telepsychiatry can make a significant impact on the delivery of mental health services, particularly to individuals with less access." This study connected a large pediatric primary care practice to remote psychiatric consultations with East Carolina University's telemedicine program. After three and a half years and 185 telepsychiatry consultations, fewer than 3 percent presented any problems.

My son was lucky: even though we live in a community where parents may wait eight months or more to see a child psychiatrist, when Michael was just seven, we were able to get a referral through a friend to one of the best child psychiatrists in Boise. Dr. P. was efficient, gruff, and direct: after my divorce, he was one of the few health care providers willing to address head-on the high-conflict behavior my ex-husband and I exhibited—with its damaging implications for Michael's care. His initial diagnosis for our son was oppositional defiant disorder, a behavioral disorder characterized by a refusal to comply with authority figures and extreme outbursts. He treated my son until 2011, when he decided to close his practice, in his words, "to focus on patients with autism." Because of chronic shortages and long wait lists in our area, we were not able to find another regular psychiatrist for two years, relying on our primary care doctor and later on a behavioral health practice physician's assistant to manage Michael's increasingly complex cocktail of medications.

One Saturday morning in 2013, I opened the newspaper to disturbing news. Following an investigation by the Idaho state medical board, Dr. P.'s license had been revoked. The investigation alleged improper sexual conduct with underage boys, including nude massages with children. My mouth went dry. This man was someone I trusted to care for my son. This man was by all accounts the best child psychiatrist in the Treasure Valley. To paraphrase Flannery O'Connor, a good child psychiatrist is hard to find. Dr. P.'s story is not an isolated incident: other child psychiatrists have also been implicated in improper relationships with their young and vulnerable patients.

## A New Way of Thinking about Treatment

As we saw in chapter 3, lack of access to quality local mental health care drives parents who have the means to seek treatment outside of their communities. And often, after so many failures and setbacks, parents are desperate to find an innovative approach to the problem of mental illness.

Juvenile bipolar disorder, my son's diagnosis, is still clouded in controversy, in no small part because of the tremendous stigma that attaches to labeling a child with a serious mental illness. Dr. Joseph Biederman and his colleagues at Massachusetts General Hospital pushed aggressively to expand diagnostic criteria for bipolar disorder to children in the 1990s; his reputation was later tarnished by the revelation that he and two Harvard Medical School colleagues accepted money from pharmaceutical companies in clear violation of the school's conflict-of-interest policies.

The dramatic increase in children discharged from the hospital with bipolar diagnoses between 1996 (1.3 per 10,000 children) and 2004 (7.3 per 10,000 children) has sometimes been linked to Biederman and Dr. Janet Wozniak, another Massachusetts General child psychiatrist, most notably by their vocal critic, child psychiatrist and professor Stuart Kaplan, whose book *Your Child Does Not Have Bipolar Disorder: How Bad Science and Good Public Relations Created the Diagnosis* characterizes this dramatic increase as an unholy "axis of capitalism" alliance among Biederman, his Harvard Medical School colleagues, and the major pharmaceutical companies. In an article for *Newsweek* castigating the diagnosis of bipolar disorder in preschoolers, Kaplan argued: "it's nearly impossible to distinguish between children alleged to have bipolar disorder and those with straightforward anger-control issues."

But what if those "straightforward anger-control issues" were anything but straightforward? What if they were actually a symptom of a serious mental illness? You won't find the Fear of Harm phenotype in the *DSM-5*. Dr. Papolos developed this descriptive subtype of juvenile bipolar disorder after examining hundreds of children like Michael, with multiple diagnoses and a history of medication failures, and wondering: is there a pattern there that others are not seeing? What the Harvard-trained psychiatrist discovered surprised him: in every one of these diagnosis-resistant children, he observed problems with thermal regulation—with how their bodies controlled, or failed to control, core body temperature. This became the key characteristic of his Fear of Harm phenotype. The second consistent characteristic that Dr. Papolos observed was behavior that looked like ODD or ADHD or both. He called his observations the Fear of Harm phenotype because patients consistently operated from a place of fear— they felt backed into a corner, which led to aggressive behavior.

As I noted, psychiatrists have been reluctant to diagnose juvenile bipolar disorder because the criteria are so unclear for children in the current *DSM*—in fact, this difficulty has led to the addition of a new controversial diagnosis in the *DSM-5*: disruptive mood dysregulation disorder (DMDD). Dr. Papolos is doing exactly the kind of work that NIMH director Thomas Insel has called for in rejecting wholesale acceptance of the latest iteration of the *DSM*. By challenging the *DSM* and looking for biomarkers—in this case, thermal regulation—Dr. Papolos has made the kind of leap of insight that characterizes medical pioneers.

Once he had identified the physical characteristics these children shared, he started looking for treatment options and found one in an unusual place. Dr. Papolos searched the literature for drugs that both cooled the body and helped to calm fear. Ketamine, which does both, was a near perfect match—near perfect, because although it is still used as an anesthetic for thousands of children each year, it has another less savory reputation as a 1990s club drug, sold under the squeaky-clean sobriquet "special

K." And yet chemically, the drug is much safer and better tolerated than atypical antipsychotics such as Zyprexa and Risperdal and Abilify. "Some antipsychotics are probably contraindicated in cases who meet criteria for Fear of Harm, because they may actually inhibit the capacity to thermo-regulate," Dr. Papolos said, when I told him how my son had failed to re-spond to Zyprexa.

As Dr. Papolos describes it, Fear of Harm is essentially a reverse ver-sion of post-traumatic stress disorder (PTSD). In PTSD, a child or an adult experiences a traumatic event and relives it in dreams. With Fear of Harm, the child experiences traumatic events in dreams—and lives with that trauma in real life. For some reason, the thermal dysregulation causes vivid and violent dreams to be encoded as memories, all because the child is too warm during REM sleep. The child then grows up in a perpetual state of fear, leading to unpredictable behaviors and occasionally violent out-bursts. This description seemed to fit my son exactly. He often described feeling "backed into a corner," or being bullied or victimized, even when I did not observe bullying behavior. And his sleep had always been troubled—even after his tonsils were removed, he continued to have vio-lent, gory nightmares, waking several times per night. "If you're being at-tacked by a shark in a dream, you feel it's an actual attack, and your body remembers it that way," Dr. Papolos said to me. "Fear and aggression are sometimes the only real emotions these children have known."

Michael also had the opportunity to talk with Dr. Papolos alone. "I felt like I could see myself in a new way," he said after their interview. "He totally explained why I felt the way I did. I always feel backed into a corner before I lash out. I feel like people are always out to get me."

## MEDICATIONS

Remember that laundry list of drugs my son has taken, in chapter 3? Maybe I'm an outlier, but I think that we should not rule out any drug that can potentially change a child's life. If medical marijuana showed promise in treating juvenile bipolar disorder (and plenty of laypeople who commented on my blog thought it would), I would sign my son up for clinical trials tomorrow. In fact, one Oregon couple has treated their son's severe autism with medical marijuana, they claim, successfully. I do not see the distinction between legal and illegal drugs as any more valid than the distinction between mental and physical illness. Many of our "legal" drugs are abused by people who self-medicate, and yet as a society, we stigmatize crack cocaine users far more than OxyContin pill poppers. Furthermore, many of our perfectly legal maintenance medications are derivatives of illegal drugs: Wellbutrin is cocaine without the high (both drugs are dopamine transporter inhibitors), and Ritalin is closely related to speed.

I discussed the controversy over medicating children in the previous chapter but it bears repeating here. Critics like Robert Whitaker have argued that medications actually cause the diseases they claim to ameliorate. In 2013, the inspector general's office at the Department of Health and Human Services began a systematic review of atypical antipsychotic prescriptions to children under the age of eighteen on Medicaid. Antipsychotics account for the largest group of drugs in the Medicaid system, costing $3.6 billion in 2008. Children on Medicaid are four times more likely to be prescribed atypical antipsychotics, with their life-altering and potentially life-shortening side effects, than children with private insurance. In 2008, 19,045 children under the age of five were given these medications under Medicaid.

The problem is twofold: first, atypical antispychotics are basically untested in children, though numerous studies suggest the long-term metabolic changes they cause may adversely affect both quality and quantity of life. Second, there are much safer drugs, chemically speaking—drugs with fewer side effects and less harmful profiles. Lithium, for example, has been used for more than fifty years and is extremely effective at mood stabilization in 60–80 percent of patients with bipolar disorder. But no one makes money off of prescribing lithium. Other drugs, like ecstasy, which has shown promise in treating post-traumatic stress disorder, and ketamine, which has been shown to stop suicidal ideation in its tracks, are classified as Schedule III controlled substances (along with hydrocodone and ana-bolic steroids) by the U.S. Drug Enforcement Administration (DEA), adding a whole new level of stigma to their use. Still, if ketamine can help my son to lead a normal life, I am willing to try it.

As of 2013, Dr. Papolos had treated seventy-four patients with nasal mist ketamine, and all but one had seen significant improvement in behav-ior and mood. Ketamine is FDA approved for limited applications in chil-dren. The nasal mist method is a treatment course of four doses total, given at three-day intervals. His first patient was a young girl who had failed to respond to any other medications or therapies. She was facing dental sur-gery, and Dr. Papolos convinced her mother to ask the dentist for ketamine as an anesthetic. "We saw immediate improvement," he said. "It was like the child underneath the fear was revealed."

But Dr. Papolos cautions that the drug is not a "magic bullet." The maladaptive coping strategies these children develop to protect them-selves take additional therapy to unlearn. He is training auxiliary thera-pists with information about Fear of Harm children so that they can help their patients to transition to acceptable and healthy behavior, once the underlying physiological cause has been treated and managed. He also does not take his patients off of mood stabilizers like lithium, but uses ketamine as a complementary therapy.

Dr. Papolos believes that his new diagnostic criteria and ketamine therapy have the potential to help as many as a million children across the United States who are currently not receiving the therapy they need. "Ketamine helps these children to feel an emotion they have never felt before," he explains. "They feel calm."

## PSYCHOTHERAPY, OCCUPATIONAL THERAPY, AND OTHER ALTERNATIVES

Most doctors would agree with Dr. Papolos that no medication is a "magic bullet" for children with mental illness. Certainly medication plays an im-portant role in the management of a chronic disorder: to return to the popular biological model, a patient with diabetes takes insulin, but the person also manages his or her diet and exercises regularly to keep the disease in check. Similarly, ancillary therapies provide tremendous benefits to children with mental illness. As I often tell my son, mental illness may be an explanation for inappropriate or dangerous behavior, but it's not an excuse. Knowing the challenges he faces, he is better equipped to develop coping strategies that work for him.

Michael sees a psychiatrist about once every six weeks to manage his medications. He sees a psychologist trained in cognitive behavior therapy (CBT) every other week. My personal experience with CBT has been overwhelmingly positive, and Michael is also learning to monitor his thinking patterns. If he catches himself early enough, he can prevent himself from dangerous and frightening rages. A typical session involves Michael playing chess with his therapist—chess provides a perfect model for him to understand the strategic nature of managing his complicated moods and the sometimes overwhelming sensory input that can lead to meltdowns. I am grateful that Michael is aware of his challenges—one potentially dangerous complication of some serious mental illnesses is anosognosia, or lack of insight. Many people with schizophrenia, for example, are unaware that their reality does not correspond to everyone else's.

Michael's favorite therapeutic activity is occupational therapy. Picture a two-story room with rope swings and a hammock, a plywood fort painted to look like a castle, and colorful giant foam blocks of various shapes. This is the main play area at the Sensory Bin, an occupational therapy clinic designed specifically for children. I watch as my son clambers up a rope ladder, then holds a rope swing in his hands, his look uncertain. "You can do it!" his occupational therapist, Andrea Moroge, a slender woman with a kind face and quick smile, encourages him. Michael closes his eyes and launches himself into space, the rope clasped tight between his fingers. A look of pure joy crosses his face as he lands in a foam pit.

I never would have thought of using occupational therapy for my son if I hadn't worked at a college that had an occupational therapist assistant program. But it has proved to be the most effective therapy to help my son navigate his world. He took the Sensory Integration and Praxis Test (SIPT) at the age of eleven—and the results were like a Rosetta Stone for me and Michael's caregivers. I could finally understand why my son struggled with things as simple as tying his shoes, organizing homework papers in a binder, and writing his name.

Sensory integration is essentially the brain's way of organizing input it receives from the senses into a usable form. Michael has problems with visual processing that make it difficult for him to write or copy information from a chalkboard. He also has severe problems with processing tactile information, which means that Michael does not use touch appropriately in social situations and may even be unsafe—for example, he may not realize that punching a wall hurts, because his brain does not process pain normally. And he has problems holding his own body up against gravity and walking across a room: his test results noted that "Michael has deficits with his walking gait pattern. It is not typical and is a dysfunction of his balance, motor coordination, and postural strength."

The SIPT examiner concluded that "Michael is having severe issues with planning and positioning his body relative to objects, people, and his own body parts. Functionally, this is seen with movements that are clumsy; poor body awareness for his surroundings, such as walking into objects, furniture, or brushing against walls; difficulty imitating new movements; difficulty knowing and changing positions and actions in group games; poor execution of his ideas; and difficulty maintaining a level of organization with his belongings, such as maintaining his backpack, folders, and work/play spaces neat and in order."

What does this look like in real life? He can't organize papers or copy notes from a whiteboard. When we were in New York, a man pushing a large trash bin cursed at Michael when my son was unable to change direction and walked straight into his path. Occupational therapy helps Michael to find new ways to address his sensory deficits. Lately we've also been working on peer group interactions. Michael will often blurt out statements that are completely inappropriate for the social situation: if you ask him whether the jeans you are wearing make you look fat, be prepared for "yes" as the answer. He is also quick to characterize anything that confuses him as "stupid," a word I hope to remove from his vocabulary.

In addition to his weekly therapies, Michael also has PSR services (psychosocial rehabilitation—an imminent name change will make this service "community-based rehabilitation services") through Idaho's Children's Mental Health Program. His PSR worker, Michelle, takes him into the community to help him navigate everything from public parks to the library to the YMCA. Though Michael was originally resistant to PSR, perhaps because his first experience with it was ordered by a juvenile justice magistrate, he and Michelle have grown close over the years. She's a no-nonsense woman with a wry sense of humor that Michael appreciates. Lately, they spend most of their time at the neighborhood park with Michael's good friend Jayden (not his real name), a twelve-year-old with autism and other developmental disabilities who shares Michael's love for Dr. Who and Rick Riordan's Percy Jackson series.

As a quick aside, I'm immensely grateful for Riordan, and also a tad jealous—as a classicist and a writer, I wish I had thought about transporting the Greek gods and their half-human offspring to modern-day New York City. Riordan's hero, Percy Jackson, is the only human son of the sea god Poseidon. He also has ADHD and doesn't quite fit into human society. Michael feels such a strong kinship with Percy that he becomes anxious when Riordan doesn't deliver the next book in the series on its promised due date. I wish the movie versions would pay more attention to Percy's diagnosis and the challenges it creates for him. Children with mental disorders need heroes like Percy Jackson.

Which brings me to another kind of alternative therapy: technology. ADHD? There's an app for that. No, really. If your child has a tablet or a smartphone, you might consider harnessing its power for good. EpicWin turns homework and chores into a role-playing game, complete with your child's own avatar and stamina points for doing the laundry. Attention Exercise, developed from Edward Hallowell's book on managing ADHD, uses simple, quick drawing tasks to help you improve your child's concentration. Another app useful for children and adults alike, 30/30, allows users to set a timer for a task and track the actual amount of time it takes to do things like homework or cleaning. Parents can also use iReward as an electronic version of the old chore chart on the fridge. There's even a Pinterest page for bipolar disorder apps.

There are myriad other alternative therapies available for children with mental illness. In addition to the special diets introduced in chapter 3, there's also equine therapy, art therapy, and music therapy, all of which seem to offer positive results to children with mental disorders. Positive reinforcement, realistic expectations, and engaging, challenging activities all help children with mental illness to manage their condition and learn appropriate ways to engage with their world.

## RESIDENTIAL TREATMENT

For some parents, residential treatment centers are the only option. But for most parents, it's an option of last resort. One of the earliest psychiatric hospitals in the West was Bedlam, an alternate pronunciation of London's Bethlem Hospital that itself became a byword for mental illness. Though it's not certain when the hospital, founded in 1247, became dedicated exclusively to psychiatric care, it has been in continuous operation in that capacity for at least six hundred years. Conditions there and in other early asylums were appalling, even by the standards of the times. Edward Wakefield described a visit in 1814 as follows: "One of the side rooms contained about ten patients, each chained by one arm to the wall; the chain allowing them merely to stand up by the bench or form fixed to the wall, or sit down on it. The nakedness of each patient was covered by a blanket only."

If you start to investigate residential treatment options—and I have to admit that I have done this on more than one occasion—what you find may not seem like much of an improvement on what Wakefield described two centuries ago. I understand our society's relentless emphasis on personal accountability and choices. But many parents desperate for solutions and uneducated about their options decide to send their children to behavioral boot camps that can do more harm than good. Unregulated and unlicensed wilderness camps and boarding schools for troubled teens are now calling themselves "therapeutic treatment centers." Children die there.

When Dana Blum sent her fourteen-year-old son Brendan to an organization called Youth Care in Utah, a state-licensed, privately operated residential facility, the single mother of two desperately needed a break, and she thought she had found a place that would keep her son, diagnosed with high-functioning autism, safe. Brendan died five months later from a treatable condition: he had experienced diarrhea and vomiting, and died from a twisted bowel without receiving medical care other than over-the-counter medication. The private facility cost her $15,000 per month. "State-run facilities generally offer services only to low-income families with children covered by Medicaid," Gina Fernandes, who told Dana and Brendan's story on Momlogic.com in 2009, explained, noting how difficult it is for middle-income families to get residential care for their children, leading them to choose private options like Youth Care.

The organization Teen Advocates USA monitors abuses of the system, reporting on for-profit groups that "thrive on children as a commodity," now more than a billion-dollar-a-year industry. If you don't have money, you have Medicaid and access to state-run residential treatment programs. But if you do have money, your only therapeutic options are often an unregulated "shadow" system that plays into the fantasy that children with mental illness are choosing to behave badly, that forty days in the wilderness will "cure" them.

But not all therapeutic treatment programs are dangerous. One of the most popular therapeutic survival camps is located in my own state, Idaho. The School of Urban and Wilderness Survival (SUWS) was founded in the early 1980s by Brigham Young University alumnus L. Jay Mitchell. The camp is based in Gooding, Idaho. Participants pay nearly $8,000 for a twenty-one-day wilderness experience with seven children and two guides. The camp uses a "search and rescue" approach to help learn new strategies for cooperation and appropriate behavior. The program was profiled in an

Idaho Public Television *Outdoor Idaho* documentary called "Desert Therapy" in April 2006.

Another for-profit enterprise, Aspen Education Group, offers four wilderness programs in North Carolina and one in Lehi, Utah. "Your child will experience the highest standards of safety and therapy in the context of one of the most powerful settings for real change—the wilderness," its website promises. The groups mix substance abusers with teens who have poor self-esteem or family conflict issues. Program graduates can move on to therapeutic boarding schools, including residential programs like Youth Care, where Brendan Blum died. No actual costs for these programs are listed on the website, but Aspen promises that "low-interest loans and other financing options mean monthly payments as low as $400–$800 per month."

Experts agree that the very worst option for a teen with a mental disorder is a military-style boot camp. And yet this "treatment" method has proven popular with upper-middle-class parents who don't know what else to do with their kids. These programs are often unlicensed and unregulated: one report investigating private residential facilities like those operated by Aspen Education Group noted that "although there is a serious lack of adequate information, it is clear from many reports that a significant number of children are being mistreated in such programs and, in some cases, are even dying in them." Even the National Association of Therapeutic Schools and Programs, an industry group, has difficulty keeping track of all the programs that are offered.

If your child has a mental disorder that requires residential treatment, it's important to explore your options and to ask the right questions. Some graduates of programs report life-changing results. But with private residential treatment options, the consensus seems to be very much "caveat emptor," and that buyer's warning may mean your child's life. Working with your state's health and welfare department can help you to find the most therapeutic and cost-effective solutions for you and your child. Anything that promises a quick fix is unlikely to be effective—and may even be dangerous—in the long run.

## COSTS, HEALTH INSURANCE, AND MEDICAID

None of this treatment comes cheap. The Centers for Disease Control estimates the annual aggregate cost of children's mental health care, including health care, juvenile justice programs, special education programs, and lost productivity, at $247 billion. Families who have a child with autism spend an average of $60,000 per year on treatment. What Michael experienced in Westport is the gold standard of treatment for children with mental illness. If you have money and access, you can receive world-class care that can make a difference in your child's life. My blog gave me access I never could have dreamed of. The money part was more difficult. Dr. Papolos does not accept insurance. As I mentioned, his consultation fee was more than half my monthly take-home pay. My insurance company would only reimburse a small fraction of that cost. And I had to fly us both to New York for treatment, missing three days of work.

All of this helps to explain why mothers of children with autism earn 56 percent less on average than mothers whose children have no disabilities. Author Jeff Howe was castigated for his honest assessment of the costs associated with raising his son who has autism, including $1,800 for diapers for his five-year-old; Autism Speaks, a national advocacy group, puts the estimated lifetime cost of raising a single child with autism at $3.2 million.

Like many solidly middle-class parents who have a child with disabilities, I cannot afford to give my child all the therapies that would help him to succeed. It took me more than a year to pay off the November 2012 $1,100 emergency room visit, a cost incurred when Michael was on a major medical health insurance plan that did not provide any coverage for mental illness. I have good insurance now through my employer, but I still have to alternate Michael's psychotherapy visits with his occupational therapy group—at a cost of $170 per month. His medications—all but one generic—cost another $100 per month. Visits with his psychiatrist are just $20; the average week-long hospital stay, with insurance, is about $900 out of pocket.

The average week-long hospital stay without insurance doesn't exist: it's called juvenile detention. One concerned dad summed up the experience of many parents in America: "Nobody would help us or help him, and his mom makes too much to qualify for health care. None of the plans would pay for any of his mental health needs, so we pay everything out of pocket. No hospital wants to take your child to help them if you have no insurance."

One woman posted a comment on my blog that she actually had to divorce the man she loved so that he could get treatment for his bipolar disorder that he desperately needed: "In our experience, only Medicaid-accepting low-income mental health clinics were able to take serious mental illness as seriously as it needs to be taken. They have been miraculous for us. In our case, we had to get divorced so he could get Medicaid. That's why he's my ex."

Medicaid does make a difference. In fact, a groundbreaking double-blind 2013 study of Oregon's Medicaid system revealed that while there were no notable improvements to physical health, mental health improved significantly: depression rates were reduced by 30 percent for those who were able to obtain services through Medicaid, suggesting that removing barriers of access to care can make a real difference in people's lives.

Any parent of a child with a serious mental illness should know one acronym: SAMHSA. It stands for Substance Abuse and Mental Health Services Administration, the agency that coordinates Medicaid and mental health care for families and that can provide help to families struggling to find care. But help is not easy to access. So you can better appreciate just how baffling this system can be, I'm going to quote directly from a May 7, 2013, SAMHSA policy memo describing the development of services that would allow children with complex mental health care needs to remain in their communities and with their families, a worthy goal. Do your best to read this entire quote without stopping: "Over the past 2 decades, 2 major federal initiatives have addressed the needs of children and youth with significant mental health conditions: Substance Abuse and Mental

Health Services Administration's (SAMHSA) Children's Mental Health Initiative (CMHI) and the Centers for Medicare and Medicaid Services (CMS) Psychiatric Residential Treatment Facility (PRTF) demonstration program."

Did you understand any of that? Seriously, it's like trying to decode Chinese characters. Colleges should start offering a degree, or at a minimum, a certificate program, in ADA (acronym decoding ability, not the Americans with Disabilities Act). When I lost my job in 2012, I also lost all private-insurance-provided mental health care services for my son. The Mental Health Parity and Addiction Equity Act of 2008 (MHPAEA) required employer-sponsored plans to create parity for mental and physical health, but it did not extend that requirement to individual plans. I could not find an affordable individual insurance plan that covered Michael's mental health care. So I did the logical thing and applied for Medicaid.

The form was complicated, and apparently I didn't do it right: I was denied. In a catch-22 familiar to many families, I made too much money as an independent contractor to qualify for services, but not nearly enough to afford a health care plan that included mental health services for my son. I've been working with Michael's CMH (Children's Mental Health) caseworker for the past two years to try to finalize an exhaustive report that would qualify him for services under Katie Beckett, a grant established for children with developmental disabilities. The report, as of this writing, is still not finalized. My point is that even for an educated, middle-class, white woman, navigating the system is hard, and it takes time. Research validates my experience: "most children who need a mental health evaluation do not receive services and Latinos and the uninsured have especially high rates of unmet need relative to other children."

## HIPAA AND MENTAL ILLNESS

Once your child turns eighteen, the barrier may not be access to care—it may be access to critical health-care information. Things can go wrong in an instant. But that single instant is the result of years of neglect and in-attention and people not wanting to talk. When we look at the most re-cent mass shootings, we see a common pattern: mostly young, bright males who were exhibiting signs of mental illness. Aaron Alexis sought treat-ment at two Veterans Affairs hospitals, where he complained of insomnia, just six weeks before shooting up the Navy Yard in Washington, D.C. Jared Loughner, who injured Arizona Congresswoman Gabrielle Giffords and killed six other bystanders, injuring twelve more, was diagnosed with schizophrenia. James Holmes, who shot up a theater in Aurora, Colorado, just a few miles from Columbine, also suffered from mental illness. So did Seung-Hui Cho, who went from one classroom to the next, killing his Virginia Tech classmates. One woman also made this list: Amy Bishop, another person with documented schizophrenia, managed to kill three of her University of Alabama colleagues at a faculty meeting before her gun jammed.

Serious mental illnesses like schizophrenia can be so destructive be-cause one of the symptoms may be a lack of awareness or insight into the disease. When your stomach hurts, you know about it. You can describe your own symptoms. But when you are suffering from schizophrenia, you believe in your own alternate reality. You're not the sick one—it's every-one else. One of the biggest challenges of mental illness is that it so often begins to manifest just at the age that young people are starting to become independent. Well-meaning laws like Health Insurance Portability and Accountability Act (HIPAA) and Family Educational Rights and Privacy Act (FERPA) prevent parents from accessing much-needed medical infor-mation until it's too late to save their children.

A former colleague of mine lost her son for exactly this reason. I got to know Veronica (not her real name) when she was the night instructor at a private career college where I taught English. Veronica's son Brian (not his real name) was an Iraq War vet, like several of our students. Brian suffered a TBI when his convoy fell prey to an IED on a dusty road in Iraq. That's traumatic brain injury and improvised explosive device, for those of you who are TLA (three-letter acronym) impaired. Brian was down in

Arizona, and the Veterans Benefits Administration kept denying him service.

"I've got to do something," Veronica told me. "He's got to get help." She went to court and tried to get guardianship, so she could have Brian committed. He was doing really crazy stuff at that point, like running naked through rail yards at night. It was only a matter of time, she said. Only a matter of time. But still the courts wouldn't have him committed. "He has to be an imminent threat to himself or others," she said, laughing bitterly. "Apparently if the train isn't actually bearing down on you, it's not 'imminent' enough."

One night Veronica wasn't there anymore. I figured something with Brian had come up and thought nothing more of it. I taught my class. "Why can't we end a sentence with a preposition?" my students asked. "Why can't we split infinitives?"

"Because you can't do it in Latin," I replied. "You can't split *esse* in Latin. And you can't end a sentence in Latin with *cum*. This is the sort of English up with which we will not put."

No one got the allusion to Winston Churchill.

A few weeks passed. Then one night, as I parked, I saw Veronica across the street.

"Liza," she called and waved. "Liza!"

I crossed the street. "Veronica, where have you been?" I asked. "And how is Brian?"

She sucked her breath in, her face tightening. "You didn't hear?" she said. "They didn't tell you?"

"Tell me what?"

"Brian. He killed himself. My baby killed himself. With my gun." The words came sharp and ragged, the existential agony of a mother who has lost her child.

"No," I said. "I didn't hear."

"I thought I was going to get him into the VA," she said. "But they denied him. He came home to my house. We had a good talk. And then the next morning, I found him. I found him! Oh, God," she gasped, "the gun was mine!"

"I'm sorry," I said. "I am so sorry." What else can you say?

I hugged her, a hard thing for me. Then I crossed the street. I taught my class about dangling and misplaced modifiers. I never saw Veronica again.

What can we do to keep bright, troubled young people from harming themselves or others? Our inattention to the problem of mental illness results in lost productivity on a massive scale. But worse, it results in lost lives. As Virginia senator Creigh Deeds tweeted after his son Gus wounded his father with a knife and then fatally shot himself, "I am alive so must live. Some wounds won't heal." No one and nothing can replace your dead child.

## McBrains and Mental Illness

It seems clear from stories like Veronica's that people with mental illness do not have a choice about their behavior. But mental illness deniers remain prominent in our society. Perhaps the most obvious example is the Citizens Commission on Human Rights (CCHR), a so-called watchdog group formed in 1969 by the Church of Scientology in conjunction with Dr. Thomas Szasz. Its stance on mental illness is clear (grammatical errors left intact): "The psychiatric/pharmaceutical industry spends billions of dollars a year in order to convince the public, legislators and the press that psychiatric disorders such as Bi-Polar Disorder, Depression, Attention Deficit Disorder (ADD/ADHD), Post Traumatic Stress Disorder, etc., are medical diseases on par with verifiable medical conditions such as cancer, diabetes and heart disease. This is simply a way to maintain their hold on a $84 billion dollar-a-year psychiatric drug industry that is based on marketing and not science."

For people who do not have children or family members with mental illness, these views have proven attractive, so much so that they are effective impediments to real change in our health care delivery model. As we saw in the chapter on stigma, if we can blame the victim, we don't have to assume responsibility for the consequences. Yet this "somebody else's problem" attitude comes at a significant cost to society as a whole.

Wherever there's a complex and widespread medical problem—cancer, obesity, and now mental illness—there are people with ideas about how to make money off of it. Brain Balance Achievement Center targets the rapidly growing population of parents of children with ADHD, autism spectrum disorders, and learning disabilities like dyslexia. The for-profit organization's treatment philosophy is based on the book *Disconnected Kids* by Dr. Robert Melillo, a chiropractor with a master's degree in neuroscience and a gift for marketing. Dr. Melillo created the Brain Balance Program as an alternative to medication and an attempt to treat the whole child, not just the presenting disorder: "No one was looking at the other problems these children had—problems that could provide clues to the underlying cause," he wrote. "But I did, and I could see that they involve every system in the body, not just the brain."

The Brain Balance Program does not use traditional medicine, medication, or psychotherapy to treat children with mental disorders. Instead, it integrates nutrition with physical and mental exercises designed to improve the child's overall health and stimulate new connections between the hemispheres of the brain. A 2010 preliminary study of 122 children with ADHD who underwent Dr. Melillo's hemispheric treatment did show a reduction in ADHD symptoms for children who completed a twelve-week program, but the study had flaws, including the absence of a control group and the affiliation of its researchers with the Brain Balance Program.

It's likely, as we saw in chapter 3, that Dr. Melillo is partially correct in his understanding of these disorders as whole-body problems rather than just brain problems, and that a deficiency in neural networks is also partially to blame. But his proposed "unified field theory" of mental disorders is too simplistic and not supported by research. The Brain Balance Program website home page trumpets (in all caps), "Newly published control study confirms success of Brain Balance Program among children with ADHD." One study alone is not sufficient to substantiate the extravagant claims the Brain Balance Program makes. And it would be interesting to compare children in the Brain Balance Program to children receiving other therapeutic treatments such as occupation therapy, treatments which are generally covered by health insurance (the Brain Balance Program is not).

But the real problem for me isn't the scientific claims; it's that to me, it seems as if Dr. Melillo is manipulating this information to make money off of families with limited resources. Like medispas and many nutrition centers, Brain Balance centers do not accept health insurance. If you look at the very bottom of the website, you'll see the word "franchise"; in fact, CNNMoney profiled Brain Balance as one of its five hottest franchises (along with School of Rock) in 2013. Brain Balance centers are similar to the Kaplan or Sylvan Learning Center model, companies that provide after-school tutoring for children who are struggling academically. Dr. Melillo has taken the Kaplan cake and frosted it with a nice neuroscience glaze.

Quasi-health-care centers designed to make money off of desperate patients are nothing new in America. We already have a slew of weight loss treatment centers that advocate everything from proprietary diet and exercise programs to exotic wrap treatments and plastic surgery. Medispas use medical procedures to coddle a clientele who want to slow down the aging process. Nutritional supplement companies are booming, despite research that says supplements are nowhere near as effective as their manufacturers claim. Even cancer has its Cancer Treatment Centers of America, a private, for-profit hospital system that offers last-resort hope to desperately ill patients and their families.

You can't find out how much Brain Balance treatment costs on the website—but this is a criticism that could be leveled at mainstream health care as well. Still, anecdotal evidence suggests that a typical course of treatment costs between $5,000 and $8,000. One friend of mine, a father of a ten-year-old with autism and ADHD who attended a Brain Balance information session, described it as "Scientology for Asperger's kids," in reference to the Church of Scientology's well-publicized abhorrence of psychiatry. But other parents report positive progress in their children. One mother described her experience with her five-year-old son on her blog: "When I walked out of that presentation in April I knew I had to take the chance. No matter what the sacrifice. No matter what the cost. If there was a chance my baby could get better, I had to try. I could not be more thankful that I did. It worked."

Though I personally would not enroll my son in a Brain Balance Program, I have a tough time criticizing any mother who makes significant sacrifices to do so and feels that it worked for her child. Some prominent science bloggers, including Emily Willingham of *A Life Less Ordinary*; Harriet Hall, MD, of *Science-Based Medicine*; and more recently, the anonymous author of *NeuroBollocks*, criticize the Brain Balance Program as pseudoscience. But at the end of the day, all that matters is your child. And the kinds of things the Brain Balance Program advocates will definitely not physically harm a child, which is more than can be said for atypical antipsychotic medications. The ultimate goal for all parents of children with mental illness is to relieve their children's suffering, to improve chances for a quality life.

## COMMUNITY-BASED CARE

I started this chapter by emphasizing everything that's wrong with the current model of mental health care in America. But some fortunate communities have developed life-changing mental health care delivery models for children and families. In San Antonio, Texas, an organization called Clarity Child Guidance Center is providing an example of truly community-based mental health care.

Clarity Child Guidance Center was founded in 1886 by thirteen caring women who wanted to take care of orphaned children. Over the years, it became clear that the children not adopted were most often children suffering with mental illness. In the 1950s, the organization went through the formal process of changing its mission to providing mental health care services to the community. A 2010 nonprofit merger brought outpatient care services to an organization that was already expert at providing acute inpatient care for children with mental illness.

"Since 2010, we have been able to meet a child at any level of treatment," said Clarity's marketing and community outreach vice president Rebecca Helterbrand when I toured the center in October 2013. Clarity provides a unique alternative to juvenile detention for children with episodic behavioral issues. Its outpatient day stabilization program was designed for exactly the kind of situation my son faced when his principal had to call the school resource officer. Instead of juvenile detention, children are able to attend a therapeutic stabilization program from 8:00 to 4:00, then go home for dinner with their families. Clarity's fifty-two-bed acute care hospital and outpatient treatment programs provided services to over eight thousand children in 2013. But that's only a fraction of the eighty thousand children in Bexar County who need mental health care.

Clarity's caregivers recognize that the family is part of the solution for children with mental illness. Family treatment and family therapy are a part of the process, as the treatment team helps family members to understand the journey their children are taking. Their biggest challenge is building awareness: "There's a long-standing belief that parents are not aware of the mental health services available in their communities, first because those services are not available, but second because of the stigma," Rebecca said. "If a child breaks her arm, parents know what to do. With mental illness, parents are afraid they will be blamed, that their parenting skills will be attacked."

Fortunately, San Antonio's medical community knows about Clarity and refers parents and children for services. The organization is also a research partner for the University of Texas Health Science Center at San Antonio, providing data for evidence-based outcomes that drive quality care. Unlike many residential treatment camps and centers, Clarity is a nonprofit: 80 percent of the children it treats are at or below the poverty level. While some of these children have Medicaid or Children's Health Insurance Program (CHIP), the center provides charity care to children throughout the region. In fact, 20 percent come from outside the San Antonio metropolitan area because there are simply no local services available. Texas's per capita spending on children's mental health is roughly $19 per child per year. The U.S. average is $80 per child per year. "We rank dead last among all states on providing funding," Rebecca noted. "But we are still able to provide excellent services to our patients and their families, in large part because of community donors."

The best part: Clarity doesn't look like a hospital. The hospital where my son goes for acute care is encircled with a chain-link fence topped with barbed wire. Visiting hours are severely limited, and parents have to leave everything—cell phones, purses, etc.—in their cars, as if they were visiting a prison. By contrast, Clarity's grounds look like a park, with all the accoutrements of childhood joy: a pleasant, shaded courtyard; a ropes course; a state-of-the-art playground; and a swimming pool. Children ask their parents, "Can we go to Clarity and play today?"

Clarity is a true community mental health provider. "If parents knew about us, they could walk off the street and get treatment," Rebecca said. "We are proud of what we do—we provide a continuum of care, but it's more than that. Our providers are constantly looking for ways to be best in class, to be innovative in the care of children."

Reward and consequence is the model used for most children in inpatient facilities. While this model—one popular example is the 1990 book *Parenting with Love and Logic*—makes sense for normal children, it can backfire with children who have mental disorders. Clarity's doctors searched for a different kind of model and created something called ClarityCare. Their model is based on a belief that children do well when they can. If they are not doing well, something is preventing them from behaving appropriately. The model emphasizes peer-to-peer collaboration rather than hierarchy between caregiver and child.

Consider a child who wakes up every day at 3:00 a.m. screaming. Under the reward and consequence model, caregivers would try to comfort the child, but they would also stress the rules and consequences: "I'm going to count to ten, and if you don't stop screaming and settle down, there will be a consequence."

The ClarityCare model assumes this child would rather be sleeping peacefully—that something is causing his behavioral problem. Rather than emphasizing rules and consequences, the model challenges caregivers to search for the reason behind the noncompliant behavior: "I owe it to this child to figure out why he is so upset." With minimal effort, the caregiver discovers that 3:00 a.m. is the time when his stepfather would come home drunk every night and wreak havoc on the family. "We could have made his situation worse by punishing him. Instead we worked collaboratively with him to understand the problem," Rebecca explained.

Even the center's seclusion rooms reflect a child-centered, collaborative mindset. All mental health treatment facilities are required by law to have a seclusion room for escalating patients. At Clarity, they've rebranded the seclusion room—often used as a threat at other facilities—as a relaxation room, a privilege children can earn. The room is cushioned with soft pillows. A light and bubble tower stands in one corner; children can adjust the color and frequency of the bubbles. Music plays, and aromatherapy is used to calm the disturbed child's senses. The room is designed to relax and soothe, rather than increase anxiety, as many traditional seclusion rooms do.

Dr. Soad Michelsen, Clarity's medical director for the past ten years, personally manages care for some of the most difficult patients. "I have never seen a situation when there is not hope for a child," Dr. Michelson, herself a mother of three, told me when I asked her what she liked most about her work. She views Clarity as an extended summer camp, a place that provides respite for children and their families. "We have never treated a child who doesn't leave us at least one step forward," she said.

Lisa Sanchez and her husband are normal working parents. They initially resisted seeking help for their son because of the cultural stigma attached to mental illness; Lisa's mother-in-law said, "Crack an egg on his head, and he'll be fine." Her husband felt they should be able to solve their child's problems without external help. Lisa fought all those negative messages and sought care for her son at Clarity. Her child is now an adult, who recently got his first job. Though she acknowledges that he will need care for his bipolar disorder and severe anxiety disorder for the rest of his life, Lisa feels that admitting he needed help, then getting the help he needed, has given her son a real chance to be happy and productive.

What mothers of children with mental illness must eventually realize is that mental health care can provide a happier ending for your child. But that happier ending is not going to be what you expected when you first held your newborn baby in your arms.

# FIVE

# EDUCATION

## *How Do Public Schools Deal with Children Who Have Mental Illness?*

> The authority of those who teach is often an obstacle
> to those who want to learn.
>
> —Cicero

On April 26, 2009, fifteen-year-old Matthew Abramowski came home from school and set his parents' house on fire. A smoke alarm alerted his mother, Diana, and his father, Joseph, who escaped with their physical lives into any parent's worst emotional nightmare. Matthew was arrested and charged as an adult with attempted murder, a crime that carried a twenty-five-year sentence. Because prosecutors claimed he had threatened to kill his parents, Diana and Joseph were not allowed to see or speak with their son. He ultimately spent seventeen months in a juvenile detention center.

Matthew Abramowski, now nineteen years old, has autism. "I felt like a piece of spit on the sidewalk," he later testified in 2013 as part of a federal case his parents brought against the two largest school districts in Idaho on his behalf. "I felt like the village animal." Student witnesses told the jury that Matthew was the victim of pervasive and unrelenting bullying, a common experience for children who have developmental or mental disorders, including Adam Lanza. Matthew is still trying to finish his high school graduation requirements. With the added burden of a felony on his record, it is unlikely that he will ever hold a job. Public education failed him in profound and life-changing ways.

Whether or not you have a child with a mental disorder, children's mental illness is your problem: in every classroom of twenty-five elementary school students, five are potentially disruptive and possibly even dangerous. One in five children in public school may have serious, often unmet learning needs. By failing to provide an appropriate learning environment for children with ADHD, juvenile bipolar disorder, oppositional defiant disorder, and autism—children like Matthew Abramowski and my son Michael—our educational system also denies an effective and appropriate education to all students. It comes at a high cost for taxpayers: in 2012, the price tag for one year of juvenile detention for a child in California was $179,400. And yet the state was forty-ninth in the nation on per pupil public school spending that same year, with an average $8,482 per student per year.

Marcie Lipsitt, the mother of a son with special needs and a forceful advocate for special education in Michigan, explained in a telephone conversation with me why this issue matters to both liberals and conservatives: "If you are a Democrat like I am, then you believe that every child has the right to the 14th Amendment [Due Process]. If I am talking to a Republican, I remind them that 99 percent of these kids can go on to become taxpayers. We are taking children who could become taxpayers and turning them into tax burdens. If we were a country that wanted to do it right, we could provide children with an appropriate education and young adults with the supports they need to succeed in the workplace."

## SCHOOL SAFETY AND ZERO TOLERANCE

Imagine an empty kindergarten classroom, colorful art projects on the walls, wooden blocks and toy cars scattered on a rug. The children have been quickly and efficiently escorted from the room by the school principal to a designated spot on the playground. In the center of the room a small red-faced, blond-haired boy stands, fists clenched, eyes screwed shut, and screams. At the age of five, Michael already required a "clear the room" crisis plan.

Will Johnson, a high school special education teacher, shared his perspective in a comment on my blog post: "I've worked with students who can be incredibly violent and destructive. These same students, like your son, are also often incredibly kind and generous. The problems underlying the school shootings are far more complex than the conversation about these shootings. Our society's failure to care for both the mentally ill and the mentally healthy, for both children and adults, is certainly deeply connected to the violence that results from mental illness." His comment hints at the unintended and terrible consequence of a nationwide "zero-tolerance" approach to children with emotional and behavioral challenges.

For most parents of children with mental illness or developmental disorders like autism, the public school system is the first place they must face hard evidence of their child's disability. And for too many children with mental illness, that first encounter with public school funnels them into a "school-to-prison" pipeline that has all but replaced therapeutic care in the United States. One study noted, "A child facing status offense charges is likely to be a child for whom school system personnel failed to provide appropriate special education services, and with whom parents have become increasingly frustrated." For children with mental illness who continue to attend public schools, bullying is a major problem—children with mental illness are likely to be bullied, but they are also likely to be the bully, especially if they have oppositional defiant disorder, according to one 2012 study.

A 2011 report from the National Education Policy Center, entitled "Discipline Policies, Successful Schools, and Racial Justice," noted that in 2006 more than 3.25 million schoolchildren were suspended at least once, and more than one hundred thousand were expelled. The data showed that children with disabilities were disproportionately affected: in some states, 19 percent of the school districts reported "significant discrepancies" in suspension rates for children with disabilities. These disparities were even more marked for nonwhite children who had disabilities—as many as 30 percent of African American children with disabilities were suspended at least once. The report also noted that 95 percent of all suspensions were for disruptive or defiant behavior.

Michael's problems began in preschool. Another child invaded the cave he had created for himself under the playground slide, and he responded by biting her. When his teacher asked him why he bit his classmate, he shrugged and responded, "I'm a biting dragon. That's what dragons do." The teacher tried to explain that the school had no problem with him being a dragon per se, but that biting dragons were not allowed. "You can be a flying dragon, or even a fire-breathing dragon," she said. "But you cannot be a biting dragon."

"But dragons bite," he insisted, unmoved by her logic. Rigid, inflexible thinking is one symptom of his illness. We found another preschool.

That moment has been replicated in various iterations throughout my son's school career. Michael often does not understand how to interact with his teachers or his peers. He says inappropriate things, laughs at the wrong time, or is too rough, without understanding why other people are bothered or annoyed with his behavior. He reports that he is unable to hear his own tone of voice, which often seems loud or monotone to others. When he was three, I was a stay-at-home mother, so I could drop everything and rescue his teacher and his classmates. But after my divorce, I realized just how hard it is to balance caregiving with work.

I think it's fair to say that I'm pretty passionate about education. I've worked for years as a college educator and administrator, and I'm the Americans with Disabilities Act accommodations coordinator at my college. I was the secretary for an International Baccalaureate business and economics charter school board, and I cofounded TeachIdaho, a mentoring and professional development organization for K–12 teachers, with Kali Kurdy, a thirty-year public school classroom veteran, and Sallie Herrold, a fellow charter school board member. And yet I view my friends who are full-time advocates for their children's educational needs with admiration, respect, and even a little fear. The phenomenon of the Asian Tiger Mothers made news in 2012 with Amy Chua's controversial book about her relentless pursuit of her children's success. In some ways, mothers of children with mental illness become Dragon Mothers. They breathe fire— and they know exactly what the public school system is required to give their children. Parents have to be advocates for their children. They have to become as savvy and educated as the school district personnel who are paid and trained in these areas of law.

But this level of advocacy breeds resentment both from school district personnel and from other parents, as I learned with my own son. Part of the reason is the cost: special education is more expensive. When IDEA was enacted, the cost of providing special education for a child with disabilities was estimated at two times as much as the cost of providing education for a child without disabilities. IDEA was designed to help the states bridge that budget gap with federal funds, with a reimbursement cap set at 40 percent of the state average per-pupil costs. But because IDEA is not fully funded, in 2012 the states were only reimbursed an average of 16 percent of their excess costs, leaving state taxpayers to pick up the rest.

The extra costs sometimes lead to other parents' and even teachers' resentment of parents with special needs children. Responding to the Debate.org question, "Do U.S. schools spend too much money on special education programs?" 56 percent said "Yes." Comments revealed concern over unfairness or wasting resources; one educator wrote, "They [special education students] get all of the latest technology and all of the support while the general education and gifted students get little to nothing."

In addition to resentment over extra resources, there's a more visceral reason parents worry about special education for children like my son: fear. When I published my opposition to a proposed law in Idaho that would deny a public education to children convicted of a violent misdemeanor or felony, one mother engaged me in a vigorous online debate, the gist of which was, "I don't want kids like your son in my daughter's classroom. Kids like your son make me feel unsafe."

Though I disagree with this woman, I honestly understand the place of fear she is coming from—and her "kick out bad kids so good kids can learn" tactics are celebrated by the media in movies like *Lean on Me*, with Morgan Freeman portraying a "tough love" school principal in inner-city Los Angeles. School shootings and fears of violence have led to "zero-tolerance" disciplinary policies in schools nationwide. According to some parents, the Success Academy charter school in Harlem earns its high standardized-test achievement rates at the cost of students whose special needs and behavioral problems might pull those averages down. The school's suspension rate in 2010–11 was 22 percent of the total student population—far too many students. One study supporting a public health approach to children's mental health noted that "within the education sector, legislation requiring schools to provide services in the case of a diagnosis requires schools to financially strap themselves. Many schools find it easier to let children drop out (often to the juvenile justice system) than seek mental health services."

Contrast that all-too-common "weed them out" approach with another school in Walla Walla, Washington, where suspension rates have dropped 85 percent in recent years. Lincoln High School principal Jim Sporleder changed his school's entire approach to discipline after a fortuitous conversation with molecular biologist Dr. John Medina, whose *New York Times* best-selling 2008 book *Brain Rules* provides interesting science-based insights into the way our brains work.

One of Dr. Medina's observations about learning caught Sporleder's attention: "Toxic stress damages kid's brains. When trauma launches kids into flight, fight or fright mode, they cannot learn. It is physiologically impossible." Lincoln High School was a school of last resort for most of its students, who definitely fit the low-income, at-risk profile. So Sporleder decided to do something different. Rather than suspend students for defiant or disruptive behavior, he started to ask them what was wrong. To his surprise, this approach usually resulted in a positive response—students admitted to challenges in their lives, then actually apologized for their behavior and changed it.

Jim Sporleder's innovative, science-based approach to discipline echoes the type of intervention we saw at Clarity Child Guidance Center in chapter 4. The model turns everything we thought we knew on its head: Children are not misbehaving because they want to misbehave. They are misbehaving because they need our help. Classroom management should focus, then, not on "weeding out" the bad kids, but on understanding how to help all children thrive. In an article pointing out the functional difficulties children with ADHD face in navigating a regular classroom, Dr. Mark Bertin noted, "Smaller classrooms that minimize distraction go a long way to helping children with ADHD, as well as all students."

And yet, New York City's public school system reported seventy thousand suspensions in the 2011–12 school year, 40 percent more than the period six years earlier. Of the 882 arrests during the school year studied, one in every six was for "resisting arrest" or "obstructing governmental administration," charges for which there is often no underlying criminal behavior. For example, the study found that black students in New York City are fourteen times more likely to be arrested because of school-based incidents than their white peers; Hispanic students are five times more likely to be arrested than whites. Special-needs children are also disproportionately affected and are four times more likely to be suspended than their peers.

One comment on my blog addressed Adam Lanza's documented negative experience with public school: "Our special education system has failed our children and their families terribly and it is critical that we address this and work toward effective change. Your letter puts a face to Adam Lanza and to his mother . . . and while my heart aches beyond belief for the children and educators who died, it also aches for Adam. The rage and the pain that must have simmered within him, the fury that must have driven him to such an act cannot be discounted in this whole terrible scenario . . . and I cannot help but wonder what the school and special education system did for him (or more importantly, did not do) all those years before now."

The Safe Schools/Healthy Students (SS/HS) Initiative enacted by Congress in 1999 after a wave of school shootings, including Columbine, provided more than $2 billion in grants to 350 school districts to create local partnerships among public schools, law enforcement, mental health, and juvenile justice agencies. One of its primary missions was to address the unmet mental health needs of at-risk students. A 2011 study of the SS/HS initiative found that grant recipients were better able to address the mental health needs of students, both at school and within the community, and had a corresponding decrease in violence.

Most Americans agree with Jim Sporleder and the Safe Schools/Healthy Students model: in a 2013 PDK/Gallup Poll, Americans supported increased access to mental health services in schools rather than armed security guards by a nearly two-to-one margin. So how can we help those five disruptive students in a classroom of twenty-five—and their teacher—to succeed?

## Free and Appropriate Public Education

All children have the right to a free and appropriate public education, or FAPE, an acronym that parents of children with any disability know well. That right is delineated in several federal laws designed to protect individuals with disabilities, including Section 504 of the Rehabilitation Act of 1973, Title II of the Americans with Disabilities Act, and the Individuals with Disabilities Education Act of 2004, or IDEA. But enforcing that right can become a full-time job for parents of children with mental illness, too often resulting in an adversarial rather than a collaborative relationship among parents, teachers, and administrators.

One of my friend's first-day-of-school Facebook posts sums up one of the most common challenges parents of children with disabilities face when trying to exercise their child's right to a public education—making sure that teachers are aware of the hard-won accommodations already in place:

> Every single year, teachers? Every year? Go ahead and read that kid's 504 plan before the first day of school. It's the law.

She's not going to draw attention to herself to ask for her accommodations. Her mental health issues cause too much anxiety to do that. Here we go again.
            —crazy mom who knows there must be a file at the school
                    just like Elaine's on that episode of "Seinfeld"


The seemingly endless accommodations skirmishes, the reams of paperwork, the tests (often the wrong ones) and memos and meetings with
bureaucratic administrators who refuse to meet your eyes all may help to
explain why increasing numbers of parents—among them Nancy Lanza—
choose to homeschool their children—1.5 million in 2007, an increase
from 850,000 in 1999 and 1.1 million in 2003.

Every parent of a child with any kind of disability should sit in on a
trial like Diana Abramowski's suit against Idaho's two largest school districts on behalf of her son, alleging that they'd failed to provide him with
the education to which he was entitled. It provides an invaluable opportunity for parents to become more aware, increase dissemination of information about types of testing, and assist parents in understanding what we
need to ask for. I attended three of the seven days of the Matthew
Abramowski trial. I heard doctors and students and teachers testify. When
the jury returned a verdict in favor of Idaho's two largest school districts
after deliberating for several hours, I was stunned: perhaps I had been
witnessing a different trial. But Charlene Quade, one of Matthew's attorneys and herself the mother of two daughters with disabilities, took the
decision in stride. "This is a complicated issue," she told me. "The laws
that require a free and appropriate public education can be tough for anyone to understand. On the positive side, this story got picked up everywhere. It's a pebble in a pond. It will create ripples lapping against the
shore, creating change."

The Abramowski case illustrates just how hard parents have to fight
for educational services for their children with mental disorders. No one
disputes that Matthew Abramowski has autism. In California, he was on
an individualized education plan that provided special services to supple-

ment his primary homeschooling education. But when the family moved from California to Idaho, things began to go very wrong, according to his mother. Matthew decided that he wanted to attend public school; Diana found herself working with his teachers, providing in-class and at-home tutoring. The Meridian School District did not feel that Matthew needed an IEP, despite his autism, so they put him on a less restrictive Section 504 plan instead.

After the fire, Diana Abramowski and her husband were not allowed to see Matthew. "We informed the police that he was autistic, and the detective said, 'I don't know what that is,'" she recalled when we spoke about the trial and the events that led up to it. "My husband and I asked three times to be with him. They took my son, they Mirandized him, he had just turned fifteen and he had a disability, and they knew it. The prosecutors' office called us in and wanted to put him away for twenty-five years. Matthew is not aggressive. He doesn't even yell. I couldn't even work with the public defender because Matthew said something like 'I'm going to kill my parents.' He was just scripting [a behavior some children with autism have, where they recite words that seem appropriate, as if from a script]. Kids make statements like that all of the time. They all say things like, 'My parents grounded me, I want to kill them.'"

After the fire, Diana started getting calls from strangers who told her that they knew Matthew had been relentlessly bullied. At the federal trial, Matthew's former classmates testified about the bullying. But as often happens in these cases, it was easier to blame the mom. The school district's attorneys portrayed Diana as a Dragon Mother who attacked the teachers and called them bad names. "I think the teachers are incredible," Diana said. "I never blamed anybody. I just said, 'You are not listening. Help me out here.'

"The one thing I always wanted was for someone to say 'I'm sorry.' Just one of those kids, one of those administrators. His whole life, he thought he was just supposed to be bullied and he just had to accept it. He was basically crying for help."

Diana is still trying to get an IEP for her son. "I had no idea what was going on," she said. "It's not a special autism he has—it's just like all the other kids. If you can't hire an attorney, there are no fair options for parents to fight the system. This happens to any parent who fights for their kids. Do they really think I'm just this mom making their lives miserable? That I want to spend my time doing this? Why would a mom do this? There's no person who wants this kind of punishment. And the jargon— it's like you've gone to Mars."

## PARENT ADVOCATES

The laws that entitle all children to a public education are complicated, flawed, and, as Diana Abramowski noted, jargon ridden. Fortunately, there are parent advocates like Marcie Lipsitt to help the rest of us make sense of them. When Lipsitt starts talking about education and children's mental health, the ideas rush over themselves like a swollen river in swirls and eddies and torrents of words, struggling to carve meaning from the canyonlike edifice of *plus ça change* public education (let's just say she is not a big fan of Michigan's public schools). "Children with psychiatric and learning disabilities are our most underserved population," she said when I contacted her in April 2013 after a colleague pointed me to a blog post Lipsitt wrote in response to mine.

Lipsitt knows what she's talking about, but like many advocates, myself included, she found her calling almost by accident, as she navigated the baffling mental health system with her own child, Andrew, who is now twenty-four. Armed with a degree in English and a native business acumen she honed working in her family's building supply business, Lipsitt talked her way into an appointment with Janet Wozniak, one of the nation's foremost experts on pediatric bipolar disorder. Lipsitt became a fund-raiser for Massachusetts General Hospital and sat on the board of the Balanced Mind Foundation, a national advocacy group, until she started to feel that the organization was moving away from a focus on clinical outcomes and research and toward what Lipsitt terms "political correctness."

I found Lipsitt by chance, when a colleague whose own children struggle with mental illness placed a blog post she had written, defending me,
on my desk one morning. Her post, "I Too Could Be Adam Lanza's Mother,
Without the Guns of Course," was a powerful affirmation that I was not
alone in my struggles.

> Liza Long's blog speaks to the deepest part of my pain and
> sorrow as I watch my child lose his childhood and move into
> an adulthood that he will struggle to navigate. Liza Long's
> blog speaks to my fear as a mother that has been frightened of
> my son on more days than I can count. I will love my son
> every day of his life and every day of my life. I will stand by his
> side and fight for his sanity and right to a small measure of the
> American Dream.

Lipsitt's baptism by immersion into the world of special education
advocacy began in 2005, when her school district "crossed the line" with
Andrew's IEP. Lipsitt did some research and decided to take the school
district to a due process hearing in January 2006. A due process hearing is
one remedy available to parents who feel that the school district has failed
to provide their child a free and appropriate education under IDEA. Unfortunately for parents who did not attend law school, the administrative
hearing process looks a whole lot like court. Parents are free to represent
themselves—but "caveat emptor" is very much the rule in this complicated legal area, where your child's education and future may be at stake.
The due process "judge" is an impartial hearing officer (IHO) who listens
to both sides, then makes a determination based on the evidence, case law,
and precedent. Parents who are not satisfied with the outcome can appeal
to federal court.

In Lipsitt's case, the due process hearings lasted until March—these
proceedings tend to drag on, because while they are ongoing, the school
district does not have to provide services. Lipsitt was asking for a costly
home-based private program for Andrew. The law requires that students

be educated in the "least restrictive environment." Because of Andrew's multiple disabilities, he could not fit into a traditional high school and couldn't learn in classes, so his least restrictive environment was costly one-on-one teaching. "We prevailed at the state level, setting a precedent for children like Andrew," Lipsitt said. "The ruling came out on my birthday at the end of July. The school district then appealed to federal court, and we finally settled at the end of September."

Finally the district agreed to drop its appeal, settle her case, and pay for Andrew's education if she would stop filing complaints. The settlement also required her to refrain from helping any other families in Birmingham with their special-needs children's requests for a period of two years. "It's the hardest piece of paper I ever signed, because I had to compromise everything I ever believed in," Lipsitt said. "I opened every can of worms. But I had to stop. We had already spent $73,000 on legal fees, and we were paying for all of Andrew's schooling. I had to do what was best for my son."

"I'm not Pollyanna. I never have been. But I really had no idea how dark and ugly special education is. People lie to you—these are the people you trust to educate and care for your children," she said, describing the adversarial relationship that often develops with the school district when parents fight for their children's education.

Lipsitt now works full-time as a special education advocate, taking clients strictly by referral. She meets the parents wherever they are in their child's journey, and there are some days when she has meetings in five separate school districts—"nothing short of insanity!" She laughed. "It's not going to be a 'Kumbaya' session with all of us smiling across the table," she added. "And yet I still get plenty of referrals from school administrators."

She calls her work "the learning curve of a lifetime," expressing her belief that IDEA was a poorly written law in 1975 when President Ford signed it, and that every reauthorization has further eroded its protections for children with mental illness. "Children are being segregated again," she said. "Too many kids today are unwelcome guests in a mainstream classroom."

The backlash in her own community that began with her due process hearing in 2006 is still ongoing. "There were parents who thought I was evil," she said. "Why would I do this to Birmingham? But we never asked the district for anything other than to try to do their best for our son. When even parents of children with disabilities don't understand or support what you are doing, that's hard. There are parents in this state who are fine with their children earning a D. I'm not that parent. My husband says it's time for the bulletproof vest."

For her own son, Lipsitt hopes that he will be able to attend community college in the coming year, though she compares the task of preparing for that to Sisyphus's endless stone rolling. "People ask me all the time why I do what I do. At the end of the day, I don't do it for people to like me. I fight for kids, and the children I meet deserve an education. The reality is that I will forever believe that children deserve to be fought for. Adam Lanza clearly was a kid who had psychiatric issues, and the school was not meeting his needs. These are very ill children. Family life with them is not like you think. You're not supposed to be afraid of your child. I am. I have the kindest, most gentle son—when his brain is working. But when it's not . . ." She trailed off. "We need services," Lipsitt said finally. "We need programs. We need to fund research. My son—and every child—deserves to have the best life possible."

## IDEA IN PRACTICE

IDEA lists thirteen separate categories under which a child might be eligible for services: of these, autism, emotional disturbance, and "other health impairment" are the categories that most often apply to children with mental illness. Michael's IEP uses emotional disturbance as its basis— "other health impairment" is the category commonly used for children diagnosed with ADHD. The "emotional disturbance" category is used more than any other to remove children from the general school population into a restrictive environment. As one study noted, "This tendency is concerning as the outcomes for students with emotional disorders are bleak."

My son's school district has chosen an increasingly popular way to manage students with behavioral and emotional challenges: remove them from mainstream classrooms. Michael's school is called the ASCENT Program, and it's basically a self-contained holding pen for children—95 percent of them boys—between the ages of twelve and twenty-three who have IEPs for emotional disturbances.

ASCENT stands rather optimistically for Alternative Students Courageously Exploring New Territory. The school district claims that this program "makes learning and socializing possible for students who have difficulty in the traditional school setting." But kids are discouraged from becoming friends with each other or socializing outside of school. After my blog went viral, a local journalist asked me, "Aren't you concerned about the stigma for your son? About what his friends, the kids he goes to school with, will think when they find out he has been to jail or Intermountain?"

"No," I answered quite simply. And I wasn't. My son's classmates have all been to jail or Intermountain Hospital, most of them multiple times. A typical day at ASCENT includes at least one lockdown for safety reasons. My son caused two or three last year himself, though so far, this year is going well for him. Michael has an IQ that qualifies him for highly gifted programs, yet on his report card, he earned an F in math last year, cognitively his strongest subject. His report card noted that "he has trouble completing the work due to the fact that he can't focus. He needs to request a quieter environment or express his struggles so that teachers can better meet his needs."

Here's where I struggle: I really like Michael's teachers, school counselor, and principal. Like Diana Abramowski, I think these teachers are courageous to engage with the most difficult children, every single day. But my son won't actually be able to graduate from high school if he can't transition out of the ASCENT Program and back into a mainstream classroom. And I cannot see how being sequestered with children who share his behavioral challenges—and much worse—is going to help him to learn to socialize in the world I hope he inhabits as an adult. Restrictive programs like these do not prepare children for college. They prepare children for prison.

Before he was transferred to ASCENT, his junior high school used an even less attractive option to manage Michael's outbursts: an isolation room. After one particularly lengthy rage, the principal found him kneeling in the corner of the small room, repetitively trying to insert his glasses into an outlet so that he could electrocute himself. Many parents of children with mental illness are afraid that budget cuts will lead to an increased use of these isolation rooms: one angry mother in Washington claimed that a special education teacher locked her second-grade daughter, who has fetal alcohol syndrome, in a windowless closet for several hours. Michael's current school actually has a padded room, its walls clad in thick green wrestling mats.

Charlene Quade, Matthew Abramowski's attorney, noted that one problematic area is teacher training. "Teachers mean well. But teachers are not trained to recognize the signs," she said. "Teachers need to make special education training part of their negotiation for bargaining. Teachers are put in a position where they are violating IDEA on behalf of their employer. They are put in a difficult position. They want to do what's best for these children, but they are not given the supports they need."

She also noted that parents who understand how testing works and which tests to ask for will likely find success in helping the school district to understand the needs of their child. "The earlier you identify the problem, the better your outcomes," she said. "We are not talking about stuff that costs millions of dollars. We are talking about some basic, inexpensive things. Early identification and intervention saves the whole economy money. In Matthew's case, at the end of the day we have a man who is developmentally disabled and requires Medicaid services. It didn't have to be that way. What does developmental mean? It means that if you start younger, you can chart a different trajectory for development."

Unfortunately, when it comes to getting much-needed services, parents are in an unequal bargaining position compared to school districts; this seems especially true for parents who come prepared with information, because administrators have a tendency to label them as troublemakers. The laws are baffling, and even if you can understand them, you can't find anyone to help you fight for your child's rights. No agency in Idaho will take a case against a school district to trial on behalf of the student. No family can afford the legal fight. Every Dragon Mother/advocate I talked to, without fail, mentioned at some point that the school district—in Florida, in California, in Texas, in Michigan, in Idaho—had advised her simply to move.

Charlene Quade has heard the same frustration that Marcie Lipsitt expressed from nearly every client. "You hear, 'They are just leeches, these parents of kids with disabilities.' But the net cost to society is more than most people can get their heads around. Children with mental illness have a relatively stable life expectancy. As taxpayers, if we don't educate these children, we will be paying for their services or they will be incarcerated. Parents spend their retirement funds; they use all of their disposable income trying to provide services that the school district should provide. Too often the schools create something more broken than what we started with."

## COMMON CORE: A CHANCE FOR CHANGE?

People don't like to talk about mental illness. But they love to talk about education reform, usually with a call for "standards," the latest example being the 2013 national debate about bipartisan-backed Common Core State Standards (CCSS) implementation and the previous handwringing about the bipartisan Titanic that was No Child Left Behind. The symptoms of this failure are very well documented in subpar standardized test results. Google "Our nation's schools are failing us," and you'll find agreement among pretty much every sector. As Stella O'Neal at the Prison Justice Project succinctly puts it, "Our nation's schools are failing our children. Black students lag behind white students from the very first day of kindergarten, a disparity that is as evident among suburban middle class children as it is among their inner city peers."

The Common Core State Standards Initiative was developed jointly by the nation's governors and state education commissioners with the goal to better prepare America's children for college and careers. How these higher standards will affect children with mental disorders is still unclear. In 2007–08, IDEA reported the following IEP percentages for children and young people aged three through twenty-one:

- Other health impairments (ADHD): 10 percent
- Emotional disturbance: 7 percent
- Autism: 4 percent

Under Common Core, school districts are encouraged to adopt a co-teaching inclusion model for most special education instruction in their general education curriculum. For this reason, Common Core actually provides a real opportunity for change and improvement for all children, including children with mental illness. Rather than focusing on rote memorization and rule-following that can prove too restrictive for children with ADHD and other mental disorders, Common Core uses universal design for learning (UDL) to allow for flexible learning environments and modalities that can be customized to a student's abilities. UDL focuses on the "what," the "how," and the "why" of content matter. Blogger Cameron Pipkin noted that special education teachers have essentially been practicing UDL in the classroom for years now, and that they are uniquely qualified to lead as Common Core is introduced to schools.

Here's an example of how a Common Core approach could benefit a child like Michael. Math coach and Maryvale Elementary School assistant principal Greg Mullenholz described in an online op-ed how his school developed an inclusion model for children with behavioral issues. By integrating special education into a regular general education classroom, his school was actually able to increase the amount of contact all students had with adult instructors. "We saw a dramatic decrease in the number of special education students being referred to the office. And less time in the office or out on suspension meant more time in the classroom. We also saw increases in academic achievement, student engagement, and overall self-confidence," he reported.

But one clinical psychologist, Dr. Gary Thompson, has expressed concerns over the types of standardized testing that Common Core will employ, and how that information will be protected:

> The issues involving psychological testing and privacy are issues that should be of concern to every parent with a child enrolled in public school. The power granted federal and state education administrators via the regulations of CCSS are unprecedented in nature. . . . Parents deserve to be clearly informed about these and other issues surrounding CCSS in a clear and straightforward manner so that they can make educated choices regarding their children's educations.

The issue is not likely to be resolved anytime soon. In the conservative blogosphere, 2013 saw "Obamacore" replace "Obamacare" as the latest example of a godless, socialist, Marxist conspiracy designed to corrupt the young: one letter to my local newspaper on the subject warned that "various brainwashing techniques will turn your David or Sarah into a little Obama—an Obamaite, using intrusive monitoring systems that terminate moral and just reasoning." With the failure of No Child Left Behind still fresh in their minds, states are taking a more cautious "wait and see" approach to Common Core State Standards. Indeed, as long-time teacher and administrator Marion Brady noted in a *Washington Post* editorial, "So much orchestrated attention is being showered on the Common Core Standards, the main reason for poor student performance is being ignored—a level of childhood poverty the consequences of which no amount of schooling can effectively counter."

## TEACH FOR AMERICA

Just as parents are often blamed for their children with mental illness, teachers are all too often blamed for their students who are failing. But a longitudinal study of two generations of students found that while more than half of children born into high-income households between 1979 and 1982 graduated from college by 2007, only 9 percent of children born into low-income households during that period were college completers. Marcie Lipsitt, the special education advocate, believes that poverty should count as a fourteenth category under IDEA. Poverty hurts children. And as we saw in earlier chapters, mental illness and poverty are clearly correlated.

One controversial but intriguing solution to the teaching crisis is Teach for America, a program that tries to level the playing field by providing poverty-stricken communities with young, bright, dedicated teachers. The Teach for America controversy involves the teachers themselves: rather than recruiting from education programs, Teach for America encourages applicants from top graduating college seniors in any field, regardless of whether they have been trained in a college of education. The program is a popular proving ground for young people, in part because it helps them to repay college loans: 18 percent of Harvard's graduating senior class applied to Teach for America, which requires an intensive summer training program and a two-year commitment to teaching in a low-income community.

I met Nicole Brisbane, the site coordinator for Teach for America, at an Idaho education seminar in 2013. As I researched this book, I had been continually struck by the sticky web that connected children in poverty to mental illness, suspension from public schools, and prison. Brisbane has been making the same connections. She was able to observe those social issues firsthand during her two years as a middle school teacher in an impoverished neighborhood in Miami, Florida.

Brisbane didn't plan to be a teacher; she planned to go to law school, which thrilled her mother. But when she heard about the Teach for America program during her senior year of college, she knew she had to apply. She was assigned to teach English and language arts to the worst-performing students in her school. Looking back on the experience, Brisbane realized that their issues were not rooted in a lack of ability to read, but rather reflected broader, tougher, systemic issues like poverty and negative experiences at home.

"I had just one student formally on an IEP," she recalled. "He was being raised by his grandmother, who was very engaged in the process and an effective advocate for her son." But access to care was a problem—the grandmother couldn't always afford the boy's ADHD medication, and Brisbane could definitely sense a difference on days when he went without it. Stigma was also a huge problem in her community: "Parents did not want their kids tested because of what could happen with special education classes, etc. Their parents didn't want labels for their children."

What parents were really afraid of was that if their children were tested for problems, they would be excused by the public school system from the accountability of getting an education, Brisbane said. If a child was labeled as having special needs, the teachers had a pass to not hold that child to the same standard. And education was the only ticket out of poverty for these children.

"When you have the challenges of poverty that are so pervasive, mental illness can become the norm rather than the exception," Brisbane observed. "I would say that my students faced so many different levels of mental health issues—growing up with no parents in a house with ten other people, wondering whether dinner would be available that night—mental health issues become normal and internalized. Behavior comes from that internalization of the challenge, and you see students acting on that belief that adults can't be trusted. People come in and out of their lives; no one is reliable."

For Brisbane's students, one consequence of this uncertain and tenuous existence was a reluctance to commit to the demands of her classroom. "There's a lot of thought around best practices for classroom management, especially in communities of poverty," Brisbane said. "I realized the truth of that quote that having high expectations without a relationship is self-righteous, but having a relationship without high expectations is self-pity. If you have not built a relationship with your students individually, it is impossible to hold them to a standard. You expect the work from them, but you have not laid the foundation for their trust." By spending time with her students in their community, Brisbane slowly built those invaluable relationships.

Fortunately, as a new teacher, Brisbane didn't have to do it alone: Teach for America provides resources for its teachers, including one-on-one mentoring. The program also provides training specific to students with special needs and mental health issues and encourages teachers to build relationships with local community mental health resources.

At Brisbane's school, there was very little opportunity for proactive planning. Teachers were left to fend for themselves in the classroom. "The administration is literally firefighting all day long," she said. "Imagine running a school where there is no cafeteria lunch or not enough for all your students, where buses will be late, where there's a community crisis so the school is on lockdown—what you end up with is a school that is operationally focused. The least of their priorities is building better teachers, which is why Teach for America's coaches are so valuable."

During her teaching experience, Brisbane came up with a novel approach to removing the stigma of mental health counseling in schools. "What if you just called it something else?" she said. "There is a stigma attached to this idea of mental health. Anytime you put the word 'mental' in it, there's a weird stigma attached. Instead, call it leadership training or personal development, provided by reaffirming and giving teachers. If it felt more like a personal coaching model, a success model, I think we could reach so many more students."

After her teaching experience, Brisbane went on to law school, where she discovered a passion for connecting education and law. She taught high school civics classes and became involved with a program called Know Your Rights, designed to help teenage youth who were targets for harassment. During her third year of law school, she worked with the public defender's office. "My experience was limited, but one of the things I observed was really young kids in handcuffs and physical restraints. I always wondered whether they were being restrained like that because of mental health issues," she said.

As a former teacher in a low-income neighborhood, Brisbane also offers this observation about the school-to-prison pipeline: "These kids have a tough personal circumstance as a child and don't have someone invested in their success. They are not trying to use this as an excuse. They genuinely struggle. Those behaviors manifest in attention-seeking ways. Thirteen-year-old boys lash out and are immediately labeled as criminals. They make poor decisions because of a lack of coaching and mentoring. We create a pipeline without stopping to think about how that stems from mental health. Our schools are not addressing these issues, even though they are the major point of contact with our students. Once you are a child and have to survive in a criminal justice facility, you create a cycle that affects minorities. School is the place where they spend the majority of their time. If we could identify these behaviors sooner and provide appropriate interventions, we could change lives."

## EDUTOPIA

Matthew Abramowski would agree with Nicole Brisbane about rebranding mental illness. He thinks that special education should be called "innovative training." Whatever we call it, it's clear that our current public school system is facing more than just a disagreement about common standards. And yet a public health approach to children's mental health runs up against the very real phenomenon of finite resources—how would we pay for all these services? Nicole Brisbane's idea, expanding existing school-based programs and providing after-school developmental care for children with mental illness, is one possible public health–based solution to this problem. As a working mother of a teenager with mental illness, it's an idea I really like.

Therapeutic after-school and summer care would provide innumerable benefits to working mothers like me. Instead of having to worry about my son every time I see a police car, I could know that he was safe, that the people around him were safe. Smaller classes, or Common Core inclusion for children with mental disorders, providing more teachers per classroom; developmental care for children with mental illness after school and on summer vacations; even more physical education and better nutrition in schools might help students with mental illness to achieve IDEA's promise of a free and appropriate public education.

On the other hand, current practices like zero tolerance and self-contained, restrictive environments for children with emotional disorders perpetuate the stigma attached to children with mental illness. As we consider the costs of providing interventions for kids like Matthew Abramowski and my son Michael, we also have to consider the costs of not providing those interventions—lost productivity, disability, and a new kind of institutionalization. Where do children go when they can't succeed in school? Too often, they go to jail.

# SIX

# CRIME AND PUNISHMENT

## WHY HAVE JAILS BECOME THE INSTITUTION OF CHOICE TO TREAT CHILDREN WITH MENTAL ILLNESS?

> "It's come at last," she thought, "the time when you can no longer stand between your children and heart-ache."
>
> —Betty Smith, *A Tree Grows in Brooklyn*

In November 2012, Michael's twelve-year-old friend Jayden (not his real name), who has autism, schizoaffective disorder, and an IQ classified as borderline, started to become frustrated with a substitute teacher in his special education classroom. He asked her to allow him to call his mother, Clarissa (not her real name), a requirement written into Jayden's IEP as part of the twenty-step behavior intervention plan the administration had agreed to follow when Jayden's classroom behavior escalated. On that day, according to Clarissa, the steps were not followed. While a substitute teacher without special education training was supervising the classroom, Jayden became increasingly frustrated, finally losing control and hurling a phone at the teacher, who sustained a bruise. She called the student resource officer. Because of the school's zero tolerance policy, Jayden, a pale, smallish boy with white-blond hair and a quiet voice, was arrested, handcuffed, and taken to the Ada County Juvenile Detention Center, where he was booked on charges of assault.

Clarissa, a former pediatric nurse who now stays home to provide full-time care and homeschooling to Jayden, figured the matter would blow over quickly—the judge would see that Jayden was disabled, that the school district had failed to follow his IEP, and that would be the end of it. "Three months later, there was a knock at the door. The court clerk staff handed me a warrant for Jayden's arrest," she said. The Ada County prosecutor had decided to press charges against her son.

The family retained a private attorney even though they were told that a public defender and a court advocate would assist them. "None of this was true, because we were in criminal court, not children's mental health court," Clarissa said. The court held two competency hearings, and in both, Jayden was found incompetent to stand trial and nonrestorable. The juvenile magistrate, dissatisfied with that finding, sent Jayden to the state residential mental health hospital in Blackfoot, Idaho, for restoration. Jayden spent nine days away from his family and, according to his mother, was questioned without parents or counsel. The hospital staff didn't even know Jayden had autism—they were perplexed by his refusal to socialize. "He was so homesick," his mom said. "He had never been away from us overnight before."

Almost a year later, Clarissa was still attending weekly two-hour court-ordered competency restoration classes with Jayden, classes designed to prepare this boy who does not even read on a fourth-grade level to stand trial for his "crime." The classes cost $45 per hour, and parents are required to pay for the fees by state statute. The family has already spent more than $11,000 on legal fees for their son's criminal defense. "Jayden's special education teacher tells me that two of her students are arrested every year, in a special education classroom of ten middle school students," Clarissa said. She held up a thick sheaf—nearly two reams of paper—with both hands. "These are the notes from Jayden's psychiatrist over the years. I tried to give them this information, but no one would take it. People don't believe that this happens—that a child who clearly has mental illness can be sent to jail. But it happens all the time."

The United States sends more of its children to jail each year than any other developed country in the world: 130,000, with an average of 70,000 on any given day. Of these children, as many as 75 percent have at least one mental disorder. The lifetime consequences for children who enter the juvenile justice system are grim: they are much less likely to complete high school and much more likely to go to prison as adults.

But the U.S. prison industry is booming, spending more than $6 billion on juvenile corrections each year. In my state (and many states), the only way parents can access much-needed mental health services is through the criminal justice system, a system where as many as 67 percent of boys and 75 percent of girls in juvenile detention have a mental disorder, and over half of all youth also have substance abuse problems. For youth who have been in residential detention for nine months or more, those rates are even higher: 88 percent of boys and 92 percent of girls in the California juvenile detention system had at least one psychiatric disorder, even after conduct disorder and oppositional defiant disorder were excluded. This prevalence of mental illness continues with the adult prison population. Rikers Island, the Los Angeles County Jail, and Cook County Jail in Illinois housed the nation's largest mental health treatment centers in 2011, proof of U.S. Representative Tim Murphy's assertion in a March 2013 congressional forum on mental health that with respect to mental illness, "deinstitutionalization was a disaster."

I've been through some tough things in my life. I lost my father to cancer. I went through a bankruptcy after my then husband lost his job when I was pregnant with our third child. I was divorced when my youngest daughter was just two. And I lost a home I loved to foreclosure in the housing bubble collapse that started in 2008. I've also lost a job I loved, under cruel and demeaning circumstances, and I've endured a cancer scare or two.

But I have never done anything harder than call the police on my own child.


## THE FIRST TIME

In the first chapter of this book, I described my feelings the first time my son went to jail, the emptiness, the fear, the crushing sense of failure. My friends sometimes accuse me of being a Pollyanna—and it's a fair criticism. If I ever find myself being sucked toward the event horizon of a black hole, I will probably make some asinine comment about how the ribbons of starlight trailing into death and darkness remind me that every cloud has a silver lining.

Yet there are some situations that defy even the most practiced optimist's spin skills. I found myself in one of them the first time I accompanied Michael to juvenile court, where I had to watch my tender-hearted eleven-year-old son try to hug his father—the boy had not seen his dad in more than a week—and watch as the man turned from his son and walked away. In his father's defense, Michael had made accusations of physical abuse; I'm sure his father wanted to avoid any appearance of impropriety. And yet, as parents, I like to think we have certain obligations to the offspring we bring into this world, obligations to provide for their physical needs, to keep them as safe as possible, to educate them about the values we hold dear. But above all, we have a duty to love them unconditionally. This is a duty that is sorely tested by mental illness.

At this point of crisis, I didn't really care whose fault it was. I was interested in solutions. I was interested in what was best for Michael. I wanted to do the best I could, as a parent, to fulfill the sacred contract with my offspring, to provide for him, to nurture him, to educate him, and above all, to love him. That day was a little death for me, as I started to comprehend that there are no silver linings in black holes. I realized I had to hang on tight to my son who was slipping away from me into darkness.

I asked Michael to tell me what juvenile detention was like, after his longest stay of more than one week. "They sat me down on a metal stool and made me fill out lots of paperwork. There were lots of bubble test questions, things like, Did I drink alcohol? Did I do drugs? I was eleven! And I'm a Mormon!" he said, his voice filled with indignation at the thought. "There were fifty questions, most of which were pointless."

After he filled out the questionnaire, Michael changed into black sweatpants and a green T-shirt, since the standard-issue orange jumpsuits were all too big for him. "They put me in a small room about the size of a bathroom. All I had was a stone slab with a mat like the ones you use in PE class, two blankets, and a pillow that wasn't really a pillow. It was this weird uncomfortable leatherlike thing that felt like it had gravel in it. My back hurt for a month after I got out," he said.

At 8:30, they dimmed the lights for bedtime, but he was never allowed to turn the lights completely off. "A lot of the time I couldn't get to sleep, so I stayed up all night reading random books. They didn't have much available. I read the Harry Potter books and the Chronicles of Narnia again. I also read some James Bond books," he said.

Michael was upset and angry, but afraid to admit to his emotions, so he kept them to himself. In the morning, they woke the inmates up at 6:00. After breakfast, they played volleyball in the gym. Michael felt out of place because of his young age (barely eleven). "All of the kids there were older than me by at least two years. The other kids were mostly in for drugs or driving under the influence. We weren't supposed to talk about what we were in for, but we did. There were a couple in for battery, which was what I was in for. There was one kid who was there for assault with a weapon and intent to kill. I think the weapon was a baseball bat," he said.

For school, the youths went into a room with two guards, even though the door was already locked from the outside. "There were lots of tables and a few old computers. They gave us binders that had worksheets. We did worksheets all day long. You couldn't ask questions. The teacher wasn't really a teacher. The teacher didn't actually teach anything," Michael said. "We went back to our 'rooms' (in other words, cells) at noon. Time was hard to keep track of there because they didn't have clocks on the walls. They had a small fenced area outside."

Michael really didn't like the food, which was served to their individual cells for breakfast, lunch, and dinner: "I'm a picky eater because I have very sensitive taste buds, but I am guessing a lot of other kids felt the same way. It was stuff like lasagna, or meatloaf that didn't taste like meatloaf. Sometimes they gave you soup. They gave you a food and called it something, but it didn't taste like that food," he explained.

He also wasn't impressed by the décor: "There were lots of white bricks everywhere, no color at all. There were cameras everywhere so they could see everything you did."

At 4:00, the teens finished with their schoolwork and had a break time at a walled-in area with tables. If everyone agreed, they could go outside. "We sat there at the tables and played card games until dinner. Technically you were allowed to play chess, but I couldn't find anyone to play with me. None of the other kids knew how," Michael said. "Once in a while the guards would play with me. One of the guards was really good. He beat me three times."

On Wednesdays, Saturdays, and Sundays, visitors could come for an hour. "You came to see me a couple of times, and we played chess," Michael remembered. "I always beat you, except for that one time you got a stalemate."

Twice-daily group therapy felt useless to Michael. "It was really dull and pointless, because none of the kids seemed to think they had done anything wrong, me included. They tried to talk to us about choices and consequences. It felt like a long lecture on why I am a bad person," he explained. "A lot of the guards thought after the second time I went back [in one month] that I would end up permanently in prison. They said I had no future other than one in prison. I thought, they have their opinions of me. I'll just prove them wrong. I want to prove them wrong."

But his court appearances were especially disturbing. "When I had to go to court, they put shackles on me. I had no idea why—I was an eleven-year-old kid! It's not like I was going to be able to take out a police officer," Michael said, again adopting a tone of righteous indignation. He preferred some juvenile court magistrates to others. "I usually had Judge M. . . . he really liked me. He was great. I didn't like the dark-haired guy. He sent me back to juvie. My public defender was really nice and did a good job. He told me I was most likely going to get out. Finally, after the fourth time I got Judge M. again, and he was noticing a pattern—that I always ended up in juvie when I was at my dad's house. So he released me into your custody and I didn't have to go back to Dad's anymore. I haven't been in juvie since then, and I don't ever want to go back."

For nearly a year after Michael's most recent and hopefully final stay in juvenile detention, he would wake up in the night screaming. He had terrible nightmares of being sentenced to death.


## CHILDREN LEFT BEHIND

Jail is not the help children like Jayden or Michael need. In chapter 5, we looked at how special education for children with mental illness too often turns into a school-to-prison pipeline—Jayden's story is a textbook example. One study found that the number of children with learning disabilities in prison was more than 30 percent.

The potential for the transformation of our prisons to de facto mental hospitals became apparent almost as soon as the hospitals started shutting their doors. In a 1995 editorial in the *American Journal of Public Health*, then National Institute of Mental Health clinician E. Fuller Torrey identified this disturbing trend. With institutions closed, patients with mental illness were increasingly becoming denizens of another institution: prison. He concluded, "Deinstitutionalization of seriously mentally ill individuals has been the largest failed social experiment in twentieth-century America. It has failed not because the vast majority of released individuals cannot live in the community, but because we did not ensure that they receive the medications and aftercare that they need to do so successfully." Torrey cited rural areas including Idaho as the worst offenders, noting that in 1990, presumably because of lack of access to care, three hundred people with mental illness were jailed for an average of five days without being charged with any crime.

In a landmark 2002 study, Teplin et al. looked at the rates of psychiatric disorders for 1,829 youths aged ten to eighteen who were detained in Cook County, Illinois. They found that a shocking 67 percent of males and 75 percent of females met criteria for one or more psychiatric disorders, concluding that "youth with psychiatric disorders pose a challenge for the juvenile justice system and, after their release, for the larger mental health system." The study's authors noted the inevitable ties between poverty and mental illness: for many of these children, jail was then and continues to be the only treatment option, because their parents are unable to obtain health insurance or because the children are ineligible for Medicaid under stricter guidelines. A 2008 meta-analysis of twenty-five studies revealed that youth in juvenile detention were ten times more likely to be diagnosed with psychosis than their general-population counterparts.

## WRONG INCENTIVES

When I think of Jayden's case, the cynic in me believes it's no coincidence that Jayden's judge who ordered the year of court restoration classes, Ada County Fourth District Juvenile Court Justice William Harrigfeld, shares a last name with Idaho Department of Juvenile Corrections director Sharon Harrigfeld. Harrigfeld noted in a 2012 Idaho legislature budget session that rates of juvenile crime were dropping. Dropping rates would result in more empty beds in juvenile detention wards, threatening Harrigfeld's already tight budget.

Both the department and its director are the targets of a 2012 whistleblower lawsuit that alleges corruption and sexual misconduct with minors at the Nampa juvenile corrections facility. Plaintiff's attorney Andrew Schoppe alleges in the complaint, "Defendants have fostered an environment which has permitted juvenile-on-juvenile sexual liaisons in the facility and even staff-on-juvenile sexual liaisons."

In a public statement on the department website's home page, defending her staff, the director wrote, "I am confident that our staff and the procedures we have in place focus on the safety and protection of juveniles in our custody and ensure that when allegations of misconduct are brought forward they are investigated and appropriate action is taken."

Collusion between judges and juvenile corrections is more common than you might think. One of the most egregious cases involved Michael Conahan and Mark A. Ciavarella, a Pennsylvania judge who was sentenced to twenty-eight years in prison for accepting $2.6 million in bribes from the owners of PA Child Care, a private, for-profit prison facility. In one case, Judge Ciavarella sentenced an African American girl to three months in prison for her Myspace posts that were critical of her assistant principal. As a response to his crime, the Pennsylvania Supreme Court overturned some four thousand convictions from Ciavarella's courtroom.

Sharon Harrigfeld, the director of the Ada County juvenile corrections system, drew a $91,520 salary in 2012. That's a lot of money in Idaho. "Our system is changing," she told legislative budget writers in a hearing to draft her annual budget. "We have seen a 74 percent increase in mental health diagnoses among our commitments; 12.5 percent of the juveniles committed to us are diagnosed with a developmental disability." Which begs the question: what are children like Jayden—that 12.5 percent—doing in jail?

## HELPING KIDS AND SAVING MONEY

As I mentioned earlier, juvenile corrections is a booming business. In 2012, the Vera Institute of Justice partnered with the Pew Center on the States to find out just how much prisons were costing taxpayers in the United States, and their results were an astonishing $39 billion, four times as much as was spent twenty years ago. Part of the problem is how juvenile corrections programs are currently incentivized. While it's cheaper to treat juvenile offenders in their own communities—$10,000 per year compared to $60,000 or more per year for state incarceration—local counties will often "outsource" youth to state institutions because they don't have to pay the cost of care directly, as they would if they were providing care within the community. And when local services don't exist, judges have no other options, even for young people convicted of nonviolent crimes.

Yet building new facilities is expensive, costing as much as $100,000 per cell, with an annual average price tag of $60,000 per child. Frustrated by rising costs and high numbers of inmates with mental illness, some states are trying new approaches to managing their prison populations. In

2005, the state of Washington was facing an anticipated need for three new prisons; instead, legislators decided to allocate funding to evidence-based programs to reduce crime. In juvenile justice, the state implemented Functional Family Therapy (FFT) and Aggression Replacement Training (ART) for youth and found that for each dollar invested, $11.66 was saved, with recidivism rates for juveniles reduced by 24 percent. Another approach proving popular and cost-effective is to "divert" nonviolent offenders to community-based care. Florida started treating its young people who had been incarcerated for substance abuse through diversion programs, reducing their costs by $36.4 million. Young people who successfully completed diversion programs were 46 percent less likely to be convicted of a future felony when compared to young people who were sent to prison.

Wisconsin tried a whole-family approach to juvenile justice. Noting that the annual cost to house a child in detention was $68,255 in 2004, the state launched a What Works Wisconsin campaign to study effective community-based programs, including Wraparound Milwaukee, which provides a single point of contact in a caseworker who helps families to coordinate resources. Average costs of service were $3,300 per youth per month, compared to $5,000 per month for incarceration. Illinois tried Redeploy Illinois to keep nonviolent juvenile offenders in their home communities, reducing incarceration rates by an average of 44 percent and saving the state $3.55 million. Precious nomenclature aside, it's clear that states interested in implementing proactive solutions to children's mental health are realizing actual savings, both in dollars and in lives.

What does this mean in human terms? Programs that work to keep children with their families and in their communities reduce rates of recidivism and violent crime. They save money, but more importantly, they save lives as children go on to become productive adults. The fear of young, violent criminals—those hollow-eyed young men who shoot up schools—created a bad policy of incarcerating children for mostly minor offenses. Laurence Steinberg, a passionate advocate for proportionality, the idea that adolescents are not as responsible for their crimes as adults are, argues in a 2008 policy paper that reallocation of funding from prisons to community interventions is the right move: "Seldom will policymakers have the opportunity to produce so much good for children and society with such minimal net expenditures."

## SINS OF THE PARENTS

Unfortunately, not all states are proactive at helping children and families. In fact, there's a disturbing knee-jerk reaction to blame parents for their children's problems, as we saw in the chapter on stigma. One grandmother posted this comment on my blog: "The system has 'rewarded' my daughter for 17 years of abuse and cleaning up pee and poop, being yelled and spit at, by accusing HER of child abuse—twice! The social worker and the police were satisfied once they came to the home and answered the accusations as 'unsubstantiated' but it hurts to give up our lives to care for him, and we only receive disdain or indifference from the system."

That disdain comes from a belief that the parents are to blame for their child's maladaptive behaviors. While parents sometimes do unfortunately neglect their children, when issues of mental health are at play, most parents are involved and engaged. Still, cities often seek to recoup the costs of crime from parents. In many cities, parents can be held liable if their children are out past curfew, with parents facing fines and up to ninety days of jail time. Yet researchers note that "we do not know if punishing the parents would have the intended effect of reducing juvenile crime."

In 2010, the Iowa Supreme Court struck down a law that held parents responsible for their children's crimes, saying it violated the parents' rights to due process under the Fourteenth Amendment. The Davenport, Iowa, "Parental Responsibility Ordinance" read in part: "Those who bring children into the world, or those who assume a parenting role, but who fail to effectively teach, train, guide, and control them, should be accountable to the community under the law." The case in question was brought by a single mother who received two citations after her seventeen-year-old son was arrested twice for marijuana use.

After the Columbine High School shootings, polls showed that 85 percent of Americans blamed the teen killers' parents. But in his book *Columbine*, journalist Dave Cullen demonstrates that far from being "bad parents," both Dylan Klebold's and Eric Harris's parents were actively engaged in their sons' lives. Claire Creffield posits that "bad luck" is the deciding factor that separates "good" from "bad" parents in horrific outlier events like Columbine or Newtown. In fact, peer groups are more likely to influence children than parents are, as Judith Rich Harris observes in *The Nurture Assumption*. One reason for the increased rates of recidivism might be that young people make friends with the wrong crowd—by definition— when they are incarcerated. A 2007 study of eight thousand young people in Florida showed a strong peer effect across many categories of offenses.

## A LAW ENFORCEMENT OFFICER'S PERSPECTIVE

Ada County Sheriff Gary Raney understands firsthand the challenges of a system that requires law enforcement officers to be first responders for families and individuals who are experiencing a mental health crisis. "We see parents doing the best they can every day—and they are so frustrated that they almost give up. There is nothing else for them to do," he said when we met at his Boise office in June 2013. Raney oversees the largest local law enforcement agency in Idaho, with 613 employees and 322 commissioned officers. Born and raised in Caldwell, Idaho, he grew up on a farm and decided to go into law enforcement in high school after job shadowing a local officer. In 2013, he had been with the Ada County Sheriff's Department for more than thirty years.

Raney views education as a large part of his job. "A lot of what we do is a craft," he said. "Getting my criminal justice degree did not teach me anything about being a cop. Mental health is a good area to show how important experience is—do you see someone acting out because they are drunk, or is it mental illness, or a combination?" For this reason, Raney likes to hire people with a background in sociology, noting that "it's hard to train people to be aware. Police work deals with every aspect of human behavior within our community."

With thirty years of experience, Raney has thought quite a bit about mental illness and the impacts it has on his day-to-day work, noting that the frequency of mental illness encounters has greatly increased throughout his tenure. "Has society changed and we changed with it, or were the levels of mental illness just suppressed?" he asked. "I'm not sure." Raney first encountered mental illness as a jail deputy in 1983, when he met Jimmy (not his real name), an African American man who suffered from bipolar disorder and schizophrenia. Jimmy was frequently in and out of jail, at a time when the only medication available to manage his condition was Thorazine. "The drug would put him to sleep, and then he was not a problem," Raney said.

Now Raney deals with mental illness on a daily basis. "Our role in dealing with social issues has expanded," he noted. "Part of that is because other services have disappeared. Mental illness treatment is harder to get, and there are fewer services. Intermountain [Hospital] only takes you if you have insurance. The whole system is reactive. People call us when there is no one else to call. And right now, for people with mental illness in crisis, there is no one else to call. Even the [Idaho] state statute still rests with law enforcement. A doctor does not have the authority to issue emergency care—but an officer on his first day on the job does."

Raney does see some hope; in his opinion, the Idaho Department of Health and Welfare does a better job maintaining mental health services in the community. And he noted that the law just changed for juveniles, so that a doctor can place them in emergency care. "It seems to my mind that we are seeing more juveniles," he said. "Like anyone in law enforcement, I ask myself, how did Adam Lanza happen?"

Idaho is a state that values rugged individualism and personal accountability. Raney blames desocialization, the advent of violent video games and television, and the increasingly dominant power of social media. "One of the worst things that ever happened was the air conditioner," he said. "Before that, you would sit on the front porch. You knew your neighbors and their kids. Social cohesion doesn't exist anymore. Families have more issues; kids have more issues. That's going to continue."

Raney has addressed his officers' role as first responders for mental illness through increased training. He looks for college social science degrees and provides new officers with in-service training. "Every officer has ninety-six hours of training in everything from suicide risk to veterans' issues to dealing with autism behaviors," he explained. "We understand that for our officers, recognizing what is happening with the person acting out could be a matter of survival. Walking up to a mental health situation when someone is acting out with violence and is threatening people, they have a split second to decide, is it criminal behavior or is it mental illness? That split-second decision leads to life or death." Raney specifically addressed the problem of "suicide by cop," noting that over half of his officer shootings fit the criteria. "I wish people understood how many incidents could easily escalate to lethal force," he said.

One of the hardest things for police officers is dealing with children. "We are trained to work with ADHD and autism," he said. "We try to de-escalate children. When we deal with an autistic person, maybe we used force appropriately by the law and the facts, but could we have de-escalated? When something is in crisis, you call 911. When you call and say your child is acting out, you're going to get the police."

For Raney, his own officers' mental health is one of the department's top priorities. "Every person, including me, goes in at least once a year for a mental health checkup," he said. "It's an innovative approach, and I'm proud of it. Every year we get a physical health checkup, but people don't want to talk to their counselor. We changed that. This program was successful both to reduce stigma and to reduce stress. Our deputies see some horrible things. It's part of the job." Raney noted that for law enforcement officers, the stress of putting on a gun each day and knowing that they might have to use it negatively affects quality of life. The Employee Assistance Program opened up communication and gave families a way to deal with the stress.

Raney believes that the criminal justice system could do a much better job at diverting children with mental health issues to treatment, but this shift will require a change in thinking: instead of waiting for a crisis and calling the police, people will have to recognize the signs before someone starts to destabilize. "That moment when we see someone destabilize, crisis intervention is important," Raney said. "But the majority of people don't want to act out or destabilize. How do we find the balance point? How do we apply services that are effective for those who do need them, and keep them out of the courts? Another problem is that even if you had the services available, most people don't call until it's too late, because they want to avoid the cost. Once law enforcement gets involved, we have a problem that is exponentially more expensive to society. Our data about outcomes is terrible in the criminal justice system."

Raney believes that crisis intervention teams hold the most promise for helping children with mental illness and their families. He pointed to the Memphis Police Department's model, which has been successfully implemented in several other communities. In 1988, the Memphis Police Department partnered with the Memphis chapter of the National Alliance on Mental Illness (NAMI) to create a specialized mental health unit within the department. The 225 officers who volunteer to be part of the Crisis Intervention Team (CIT) are specially trained to handle mental illness and provide coverage twenty-four hours per day, seven days per week.

The "Memphis Model" proved so effective that several other cities have patterned programs after it—there are now more than four hundred CIT programs in the United States. One study of a CIT program in Georgia showed marked positive changes in officers' attitudes toward people with mental illness. Other studies noted lower arrest rates as people with mental illness were referred to treatment rather than taken to jail.

Raney thinks this type of multidisciplinary approach to mental illness is the right answer: "Government, nonprofits, private sector—the best answer is a combination of all three," he said, noting that the solution won't come all at once. "We don't like the position we are in [as first responders] but we accept it because we are the only solution. We are who people call. It's a very difficult dynamic. Technology, education, all of these can help. We could provide crisis intervention face-to-face with telepsychiatry and an iPhone. Right now, if we can't stabilize the incident, if we have to put them on the ground in handcuffs, they are going to jail. And when they are released, it's with seven days of meds and no access to care. It's a cycle. We can—no, we will—do better."

## DANGEROUS, UNPREDICTABLE MADMEN

Sometimes, despite attempts by family to intervene, the crisis moment cannot be prevented, with devastating consequences. Karl Wurtzel (not his real name, and I have changed identifying details but not the substance of this story at the request of Karl's family) was an all-American kid in an all-American family. The youngest of three children, Karl grew up in an affluent East Coast suburb. His father, Joe, was in finance; his mother, Maria, owned a home-nursing business. Like his siblings, Karl was bright and successful in high school, where he earned top grades and was the star quarterback. Former teachers and classmates described him as bright and charismatic. He played four years of football in college, then enrolled in law school.

No one is quite sure when the trouble began. But Karl began to change. The formerly affable youngest son turned grandiose, paranoid, secretive. Raised Catholic, be became obsessed with Judaism and converted. He also became obsessed with guns and knives, stockpiling them in his apartment. One night, he attacked his father and mother with a hunting knife, fatally wounding them. He had threatened to commit suicide just days before. Diagnosed with schizophrenia, Karl has been declared unfit to stand trial three times since his initial arrest. He refuses to take his medications. One of Karl's family members shared her story with me:

> While Karl never really lashed out in a violent manner prior to stabbing his parents to death, it was very clear to our immediate family that he was extremely ill. After one particular psychotic episode, Karl was involuntarily hospitalized and

forcibly medicated. His team of psychiatrists petitioned a judge here in our home of New York to mandate Karl be placed under a program called Kendra's Law, which would legally require him to seek treatment and medication. If he did not comply, he would again be hospitalized. Our family felt this would be our prayers answered, and Karl would finally receive treatment. But inexplicably, the judge denied the doctors' request. Less than one year after that, [Joe and Maria] were dead.

Since we suffered this loss, our eyes were suddenly opened to how many other families are also suffering. Karl's parents felt they had nowhere to turn, no place to seek help. His mother was desperate to help her son: she could not bear the thought of him out on the streets, in jail, or committing suicide. I can only wonder what Adam Lanza's mother went through in her last few years, the agony and silent suffering she endured . . . many Americans have no idea what it is like to live with, and love, a seriously mentally ill individual. Something has got to change.

In many ways, Karl's story exemplifies why we are so afraid of people with mental illness, and our fears are not entirely unfounded. People with schizophrenia are much more likely than the general population to become violent, especially if they are also substance abusers. But the percentage of all violent crime attributable to schizophrenia is actually quite small—less than 10 percent—and the chances that someone with schizophrenia will commit murder are even smaller, one in three thousand for men, and one in thirty-three thousand for women.

In fact, most people with mental illness do not become Adam Lanza, but "grow out of it," as one young man shared on my blog: "I couldn't ever reach out to my parents, teachers, or friends. . . . I could have been one of those guys that cracked, grabbed a gun and went berserk. I won't touch guns, period. Won't go near them. I'm terrified of them. But at 19? I'm glad

I never had one around me." Indeed, one study concluded: "Less focus on the relative risk and more on the absolute risk of violence posed to society by people with schizophrenia would serve to reduce the associated stigma." In other words, you're much more likely to suffer violence at the hands of a sane person.

People with bipolar disorder, which I now know my son Michael has, are also much more likely than the general population to commit a violent crime, according to the results of a longitudinal study published in 2010. As with schizophrenia, comorbid substance abuse was usually associated with criminal behavior. But a Danish study of a birth cohort ruled out comorbid substance abuse and socioeconomic factors, finding that hospitalization for a mental disorder was a major predictor of violent behavior: the 2.2 percent of the men in the cohort who were hospitalized committed 10 percent of all violent crimes committed by all men; the 2.6 percent of the women committed 16 percent of all violent crimes committed by all women. Though some fear that associating violence with mental illness will increase the already pervasive stigma, I believe that we must acknowledge these uncomfortable truths.

As I said in my blog, for several years, the only times I have felt completely safe were when Michael was incarcerated or hospitalized. That's the crux of our discomfort with people who have mental illness: though in reality, safety is always an illusion, we want to think we have control over our lives, our destinies. A single individual can shatter multiple lives in an instant. There are warning signs, but because we don't want to think about or talk about mental illness, we don't want to think about or talk about the warning signs, either. Adam Lanza's mother was screaming for help. Jared Loughner's college dismissed him because the administrators thought he was dangerous. James Holmes threatened people in his academic department. Seung-Hui Cho actually rehearsed the Virginia Tech killings in broad daylight the day before his killing spree—people saw him, but no one bothered to report him.

Then there's Amy Bishop, who at the age of eighteen "accidentally" shot and killed her brother. Her family hoped she would never kill again.

They were wrong. Amy, a biology professor whose behavior fits the criteria for paranoid schizophrenia, opened fire at a faculty meeting in 2010 after she was denied tenure, killing three colleagues and wounding three others. The University of Alabama at Huntsville, where Bishop worked, now faces wrongful death lawsuits that allege administrators knew she posed a threat, that they protected themselves by requesting a police escort if Bishop was seen on campus, but that they did not protect the faculty members who were killed and wounded. In her confession, she reveals a lack of insight common to people who suffer from serious mental illness: "I cannot comprehend how I did this or why I did this, and it feels as though I am reading about some other person, but the overwhelming evidence is that the person that I am reading about is me."

## INEFFECTIVE LAWS

Karl Wurtzel's and Amy Bishop's are just two of many tragic stories of violence that could have been prevented with existing laws and with earlier intervention. In both cases, family members, friends, colleagues saw signs that something was wrong. Karl's parents tried to have him committed using Kendra's Law. Why can't these laws be enforced to protect both people with mental illness and those they might harm? And what are the effects of "outsourcing" mental health crises to law enforcement? How do police officers feel about their de facto role as the nation's mental health first-line providers?

In his unpublished but widely circulated 2011 master's thesis for the Naval Postgraduate School, Michael Biasotti, 2012 president of the New York State Association of Chiefs of Police and a career law enforcement officer, surveyed 2,406 other senior officials nationwide about the impact mental illness had on their resources. He found that a majority of respondents believed that state laws about mental illness were poorly understood or too complicated to put into practice. Additionally, transportation and security were seen as "a major consumer of law resources nationally." Of those surveyed, over 57 percent reported lack of availability of services as a significant obstacle to arranging care for mentally ill, with only slightly under 12 percent reporting that there were no obstacles to care in their communities.

Biasotti summarized the potentially dangerous effects of these obstacles to care on families: "Because immediate family members most commonly call for emergency services to intervene in a psychiatric emergency and are typically rebuffed pending the development of danger, family members are often at risk of becoming victims of violence, and the individual in crisis is left at risk of self-harm."

One respondent commented, "Lots of services are available but [there is] no single point of contact for 'admission' into the system. [It] requires law enforcement to understand the variety of services available to be able to plug the mentally ill person into the system."

In fact, as Biasotti's data clearly show, the locus of care for both children and adults with mental illness has become the criminal justice system; 63 percent of respondents reported that the amount of time spent on mental illness had increased over the course of their careers, and nearly 18 percent said the time had "substantially increased," reflecting one of deinstitutionalization's unintended consequences (another is the dramatic increase of adults and children with serious mental illness who are now collecting government disability checks).

Biasotti argues for the national implementation of assisted outpatient treatment (AOT) laws to restore mental health services for those most at risk to the community and reclaim prisons (and law enforcement resources) for criminals. AOT laws allow courts to monitor patients' compliance with treatment programs and provide a cost-effective solution to the mental health crisis that increasingly dominates local law enforcement budgets and manpower.

As of 2012, forty-four states had already adopted these laws. New York's 1999 law, commonly referred to as "Kendra's Law" for Kendra Webdale, a young woman who was pushed in front of a subway train by a man who had schizophrenia and was off his medications, was evaluated in 2009 and found to be effective in reducing hospitalization rates from 74 percent to 36 percent and also reducing the length of time spent in the hospital.

Some argue, however, that AOT laws are racially biased and deprive people of their civil liberties without due process. Psychiatrist John Gro-hol argues against the laws: "If someone were dying from cancer or heart disease, they have an absolute right to refuse medical treatment for their ailment. So why is it that people with mental disorders can have that similar right taken away from them?"

And this is where we have to return to the balance of safety and free-dom. We want the brain to be "just another organ," mental illness to be the above-the-neck equivalent to cancer or diabetes. But unlike the patient with cancer or diabetes who refuses treatment, the patient with mental illness who refuses treatment has the capacity to harm not only himself but others. And anosognosia—that biologically based lack of insight—is a symptom of mental illness for a significant minority of patients. In other words, Karl Wurtzel, Amy Bishop, Jared Loughner, or James Holmes may not be aware that anything is wrong with stabbing parents or shooting colleagues or open-ing fire on a congresswoman or spraying a movie theater with bullets. This is the challenge that Robert Whitaker's book *Anatomy of an Epidemic* ig-nores. As D. J. Jaffe, executive director of advocacy organization Mental Illness Policy Org., wrote in his review of the book, "Among the facts he [Whitaker] ignores are people with severe mental illness in jails, in prisons, homeless and psychotic." People like Wurtzel, Bishop, Loughner, Holmes.

Do people with severe mental illness and repeated violent behavioral episodes have the right to refuse medication? Perhaps they do—but by doing so, they violate a fundamental premise of the social contract. The goal of assisted outpatient treatment laws is to release people with mental illness from two prisons: the physical barred cells that have replaced hos-pital wards, and the mental prison of an unsound mind.

## SAFETY FIRST

When I teach English, the subject of my blog often comes up. One of my students, a single mother of two young boys, raised her hand and said, "I don't want this to come out wrong. But what should I teach my children to do if they see a kid like yours in a rage? How should I tell them to handle a kid with mental illness?"

It's a tough question. My response was, is, and always will be, "Teach them to stay safe." The question of how to stay safe, especially for children, is a tough one. Obviously we shouldn't bully our peers and we shouldn't back anyone into a corner. But if a child doesn't feel safe, the child should immediately leave the situation and seek a responsible adult.

Too often, for me and for thousands of other families across the United States, staying safe involves law enforcement's help. But I also told my student that tolerance and respect were invaluable tools for helping kids like Michael. A better understanding of children and their needs, of how to allow them the space to stabilize, is really the most effective strategy. Kids with sensory integration issues are easy targets for people who like to "poke the bear," and Michael is no exception. His younger brother, Jonathan, has an innate gift for doing just the thing that sets Michael off. But Michael tries harder than my other children to keep his emotions in check. He knows firsthand how bad the consequences can be. And he has good strategies and readily available mood stabilizers like trazodone, the person with bipolar disorder's equivalent to an EpiPen for the brain. Children with mental disorders are usually on detailed behavior plans like Jayden's—usually, when the behavior plans are followed, everyone stays safe, and the child is able to de-escalate successfully.

Michael's four short stays in juvenile detention, coupled with losing the ability to be with his younger siblings for nearly a year, have definitely made an impression on him. Last summer, he was riding his bike home from the park near our home when he saw some teenagers break into his church. Because he is impulsive, a symptom of bipolar disorder, he didn't think about the consequences of following them inside. "I was just trying to make sure they didn't steal anything or damage the property," he said. A more levelheaded response would have been to alert a neighbor or to ride home and call 911. Michael is impulsive but creative: he convinced the two intruders that there was a planned meeting in just a few minutes and that they would be caught if they didn't leave right away.

And they were caught—all three of them—when they exited the building. Fortunately for Michael, the two teens confessed and corroborated his version of the story. The police officer knew Michael well and called to tell me how polite and cooperative my son had been. But when Michael got home a few minutes later, he was trembling. "I don't ever want to be bad or get in trouble again," he said, tears suddenly gushing from his eyes as he gave me an awkward hug. "I can't go back to juvie."

Parents of children with mental illness struggle to live day to day. Many can't get health care; they can't get the educational services they need. And then one day their son or daughter commits a crime, and everything changes, as this comment on my blog shows:

> We were investigating residential schools for my son, when he committed a crime that is now being prosecuted. It was 3 days after his 14th birthday, which changes everything in our state (from a legal perspective). Now, not only are we trying to help him and advocate for him, but paying legal bills and dealing with court stuff too. Oh, and we have THREE younger kids, ages 11, 9 and 3. I was laid off from my job back in August (from spending so much time on kid-related stuff), so no more benefits so the kids are on Medicaid. Marriage is in tatters, but can't make any decisions about that, since dealing with this mess alone is just not an option right now.

Returning to my student's question about safety, it's the same question Karl Wurtzel's parents and Amy Bishop's colleagues probably asked themselves. It's a question I ask myself. And indeed, there are some positive ways to interact with people who have a mental illness and are in crisis—and these positive interactions can be taught, as Sheriff Gary Raney explained. Ordinary citizens like Antoinette Tuff, an elementary school bookkeeper, can singlehandedly prevent a tragedy. Tuff stopped a twenty-year-old man armed with an AK-47 semiautomatic assault rifle and five hundred rounds of ammunition who had entered her elementary school with bad intentions. The young man, who has bipolar disorder, apparently wanted to commit suicide by cop. He told Tuff that he was not taking his medications. Because Tuff was able to see Michael Hill first as a human being, not as an "unpredictable madman," she was able to help him by sharing details of her own struggles with hard times. Hill surrendered to police and asked Tuff to apologize to the schoolchildren.

## A BETTER WAY TO TREAT OUR CHILDREN

There's no question that we are using the criminal justice system to "treat" mental illness, at great cost to children, families, and communities. What if we could provide interventions to at-risk children before they enter the criminal justice system? The risk factors—genetics, environment, socioeconomic status—are clear. Rather than adhering to zero-tolerance policies that put at-risk students at an even greater risk of going to jail, why can't we provide intensive behavioral intervention through the public schools?

One study looking at the effectiveness of applied behavior analysis (ABA) or early intensive behavioral intervention (EIBI—basically ABA for young children) found that the state of Texas could potentially save more than $2 billion on its education budget alone by providing early intervention to children like Jayden: $208,500 per child over the course of eighteen years of public education. Investment in early intensive intervention and parent training could also shave billions of dollars off of the costs of incarceration and recidivism.

But at the end of the day, it's about children, not money. Though economic arguments are compelling, it's the human capital that should drive the conversation. Children like Jayden and my son don't belong in jail, period. Young adults like Karl Wurtzel deserve treatment that will help them to manage their illness before it's too late. Getting our children who have mental illness out of jail and into treatment helps to restore our faith in the basic foundational American principles all children learn and want to believe can be theirs: life, liberty, and the pursuit of happiness.

# SEVEN

# FAMILY

## How Does Having a Child with Mental Illness Affect the Family?

All happy families are alike; each unhappy family is unhappy in its own way.

—Leo Tolstoy, *Anna Karenina*

On September 3, 2013, Kelli Stapleton, a forty-five-year-old former molecular biologist and mother of three, left her home in rural northern Michigan with her fourteen-year-old daughter, Isabelle (nicknamed Issy), who has autism. Kelli did not expect either of them to return. After Kelli's husband, Matt, alerted law enforcement that something might be wrong, police found Kelli and her daughter unconscious inside the family van, where coals were still smoldering on the carpet, creating poisonous, suffocating carbon monoxide. Both Kelli and Issy survived, but Kelli was charged with attempted murder for her desperate attempt to die with her daughter.

For several years, Kelli has written a blog called *The Status Woe*, chronicling her family's difficult journey with a daughter who has autism. In the summer of 2013, Kelli posted a chilling video filmed at Great Lakes Center for Autism Treatment and Research, a residential program where Issy received intensive treatment for a few months, documenting the mother's disastrous first attempt to implement Issy's restrictive behavior plan. In the video, Issy was so physically aggressive toward her mother that she had to be restrained. Both of Issy's caregivers sustained cuts and bruises and were bleeding at the end of the session. The stress of living with a physically violent child took its toll on the entire family, but especially on Kelli, who, like many mothers, blamed herself. "I'm sure I ruined her somewhere along the way," she wrote.

On September 3, 2013, Kelli shared the devastating news that her carefully crafted education plans for her daughter had fallen apart—rather than being able to have Issy attend the local school where her father was the principal, Issy's mother would have to drive her daughter more than two hours each day to a school in Kalamazoo. "I have to admit that I'm suffering from a severe case of battle fatigue," she wrote on the day she decided to kill herself and her daughter.

Earlier that year, Kelli had described her frustration with the multiple systems that had failed her and her family. "I have talked to doctors, psychologists, lawyers, insurance companies and no one is helping us," she wrote. "My husband has a good job and has great benefits. But through loopholes and other nonsense, we can't get help for our daughter through insurance." She also expressed the sense of loss she felt as she contemplated her daughter's future and shared her frustrations at the many sacrifices her husband and other children had to make.

When I posted this tragic story, along with a link to Kelli's blog, on my Facebook page, one of my friends wrote in support of this mom and her family, "I hope the judge will use this blog to exonerate the mother." I sincerely doubt that will happen: it's much more likely that Kelli's real-time chronicle of her desperate attempts to get help for Issy and their family will be used as Exhibit A that she was a bad mother rather than an indictment of a society that fails to help struggling families.

A 1999 NAMI special report entitled "Families on the Brink: The Impact of Ignoring Children with Serious Mental Illness" identified many of the same stressors that plague families like Kelli Stapleton's—and mine—today. This national survey of parents was compiled in response to tragic school shootings including Columbine, and it illustrates just how much the French phrase *plus ça change, plus c'est la même chose* ("the more things change, the more they stay the same") applies to children's mental health. NAMI's then executive director Laurie Flynn gave a rousing call to action: "these are the voices of mothers and fathers who must try to comprehend why their loved one, their child, has a brain disorder, but . . . they find themselves all too often having to fight for every shred of medical attention, school system support, and acceptance from their neighbors and friends. In the face of this struggle, they confront the unimaginable but all-too-real risks of family dissolution, financial bankruptcy, wrongful imprisonment of their child, and even the prospect of having to give up custody of their child just to get him or her treatment. We cannot, as a nation, permit this tragedy to persist."

*Plus ça change.*

In 1999, families who had children with mental illness faced crushing stigma. They still do. In 1999, parents often had to use the criminal justice system to get mental health treatment for their children. They still do. In 1999, parents had to fight school districts to get free and appropriate education for their children with mental illness. They still do. In 1999, parents sometimes had to give up custody of their children with mental illness just so the children could get treatment. They still do. And in 1999, society blamed parents. We still do.

Dr. Thomas Insel, the NIMH director, has said of mental illness that "these become not just individual disorders, they become family problems." Indeed, as I have seen with my own children, the entire family experiences the stresses and challenges of a child's mental illness. In this chapter, we'll explore how a child with mental illness dramatically shapes—for good and ill—the dynamics of his or her family.


## SIBLING RIVALRY, OR SOMETHING WORSE?

Our family likes to play board games, and we are all competitive. One night after my blog went viral, as we sat around the table playing Frank's Zoo, a food chain ecosystem card game with goldfish and mice at the bottom and killer whales and lions at the top, I asked James, Jonathan, and Anna what some of their biggest challenges were in dealing with Michael. Michael wasn't home that night—he had a scouting activity. While Michael and his older brother, James, have lived with me full-time since 2011, Anna and Jonathan continued with a "week on, week off" schedule, meaning they alternated weeks at their dad's house and my house—until my blog went viral and their father was granted temporary sole physical custody, ostensibly to ensure their safety. At this writing, we're baby-stepping back to more time together, thanks to a parenting coordinator who appreciates how much the children enjoy each other's company. But at this writing, we still haven't been able to return to the previous schedule of alternating weeks. Ultimately, my children's custody will be decided in the courts, and it's already been more than nine months since they were taken from me against my wishes.

"He's changed." Anna nodded when I asked her about her brother. She twirled a strand of blond hair around one finger. "I used to be scared. I was scared he would hurt me. He would throw fits and scream the meanest things! Things like, 'I'm gonna kill you!'"

"He never screamed that at you, though," I said.

"No," Jonathan chimed in. "Anna was scared but I wasn't. I never thought he would hurt me. And besides, I knew what we were supposed to do—run to your room or the car and lock the door. We would sit and play our iPods until the police came or he calmed down. Now he doesn't blow up anymore. He is awesome. He plays video games and hangs out with me. He used to hate Minecraft but now he doesn't."

"He is a lot happier and nicer," Anna said.

"It was really hard to not be with you guys, though," Jonathan said. "I want things to be the way they were before, when we could see you more."

My ten-year-old, Jonathan, puts on a brave face. He was scared. We all were scared. Siblings of a child with mental illness have an often tenuous, uncertain existence. And yet out of that uncertainty, great resilience and strong bonds can be forged. When asked about the quality of their children's relationships, parent reports were more negative than child self-reports. As the researchers said, "The sibling relationship is paradoxical, incorporating both conflict and companionship."

My oldest son James's relationship with his younger brother has been competitive since Michael was born (at the time of this writing, James is sixteen; Michael fourteen; Jonathan ten; and Anna eight). But in many ways, they understand each other better than any other people can. There is no question that Michael takes up the most physical, emotional, and financial resources—this is a common concern in families of children with any kind of disability. But when the older two boys came to live with me, they struck a truce, one that they largely honor, aside from the occasional age-appropriate spats over Xbox time.

James spends more time with his younger siblings than many sixteen-year-olds I know, balancing a demanding course load with leadership and family responsibilities. But he can still show occasional resentment and even contempt toward Michael, sentiments Michael readily returns when provoked. For me, what others might see as "ordinary" sibling rivalry always contains an element of danger. I never know when a simple argument will escalate into violence. Michael often describes feeling backed into a corner by the world in general—he can be quite specific when he describes his perceptions of persecution by his older brother. But as James once said in frustration, "Look, Michael, no one wants to make you mad. We all do everything we can to avoid making you mad."

Many families who have a child with a mental disorder describe similar feelings of walking on eggshells. In most cases, the child with the mental illness dictates the family's dynamics in both subtle and obvious ways. Researchers have found correlations between children with mental illness and sibling behavioral issues—siblings of children with autism may be more at risk for behavioral problems than other children, for example.

There are several sibling support networks online and within communities, including the Sibling Support Project, which has created a scalable Sibshop model for eight- to thirteen-year-old siblings of children with developmental disabilities that can be implemented locally. The Idaho Federation of Families for Children's Mental Health participates in this program; as its executive director, Stephen Graci, described the workshops to me: "They are basically workshops for children with siblings who have special needs. They are designed to create opportunities for kids to obtain peer support and education within a recreational context. These workshops promote relationship building between siblings through a variety of games and activities." Graci went on to say, "It's definitely not about identifying pathology or suggesting that siblings are maladjusted because of their family experiences. If given the chance, brothers and sisters have much to offer one another."

Many siblings have posted comments on my blog about the challenges of growing up with a family member who has mental illness—and the even more frightening fear of losing that sibling to substance abuse or suicide. One young woman wrote, "I am one of your daughters. My brother was in and out of hospitals and juvenile detention, attempted suicide in our home, threatened to kill my family, oh and all the while our father lived overseas. He was terrifying to live with. When you mentioned the safety plan I started crying because we had one too, but we got lucky. My brother is 22 now and while I still feel like his brilliance is wasted on his parade of short term jobs, I am proud and relieved."

A young man shared a more tragic story: "I grew up with a mentally ill sibling. My parents had money. They had insurance. There were still no resources available for them. They went through hell, my brother was never officially diagnosed with anything except an 'unspecified thought disorder' and died in an alcohol/drug related incident some years ago."

Describing how siblings "normalize" the frightening behavior that comes to define their existence, one young woman wrote to me:

> I can't believe it. You just described my brother. They say he's aspergers, but I don't know if that accounts for all of it. He's normally really sweet, sensitive, and very very smart, but when he snaps, he curses, hurts people, throws things, threatens suicide, and pulls knives. I have scars from where he's scratched or strangled me. You grow up in a household with

someone like that and it starts to seem normal. My brother is an adult now, and we can't do anything anymore because he's legally independent. He went off all of his medications and is scarier than ever. I know that he's EXACTLY the sort of person that NEEDS more supervision and help. Sadly, he doesn't believe there is anything wrong with him, and he blames my mother, saying that she "labelled him" as special needs and ruined his life. He will not seek help. He will not even try to change. I don't know if there is anything anyone can do as long as he is in denial. Everyone here giving you grief doesn't understand what it is like to grow up with a family member who acts out violently from mental illness. You are doing exactly what you have to and you are very brave.

The experience of living with a child who has mental illness means that my family's stories are probably not your family's stories. You might tell stories about the time you went to Disneyland and lost your three-year-old for fifteen minutes. Our stories are different. "Hey, Mom, remember that time Michael lost it at you when you picked me up from soccer practice and he was choking you in the car, and we were right by the hospital, and it took three guys to drag him back to the emergency room?" James said one night.

"I remember that," Michael chimed in. "I don't remember getting mad, but I do remember being in the hospital and they had me in that funny thing so I couldn't move my arms, and they gave me a shot, and I was like, 'Come on, Mom! Let's make a break for it! We can get away!'"

"Was that the night we were in the waiting room with the fish tank a really, really, really long time with James, until our neighbor came and took us home?" Jonathan said.

"I remember he bought us chicken nuggets because we didn't have dinner," Anna adds. "And you got home real late. I was sleeping in your bed."

We all laugh about this story, because in hindsight, the experiences

are so painfully absurd that laughter seems like the only appropriate response. One thing I remember is the hospital bill.

## FAMILIES BY THE NUMBERS

The 1999 NAMI report about families like mine received a nationwide
survey response of 756 families and identified some troubling trends: 50
percent of parents surveyed reported that they worried about physical aggression or violence from their child, and 36 percent reported that their
children had entered the juvenile justice system. Nearly 15 percent of
parents also reported that their children were physically or sexually abused
while in the hospital, residential treatment center, or jail—we have seen
that theme play out throughout this book.

More troubling statistics that probably remain true today:

- Nearly 50 percent of parents reported that neighbors and
  friends shunned them, and that they were blamed for their
  children's illness.
- For 55 percent of families, one partner had to quit or take an-
  other job so that the child could have care.
- Nearly 60 percent could identify with Pam Kazmaier or Kelli
  Stapleton: they felt pushed to the point of no return.
- Seventy percent reported severe marital stress.
- Eighty percent reported negative impact to siblings.

One response indicates why 37 percent of parents did not feel mental
health professionals had much to offer: "I know that with my son I constantly went back to the pediatrician saying he's having trouble sleeping,
with his behavior, connecting to other children—all of those things. He
kept examining him physically and then he ran every possible test and
said, 'He's fine. He's healthy.' And I said, 'Then, what?' And he would say,
'I don't know.' He gave me the names of some psychiatrists and psycholo-

gists after I pressed for them. I took [my son] to a psychiatrist who was an older man. . . . He said if we, the parents, stopped fighting with each other, [my son] would be fine. It was our fault."

"It was our fault." As I've noted throughout this book, most parents of a child with a mental illness have heard that phrase at least once and perhaps many times on their long journey to find treatment.

## A TALE OF THREE TEENAGERS

Unlike me and most of the parents I have quoted in this book, Angela Lindig is "one hundred percent" comfortable with using her children's real names. Angela and her husband, Darin, have three teenagers, Amber, seventeen; Ryan, sixteen; and Elise, fourteen. Any parent would agree that parenting three teenagers presents unique challenges. But the Lindigs have an exponentially more difficult time than most parents: their three teenagers all have disabilities, including mental illness.

Amber showed significant developmental delays as an infant and was ultimately diagnosed with Rett syndrome, a rare genetic mutation that affects brain function and almost always occurs in girls. Ryan was diagnosed with ADHD at age seven. And Elise, adopted from Romania at the age of three, has reactive attachment disorder (RAD), a condition that causes inappropriate social behavior and sometimes arises when children are not able to bond to their caregivers. Elise also has bipolar disorder, ADHD, and generalized anxiety disorder. After years of nearly constant bladder accidents, Elise was diagnosed with spina bifida (its name is from the Latin for "split spine"), a congenital birth defect that prevents her from feeling the sensation of needing to urinate. "She can't run, laugh, or even walk without an accident," Angela said. "The psychiatric part of that is that she doesn't care. She doesn't care if she sits in urine."

Ironically, the Lindigs adopted Elise to minimize their risks of having another child with a disability. "We still didn't have a diagnosis for Amber at that point, but we knew something was wrong, and it was probably genetic," Angela said. "We went to Romania because we had concerns about the multiple placements that usually occur in the United States for foster children, and we were concerned about attachment issues. We were so naïve." In fact, Angela's concerns about attachment extend to children from Romania and many other parts of the world. A relatively uncommon disorder in the general pediatric population, reactive attachment disorder is a common diagnosis for children who were raised in institutions and adopted from foreign countries.

Still, of all her children's disabilities, Ryan's ADHD was the hardest proverbial pill for Angela to swallow. "With Amber, we were able to go through the natural stages of grieving and acceptance," she explained. "Ryan bypassed his sister so fast in development that we would joke that he required no training. Elise's problems took longer to understand—at first we thought it was a language barrier issue. By the time she was four, we knew it was something worse. At the same time we were getting a diagnosis for Elise, I started wondering about Ryan. He was the kid in school who was next to his desk, under his desk, at someone else's desk, at the pencil sharpener—anywhere but his own desk. But he was so bright that he flew under the radar, especially with such significant issues for the siblings on both sides of him. All three of my children come with labels behind their names. It is what it is."

Their children's multiple disabilities have inevitably affected the family. Ryan is currently in counseling for anger management because Elise is so frustrating to live with and because the whole family has to make sacrifices to accommodate her issues. "It is different with Amber because her issues are different. There isn't the same grudge there," Angela said, noting how painful it can be for a sibling or a caregiver to admit to feeling frustration or anger. "You feel guilty," she said, echoing the sentiments of every caregiver. Elise tried to burn the house down when she was seven; now she lies and steals. She is also a beautiful, charming child when you meet her for just a few minutes. But she does not have the privileges or social abilities of a typical fourteen-year-old.

Elise's maladaptive behavior took a toll on Darin and Angela's marriage. "We had no issues even after Amber was born, but when Elise came along, that first year, we were at complete odds with extended family and with each other about how to discipline, how to parent," Angela said. "Nothing that we knew about parenting worked with this child, and we could not agree. Darin didn't like my methods, but he had no solutions. We would argue. Finally, I said, 'I am not going to let this child destroy twelve years of a good marriage. We are going to figure this out.' I had fantasies about him leaving and taking her with him. I wanted out, but what I wanted out of was the situation, not the marriage."

Angela and Darin came to the difficult decision that only one of them could be Elise's caregiver. For several years, Angela was Elise's only "parent." Darin did not weigh in on any parenting decisions, so that Elise could not triangulate. It worked, and they were slowly able to reintegrate Darin into the parenting process, which is now shared and equal.

Even something as simple as a night out is a major production for Darin and Angela. "We have created an interesting system," she said. "Ryan is in charge. We only go for short amounts of time to make sure Elise doesn't do anything. Elise helps Amber go to the bathroom—yes, there's some irony there." She laughed. "Ryan makes sure Elise goes to the bathroom. Ryan has a cell phone and calls me if anything goes wrong. Now we feel like we can go for a thirty-minute run together or out to dinner for an hour after work. We stay close to home. In two years, when Ryan goes to college, I don't know what I will do. Caregivers are so hard to find."

That's one thing most people don't realize. When you have a child with mental illness, you'll be paying for child care well beyond the normal twelve years. In eighth grade, Michael still goes to a day care provider after school. And parents want someone who is qualified to deal with their child, not just a sixteen-year-old babysitter trying to make extra spending money.

Because her parenting experience was so dominated by her children's disabilities, Angela became first an accidental and then a professional ad-vocate. She is the executive director of Idaho Parents Unlimited, a state-wide organization with a staff of nine that provides training and resources to more than five thousand families per year. "Considering how rural we are, accessing families is not always easy," she noted. "We think we do a good job."

Angela's career in advocacy began when she testified to the Idaho state legislature to provide a parent perspective supporting a birth-through-age-three program that Amber was enrolled in. Though she was scared, that experience made her realize how powerful her voice could be. "I thought, I have a big mouth," she said. "If I don't speak up, what about all the people who can't?" She was subsequently asked to serve on a regional early-childhood committee and helped to develop the early stages portion of Idaho's Department of Health and Welfare child website.

One day, she read about universally accessible playgrounds in a *Family Circle* magazine article, and an idea began to nibble at her mind. "It kept coming back to me," she said. "I thought, what am I going to do? I'm just a mom. Somebody who is somebody should do something."

Then Angela realized that she was that somebody, and that she could do something. She gathered influential community members around her kitchen table and started a process that culminated with the Adventure Island Playground in Meridian, Idaho's first universally accessible playground. Ron Mace, an architect and wheelchair user, gets credit for the term "universal design"—the concept behind it being that products and environments should be designed for everyone, including people with physical and mental disabilities. "I did not know how big or difficult this project would be," Angela said. "It was hard for people to grasp. They kept thinking it would be a playground just for kids with disabilities. That's not the point at all. It's a playground for everyone."

For the record, the Adventure Island Playground is my children's favorite playground in a city full of playgrounds. Elements include xylophones and drums; a wheelchair-accessible water feature with specially designed sprinklers and a large bucket to "dump" on unsuspecting friends; rocks; and ramp-accessible play structures. Swings are specially designed for children with disabilities, but they are fun for every child. The playground was the result of a community partnership that brought nonprofits, parents, and the medical community together. The park's website spells out its vision: "Imagine children with wheelchairs or those with sensory, visual or cognitive disabilities, playing side by side with their able bodied peers." Adventure Island Playground is a park for all children. And when parents and children share this space, they learn to appreciate each other's stories.

After her success with the playground, Angela served on state councils, then started working at Idaho Parents Unlimited. "I was an accidental advocate," she said. "That's probably true for most of us. None of us who have children with mental disorders set out to have those children (unless we intentionally adopted them). We find ourselves in this place by accident, not by choice. But then we have to say, what am I going to do with this?"

As hard as some of her days are, Angela would not trade the experience. "Amber is such a joyful child—she exudes happiness," Angela said. "And Ryan is so smart. It's a lot harder with Elise. She is polite and charming, and people like her, but from a parenting standpoint, she has no ability to be attached—I have to come to grips with the fact that I am not going to get that give-and-take with her."

When Elise was six, Angela reached a point of desperation and drove her daughter to Hope House, a faith-based residence in Marsing, Idaho, for children between the ages of six and eighteen who are unable to live with their families. The residential program currently costs $1,500 per month, some of which is usually offset by Social Security payments. Many of these children, like Elise, come from orphanages in other countries. "I cried the whole way home because I couldn't give up my six-year-old," Angela said. "So I brought her home. When she was seven and tried to burn down our house, I drew a line in the sand—but in the end, I didn't want to give up my seven-year-old. I wanted my daughter. We decided to keep Elise with us, in our home. We can still develop a healthy relationship, and right now she is doing well. She is motivated and trying. Last weekend she actually made a list of chores and started doing them."

Angela always gives the same advice to parents of children with disabilities and mental illness. "You have to be good to yourself," she says. "For me, that means keeping a sense of humor. I use humor in dealing with Elise's issues—she gets my sarcasm." Angela encourages parents to surround themselves with people who will support them. "This is chronic, and some of your friends and family will not be able to handle that. They will start to distance themselves from you. Your friendships are going to change. I am always amazed when people are willing to come camping with the Lindigs. But we have fun. We didn't choose this life, but this is who we are."

## THE BALANCING ACT

Angela and Darin Lindig have managed to balance work, life, and children with disabilities. But few families can have it all. If you have a child with mental illness, flexibility is critical. And if you're doing it alone, as I am, your options are even more limited. If your child has a mental illness, you'll find that balancing work and caregiving is a task equal in complexity (and futility) to planning a military incursion in Russia during the winter. As they try to juggle appointments with doctors, therapists, caseworkers, teachers, and probation officers, most families with two parents ultimately find that one parent has to stay home. In my case, I'm on my own, so staying home is not an option. I had to make some hard choices about my son's therapies last year, losing an occupational therapist and talk therapist who had worked with my son for years because I simply could not afford the driving time—more than ten hours per week—or the $400 per month out-of-pocket expense when my insurance company decided not to include our beloved occupational therapist in its provider network.

In a direct affront to the myth of the welfare queen, many single mothers are actually forced to go on welfare so that they can get services and provide care for their children. Sometimes parents are encouraged to quit their jobs, go on welfare, and collect Supplemental Security Income (SSI) for their children, just so their children can have access to mental health care. One parent shared that experience in a comment on my blog: "Mine was in [residential treatment] for a year and then the county decided they didn't want to pay for it anymore and took him out, sent him home with no plan whatsoever and now I am forced to homeschool him because the school doesn't want to deal with him. And people criticize us for taking SSI. *When exactly are we able to work?*" (Emphasis added.)

The public radio program *This American Life* has shared the stories of families who depend on the SSI benefits their children receive for mental health issues. In a classic and tragic catch-22, those same children cannot "recover," or their families may be plunged even further into poverty. To me, this enforced poverty, coupled with the school-to-prison pipeline, is the clearest evidence of how badly the current system is broken. Current funding models condemn children and families to lives of poverty and forced disability.

It goes without saying that caregivers need flexible work arrangements. While there are laws to protect caregivers, including the Family and Medical Leave Act (FMLA), which allows workers to take unpaid time off to care for family members, they are not practical for many workers—how many of us can just leave work for six weeks? Caregivers also have protected status under federal law, meaning that they can sue for wrongful termination if they are fired because they had to provide care. But these cases, as I learned from personal experience, can be difficult to prove, especially in right-to-work states like Idaho, where an employer can terminate you for no reason at all. Workers find themselves taking on extra projects or working longer hours in the hope of preserving their jobs (and their health insurance).

Even with private health insurance, many families find that the care of their child is cost prohibitive. Often the only way families of children with mental illness can afford treatment is to get on Medicaid. According to NAMI, Medicaid is the most common form of funding for mental health services for children and adults, accounting for more than 50 percent of overall public health spending in 2005. But middle-class families like the Stapletons, the Lindigs, and my own family often cannot qualify for Medicaid services. Kelli Stapleton laid out the awful equation on her blog as she explored options for funding her daughter's care. According to Kelli, these were the only ways that Issy could qualify for services under Medicaid:

1. Mom divorces Dad. Child might qualify.
2. Dad loses his job.
3. Dad dies.
4. Both parents relinquish parental rights to the state.

Some people divorce their spouses, not because they don't love them, but because there is no other way to get help for their children. In other cases, parents sign over custody of their children to the state. Yes, you read that correctly. I know you don't want to believe this. I do not want to believe this. But it's true. In "A Family's Guide to the Child Welfare System," the mother of a child named John shares her poignant story: "I remember crying for days and shutting down from the outside world. John needed residential treatment, and in our state to get help with paying for residential placement, you have to relinquish physical custody to the DHHR [Department of Health and Human Resources]. Although I had a Medicaid card that would pay for John's treatment, in our state it would not pay for a bed for him to sleep in."

A 2003 U.S. Government Accounting [now Accountability] Office (GAO) study of nineteen states revealed that at least 12,700 children were placed in the child welfare system or juvenile justice system to receive mental health care. Parents do have other options: in some states, a Katie Beckett grant, named for a girl who inspired changes to the rules for parents and children with disabilities by allowing children to collect SSI benefits despite their parents' earnings, can sometimes be used to offset the cost of care for children with mental or physical disabilities. But you need a very specific diagnosis to be able to qualify for a grant, which is why

Michael's caseworker pushed for a pervasive developmental disorder diagnosis for him.

The Bazelon Center for Mental Health Law, a national advocacy organization headquartered in Washington, D.C., is one place where families can learn about options for supportive services. "Parents should never have to give up custody to secure crucially needed mental health services for a child," the website states. "Parents forced to make this devastating choice are victims of an irrational and wholly inadequate system of insurance coverage." The center advocates for federal, state, and local policy shifts that will provide wraparound care to children and families. Wraparound care describes all the ancillary services children like Issy Stapleton or my son Michael need to remain with their families and in their communities. It's a cost-effective solution when compared with residential care or juvenile detention, and these services help to keep families together.

A 1999 joint report between the Bazelon Center and the Federation of Families for Children's Mental Health summarized the problem: "children with serious emotional disturbance do not have access to adequate mental health services and supports in their communities, and many families are forced to give up custody to the child welfare system to get help." According to the report, at least half of the states reported custody transfer issues for parents of children with mental illness. The NAMI report I referenced at the beginning of this chapter also found that one in four parents had been advised to relinquish custody of their child to the state. The solution, expressed by policy makers and advocates everywhere: increased access to home- and community-based care for children and their families.

*Plus ça change.*

## DIVORCE

Unfortunately, not every family is able to handle the stress of parenting a child with mental illness as well as the Lindigs do; too often, marriages dissolve. "A child with life-threatening illness can galvanize a family, even a whole community, to pull together to help her get the best care possible. But when children have psychiatric disorders, the effect is often, sadly, different," notes Dr. Harold Koplewicz, director of Child Mind Institute. One study showed a greater risk of divorce for parents of a child with an autism spectrum disorder—23.5 percent versus 13.8 percent for the control group. In contrast, childhood cancer does not result in higher divorce rates. In my own case, Michael's illness predated the problems that led to the end of my marriage. It was not Michael's fault. But the postdivorce period has proven nearly impossible to navigate, with the sad result that Michael's father is no longer able to participate in his son's life. Divorce is not easy in any circumstances. But when a child with mental illness is involved, and when the divorce is high in conflict, all kinds of problems can ensue.

Women generally bear the brunt of economic pain in divorce, and I was no exception. What are the consequences of divorce for women with young children? The statistics are grim: According to a 2011 U.S. Census Bureau report, divorced mothers are twice as likely as divorced fathers to live in poverty. More than 20 percent of single mothers receive welfare benefits. Over 35 percent of single mothers receiving child support are below the poverty line eighteen months after divorcing, while only 10 percent of noncustodial fathers earn less than poverty-level incomes. A 2013 Gallup Poll revealed that 31 percent of single parents had struggled to buy food in the past twelve months.

What are your chances of getting a divorce? While not quite as bad as that oft-touted 50 percent statistic, at my socioeconomic status and education level, I still had a one-in-four chance of going through a divorce, and single-parent households are increasingly the norm rather than the exception. In 2008, 21.7 percent of all households with children were headed by a single parent. Though they still suffer more than men, women who are employed at the time of divorce do not suffer nearly as badly as their unemployed counterparts, and neither do their children. I am raising my daughter in a religious tradition that values so-called traditional marriage and family, where the father provides economic support and the

mother is the primary "nurturer." Anna is a bright, inquisitive child who
will have the chance to be anything she wants to be when she grows up.
But now, when she says she wants to be a mommy, I say, "That's great! You
will be a wonderful mom. But what do you want to do for work?"

Because having done both, I can say that stay-at-home moms have it
much harder than working moms do. Especially after a divorce, and especially when a child with mental illness is involved. In a longitudinal study
of risk factors for children with mental illness, researchers discovered that
divorce and mental disorders—most commonly anxiety, behavior problems, and substance abuse—were correlated for children. That correlation
is not necessarily causal, since a number of factors are at play (families may
be more at risk for divorce, for example, because the parents have mental
illness, and that mental illness manifests in their children). But the correlation exists. High-conflict divorces like mine are especially toxic for
children with mental illness. Children with bipolar disorder, like Elise and
Michael, often attempt to manipulate and triangulate, further estranging
the parents.

The 1988 National Interview Survey on Child Health noted that
children living with single mothers were more likely to have been treated
for emotional or behavioral problems in the preceding year. A 2009 longitudinal study of adolescent disorders noted a similar correlation: "With
respect to parental characteristics, the prevalence rates of anxiety disorders, substance use disorders and behavior disorders were higher for respondents whose parents were divorced or separated." While divorce has
become a fact of life in our society, its negative implications for children's
mental health cannot be ignored.

Divorced parents have a hard time agreeing about anything; a difficult
child's care may be especially problematic. Dr. Alan Ravitz, a child and
adolescent psychiatrist, notes that parents who can't agree can prevent a
child from getting needed care. "If the conflict between the parents is such
that there is a reflexive unthinking rejection of what the other parent has
to say, then the child always suffers because the child never gets the treatment that he needs," he says. In such cases, sometimes courts have to step

in with child advocates or parenting coordinators who make decisions about the child's care when the parents are unable to compromise.

## FAMILY THERAPY

One promising treatment for families like mine is family therapy. Meghan Shaver, a clinician from the University of Pittsburgh, contacted me to describe a novel therapy called Alternatives for Families: A Cognitive-Behavioral Therapy (AF-CBT). This evidence-based program, designed to provide alternatives to physical discipline for parents of children with behavioral problems, was developed in the early 2000s by David Kolko, a nationally respected professor of psychiatry, psychology, and pediatrics at the University of Pittsburgh. The program works on clear communication of expectations and positive discipline methods.

A precursor to models like AF-CBT was Functional Family Therapy (FFT) (also called Family Preservation), developed in the 1970s as a means to ameliorate family conditions for juvenile offenders. Often, participation is court-ordered when a child enters the juvenile justice system. Many of these families are unlikable (I would put my own in that category—I like to joke that every judge in Ada County is afraid of us); all want "quick fixes" for their delinquent kids (who wouldn't?). The goal of Functional Family Therapy is to keep children out of juvenile detention and with their families: "Over the past 30 years, FFT providers have learned that they must do more than simply stop bad behaviors; they must motivate families to change by uncovering family members' unique strengths, helping families build on these strengths in ways that enhance self-respect, and offering families specific ways to improve."

Though there are no quick fixes, the University of Pittsburgh model is evidence based, meaning that clinicians and researchers are tracking outcomes and seeing measurable results. Kolko started Partnerships for Families to test his work in cognitive behavior therapy in the community, turning theory into a working therapeutic treatment for children and families. Shaver, the community liaison for Partnerships for Families, noted in a telephone conversation that "Every single client wanted to be a better parent. No parent says, 'Today is the day I want to mess my kids up.'" That philosophy—that parents want to succeed—is the driver behind AF-CBT. "It's about building skills," Shaver said.

Partnerships for Families' goals are to provide training to practitioners about effective discipline techniques that reduce problem behaviors and improve the quality of parent-child relationships. "Often, we determine what treatments work well in the very controlled settings of university- and hospital-based clinics, but we don't always investigate how well those therapies work in the real world," said Dr. Kolko, principal investigator of the study. "In developing our treatment, it was important to bring what we have learned about helping parents and children to partners in the community who deal with these issues every day." AF-CBT is rated a 3, which is a "promising practice," by the California Evidence Based Clearinghouse for Child Welfare. By giving parents the skills to model appropriate behaviors and to communicate effectively, AF-CBT reduces aggression and maladaptive behaviors in both children and parents. "It's about setting up everyone to be successful," Shaver explained. "Our goal is to make the family function in a way to stay stable, to reduce conflict, and to alleviate the stress on children and parents."

Parent-Child Interaction Therapy (PCIT) is another evidence-based treatment designed to improve the quality of the parent-child relationship. Specifically addressing the unique and often exhausting behaviors of children with chronic illness, developmental disorders, and mental retardation, PCIT has also been shown to alleviate symptoms of depression in preschoolers. "I love my child, but I just don't like him very much" is a common complaint from parents of children with behavioral disorders; parents often blame themselves and may be prone to developing mental health issues of their own.

Developed by Dr. Sheila Eyberg and Dr. Constance Hanf in the late 1980s, PCIT built on Hanf's model of two stages of positive reinforcement treatment. In the first stage, parents learn to reinforce their children's positive behaviors and ignore negative ones. In the second stage, mothers give clear directions and reward children with praise or punish with time-outs. Eyberg incorporated hands-on techniques, including positive play, because "play is the primary medium through which children develop problem-solving skills and work through developmental problems."

At the Child Mind Institute in New York, Dr. Melanie Fernandez, a board-certified psychologist and expert in PCIT, provides one-on-one coaching to parents through a one-way mirror and an earbud as they interact with children. Fernandez studied with Eyberg at the University of Florida and now trains other therapists in PCIT. She breaks down effective parenting of children with behavioral disorders into ABCs. A stands for the antecedents, or things that come before an unwanted behavior. These might include hunger, fatigue, or other triggers that cause meltdowns. B stands for the behavior itself. Fernandez encourages parents to be very specific about identifying problem behaviors—not "acting up," but "running around the room," for example. And C stands for consequences, which should always be natural, logical, and immediate, since "a huge consequence can be demoralizing, so that children give up even trying to behave."

A typical treatment plan begins with an initial phase of two to four sessions. During the first two sessions, Fernandez meets with parents to explain the skills that the parents will learn. In subsequent sessions, children come in with their parents so that the parents can practice the skills with coaching from an expert. "Home practice is an essential part of the program," Dr. Fernandez explained to me in a telephone interview

Parents learn about positive reinforcing and active ignoring. "When we see attention-seeking behaviors, destructive or aggressive behaviors, yelling, screaming, rough play, parents learn to ignore it," Dr. Fernandez explained. "I don't love the term because it sounds like tolerating. It's not. It is making a deliberate decision to remove your attention from the behavior by withholding eye and verbal contact. The moment appropriate behavior resumes, you reengage the child and thank and encourage them. It's a tough technique—you know you are doing it correctly when the behavior initially gets worse. It tends to get worse before it gets better. But it does get better."

The second phase is the discipline phase, where parents learn how to present expectations and instructions most effectively. "There are ways that you can increase or decrease the likelihood that a child will comply," Fernandez explained. "We coach parents in giving commands during play. Play is the lowest degree of difficulty when you are working with children. It's not as hard to ask a child to hand you the red block as it is to say 'Please go get dressed.'"

Once parents are successful in play situations, they extrapolate to real-life, even working on public outings. "Once the parent has mastered the skill and the child listens very consistently, we will go to Grand Central Terminal or to the park or the grocery store to help parents use the techniques from both phases. Our goal is to set both parent and child up for success," Fernandez said.

A typical treatment plan includes anywhere from thirteen to sixteen sessions. PCIT can work well for children with oppositional defiant disorder or attention-deficit/hyperactivity disorder. Children as young as two can begin treatment, but the cut-off age is six years, eleven months. "Older children are a challenge because PCIT involves some physical involvement with the child, and an eight-year-old is harder to transport. It becomes less safe for everyone," Fernandez explained. "That's why early recognition and intervention is so important."

While parents should not be blamed for their children's mental illness, Functional Family Therapy, AF-CBT, and PCIT can all help to empower families to manage the stress of daily life and difficult behaviors. But as Kelli Stapleton noted, consistent application of these therapies—and consistency is crucial to success—can be exhausting. Parents sometimes feel that they have no margin for error. And in divorced families, some level of inconsistency or triangulation is probably inevitable. Though it's hard to parent Michael on my own, I can understand why it's ultimately best for him—and for our family.

## FAMILY SECRETS, FAMILY STRENGTHS

As we saw in chapter 2, stigma also dictates how much a family is willing to share with the outside world, since families—and especially parents— are often blamed for the behavior of the child who has mental illness. Author Michael Schofield shared his daughter's story and their family's life with the world to reinforce the positive message that "denial is not going to help Jani or any of the other mentally ill and schizophrenic children I have come to know." In his book, *January First*, he wrote words that felt familiar to my experience:

> When our story became public, hundreds of families emailed me, all telling a variation of the same message: "We thought we were alone." . . . Nevertheless, from my blog posts they drew conclusions, based on what they believe, that I abused my daughter and that the true cause of Jani's condition rests in her parents and how she was raised.

Though stigma can isolate families, some families develop resilience as a result of living with a child who has mental illness: In one study that asked about strengths that emerged from mental illness, "Family resilience was reported by 87.8% of participants. Personal resilience was reported by 99.2% of participants." A 1996 qualitative study of eighty-five families yielded the expected result that families coping with a severe mental illness have significantly more stressors than normative families, but it also provided some unexpected positives: these families also have clear strengths related to family coping, adaptability, and conflict management. Though mental illness affected every aspect of family life and relationships, from finances to employment to social life, marriage status, and physical health, support groups like Federation of Families helped to reduce the sense of social isolation.

Every family of a child with mental illness has experienced some kind of stigma, some kind of intentional cruelty. And yet families—and family therapy—may hold the key to successfully managing mental illness. Before we can provide effective supports to families of children with mental illness, we have to be able to talk about the problem. We have to end stigma. My journey to help my son began and ends with stigma. In the essay that started this journey, I wrote, "It's time to talk about mental illness." I hope that in hindsight, we view 2013 as a tipping point year, as the time when people finally stopped seeing mental illness as different from physical illness—when people could finally share their stories.

As I was preparing to give a TEDx San Antonio speech in October 2013, I asked Michael if he would be comfortable with me sharing the picture of him as an eight-year-old, looking at a butterfly. I believe it was that picture—a beautiful, blond boy—as much as the inflammatory title "I Am Adam Lanza's Mother," that made my blog post go viral. When I look at this picture, I see the shadows our family was already experiencing, the missed diagnoses, the medications, the false hopes. When I wrote the words "I Am Adam Lanza's Mother," I was not comparing my son to a rampage killer. I was trying to make the point that no mother holds her beautiful newborn child in her arms and says, "I hope that you grow up to a life of pain. I hope that you grow up bullied and afraid. I hope that you lash out and hurt others in unforgivable ways."

Mothers of children with mental illness want for their children what all parents want: they want their children to be happy. We already have effective treatments and interventions—but families like those you met in this book are often not able to get these treatments, in part because of lack of access, but more often because of stigma and fear. We know what works. We even know how to pay for it. But until we can talk about mental illness—until we overcome stigma and fear—we will continue the destructive and painful cycle of prison, substance abuse, and unpredictable (but all too predictable) violence, as families and children suffer in shame and silence.

# HAPPY ENDINGS

And to me also, who appreciate life, the butterflies, and soap-bubbles, and whatever is like them amongst us, seem most to enjoy happiness.

—Friedrich Nietzsche, *Thus Spoke Zarathustra*

One Sunday in late May 2013, Ed and I backpacked six miles along a narrow trail that rises high above the Snake River, the natural border between eastern Oregon and western Idaho. The gash carved in black basalt by the cool, wide, green Snake is deeper in some places than the Grand Canyon. Our destination was the historic Kirkwood Ranch, former homestead of Len and Grace Jordan, a neat, white clapboard structure surrounded by a green lawn and a well-kept garden. Grace and Len moved to this remote spot with their three young children during the Great Depression; Len, the future governor of Idaho, ran a sheep-ranching outfit while Grace raised the children, tended the garden, and learned to live off the land.

It was a weekend of respite for all of us. Michael was with his day care provider; James stayed with friends. For two whole days, I was free to explore Carter Mansion, an old five-room tin and log moonshiner's cabin, so named for its high-class plastered walls, to search for Native American artifacts, and to dip my toes and splash my face in the Snake's refreshing water. I was free to sit on the bank where we pitched our tent and watch the sun set while I immersed myself in Grace's lovely modern pioneer memoir, *Home below Hell's Canyon*.

But we almost didn't make it to our destination. The night before, as we drove up the winding dirt road to the trailhead campsite at Pittsburg Landing, a sweetly acrid smell made me cry out: the car engine was over-heating. We let the engine cool for several minutes on the closest turnout, watching in quiet joy as the sky exploded in pinks and golds above the hills greened with spring rain. A herd of deer was grazing in a meadow just below us, flicking their white tails and glancing casually at us with their liquid eyes before returning to their supper.

When the car overheated again a few minutes later, we decided to turn around. We made camp at the bottom of the hill and watched the stars come out, until the Milky Way stretched across the black sky, a cloud of stars. "The detours aren't always a bad thing," Ed murmured as we looked up in wonder. "We never would have seen those deer, or that sun-set, or these stars, if the car hadn't quit."

"Not bad at all," I replied.

And that's how I feel about my life. I had a plan. I was prepared. Plans changed. But the detours have provided unexpected joys.

Random coins have special meaning to me. When a penny appears on the sidewalk at my feet, or a dime sits on the bus seat beside me, something in my lizard brain says, *Pay attention*. I am fully aware that our minds see patterns where none exist. The fact that I attribute meaning to spare change amuses me—it's my own personal form of augury, a less messy alternative to reading sheep entrails, less complicated than charting the movements of birds across the sky. I view this behavior as relatively harmless, a way to give false but comforting meaning to the otherwise random chaos of life.

I've learned to embrace the chaos. Living with a son who has mental illness has taught me what Zen masters spend their whole lives learning: to let go. There is an exquisite freedom that comes with living in the present tense, with appreciating moments as they happen, because you can't predict what the future will bring. There's a certain happiness in this present-tense existence, a certain freedom, even as I wonder how I will afford Michael's medical bills or whether he'll be able to attend a regular high school next year.

It is, as they say, what it is.

## A Final Word about Guns

After Newtown, I wrote a line that has been taken out of context: "It's easy to talk about guns. But it's time to talk about mental illness." I think it's still time to talk about mental illness. And though I disagree with the president on many other subjects, I applaud the Obama administration for dedicating research funds to this vital national crisis and for making parity between physical and mental health a key component of the Affordable Care Act of 2010. After meeting with the families of the Sandy Hook victims one year after the tragedy, Vice President Joe Biden, whose initial response to the tragedy was to push for tighter gun control, announced a $100 million increase in funding to help people access mental health services.

But when people ask me about guns, I have to say while it may be easy to talk about them, the issue itself is complex. No matter how you interpret events like Newtown, it's clear that guns are part of the problem for people with mental illness, and for society as a whole. The official report about the school shooting at Sandy Hook Elementary School could be summarized in five words: no answers, lots of guns. Lanza's mental illness was certainly a factor; as the report notes, "the shooter had significant mental health issues that affected his ability to live a normal life and to interact with others, even those to whom he should have been close." Like his mother.

I've learned this year that I am not Adam Lanza's mother. While I still feel a great deal of empathy for Nancy Lanza, who surely loved her son as I love mine, we are different in two important ways. First, by acknowledging the seriousness of my son's condition, I am empowered to do everything I can to ensure he gets the treatment he needs.

Second, I don't own guns, and I never will.

Some have speculated that perhaps guns were a way for Nancy Lanza to connect with her son. My son and I share some common interests too: writing, Greek mythology, and history. As far as I know, a love of history never killed anyone.

In August 2013, just days before our college's summer commencement

ceremonies, I lost a former student, who shot himself the day after completing his externship. He was just nineteen—popular, outgoing, a regular
Richard Cory. No one saw it coming.

I live in Idaho. I like to hunt. I think it's great good fun to shoot up
aluminum cans with a BB gun. But as I think about this tremendous loss,
the hole my former student's death has created in his family and in our
community, I'm reminded that Idaho has one of the highest per capita
suicide rates in the nation because we have the trifecta of suicide risk
factors: that rugged, "pull yourself up by your bootstraps" individualism,
lack of access to mental health care, and of course, easy access to firearms.

In my former student's age group, suicide is the second most common
cause of death, after accident. As I said before, more than 4,600 young
people aged ten to twenty-four complete suicide each year. Of those
deaths, 45 percent involve guns. Men are far more likely than women to
complete suicide, but women are more likely to attempt suicide. For suicides involving a firearm, 85 percent are fatal. A quick impulse to escape
can translate too easily with the pull of a trigger into a permanent, irrevo-
cable act.

But what is the solution? Our nation is facing a crisis in mental health
care. Background checks for guns seem like a good idea, but by making
access to firearms more difficult in that way, we may unintentionally prevent people who have mental illness from admitting that they need help,
especially in western states like Idaho or Texas, where the gun culture is a
part of everyday life.

As I was completing this book in September 2013, another horrific
mass shooting occurred, in the Naval Yard in Washington, D.C. Aaron
Alexis had all the right clearances. He bought his gun legally. He also had
a long-standing and well-documented history of mental illness; indeed, he
sought help in the weeks leading up to the shooting from two different
Veterans Affairs hospitals, where he reported difficulty sleeping. He told
police in Rhode Island that men were following him and that he was
hearing voices. But like too many others, Alexis was not given the help he
needed.

We do not treat our citizens who have mental illness with anything close to dignity. Instead of giving them treatment, we put them in jail, or let them live homeless on the streets. I'm not sure what the solution is. But I know that personal relationships and education are critical to reducing this tragic loss of life that occurs all too often when loaded guns meet situational and solvable life circumstances. The National Rifle Association is fond of saying that "guns don't kill people." But people with guns kill themselves, in far too many numbers. Sometimes they take innocent first graders or colleagues or movie watchers or family members with them. We can't ignore this problem as a society.

## Picture Perfect

I am truly fortunate to be secure in my children's love for me. I can't give them a picture-perfect childhood. But I can give them the foundation of unconditional love, the same foundation my parents gave to me. Even though my family isn't perfect, we are, on the whole, happy.

As a parent who went very public with my son's mental illness, I must confess that I still worry about the larger concerns of privacy for our children. We post pictures of our children on Facebook, we share their clever quips, their joys, their sorrows, without really thinking about the consequences. But the technology that changed us so quickly, that enabled a single blogger to share a cry for help with the world, is already a part of our children's lives.

While my generation debates whether or not to share pictures of our family vacations on Facebook, my children have already moved to new platforms, fleeing, as the young always do, the spaces where their parents congregate in hopes of finding their own space. The younger generation's response to privacy concerns is to use more fleeting technology like Snapchat, or to create online personae, whose anonymity emboldens them to say otherwise unspeakable things.

In the end, I have decided that for myself and for my family, advocacy requires to some extent the sacrifice of privacy in the name of promoting greater awareness and understanding. But though you would never recognize me or my children in a grocery store, I am still hesitant to use Michael's real name. His voice is his to share when he is ready. I know that he can and most likely will be a powerful self-advocate, that he will use his remarkable insight to articulate his ideas for change. As he received an award from the Idaho Federation of Families for his advocacy work, Michael told those gathered, "I'm not a politician. I don't know how to give speeches. But I do know that the stigma of mental illness has got to stop."


## PRIVACY AND STIGMA

As I think about privacy and stigma, I'm reminded of things that were once private but are now shouted from rooftops. Christianity was incubated in underground catacombs, its followers identifying each other with an obscure symbol, a fish (ichthus), scratched and easily erased in sand. For millennia, lepers were sent away to colonies and shunned. For years, people didn't speak of breast cancer—now pink ribbons festoon everything from muffin pans to Hershey's Kisses every October. In the 1990s, Bill Clinton told gay members of the military, "Don't ask, don't tell." Less than twenty years later, the military extended full benefits to gay spouses.

Things can change that quickly. All it takes is for people to accept their friends, their children's classmates, and yes, their own children, their parents, their siblings who suffer from a chronic and manageable disease. One of the first and most powerful steps is to acknowledge the personhood of people with mental illness. I've tried very hard throughout this book to use person-centered language when discussing mental illness. My son is not bipolar. He is Michael. And Michael has bipolar disorder. Journalists, medical providers, teachers, and friends can all take this important first step to recognizing the intrinsic equality of people who have mental illness. Language reflects our values, and we should value the worth of people who have mental illness as much as we value any person.

I was criticized for speaking in public about what some people thought should remain private. I maintain that I am still a private person. I choose what I share—and what I don't. Each of us needs our secrets. You have yours, and I have mine.

But the fact that my son has bipolar disorder is not and should not be a secret. His illness is nothing for him, or me, to be ashamed of. It is not an excuse to deny him an education, or meaningful work, or a bright future. I wish for my child all the things any parent wishes. Nancy Lanza, Susan Klebold, Arlene Holmes wished those things for their children, too.

When I began this book, I still did not have answers. Like many parents, I was living without hope, in fear for my son and my family. What a difference a diagnosis makes! As I have written this book, I have also finally seen positive and hopefully lasting changes in my son's mental health. The diagnosis of bipolar disorder, the incorporation of lithium, the continued use of consistent positive parenting techniques, the addition of respite care—all of these have contributed to dramatic improvements in my son's and my quality of life. After several painful months apart, Michael once again has consistent contact with his younger siblings, whose love and support for their brother is a model for how all children should treat their siblings who have mental illness. Though our separation has been difficult, it has made us appreciate all the more just how special our family is, how fortunate, despite our misfortunes, we are to have each other.

As I said in the beginning, I wrote this book for two audiences. If you do not have a child with mental illness, I hope this book has helped you to understand what one in five children in America and their parents must go through to obtain treatment. And I hope you'll look at that child acting out on the playground or in the classroom with different, more compassionate eyes. Social stigma is a powerful force. When an Adam Lanza or James Holmes or Jared Loughner tears apart our cherished notions of safety for ourselves and our children, we need to remember that society as a whole shares at least some blame for refusing to provide help when help was asked for. Martin Drell, MD, president of the American Academy of

Child and Adolescent Psychiatry, said in the organization's 2012 annual report, "We're at the perfect intersection of events—children's mental health may never be more important in our nation's history than right now." That statement seems even more true today, after Sandy Hook.

If you're a parent of a child with mental illness, I hope this book has offered you hope, a sense of community, and an inspiration to share your own story. It was not an easy book to write, especially as I was living it. But as I looked at trends—the school-to-prison pipeline, the association of mental illness with poverty, the stresses of single parenthood—I realized that we have the opportunity to create real and lasting change in our society, with relatively little expense, by reallocating resources and providing early and effective interventions at home, in schools, and in treatment. As parents like me speak out and share our stories, parents of children with mental illness can and will find the help they need for their children. We are not alone. Our pictures may not be perfect, but our families—and our children—can be happy, whole, and well.

# ACKNOWLEDGMENTS

This book would never have happened without Nathaniel Hoffman, longtime friend, fellow writer, and editor of Boise State University's online journal the *Blue Review*. Nate talked me into putting my name on my anonymous story and changed the title to "I Am Adam Lanza's Mother." The rest is Internet history. My agent, Lisa Kopel, understood me and the importance of this book from the start and provided expert advice and support throughout the process. Howard Bragman helped me to navigate the unfamiliar and often overwhelming modern media world. My editor Caroline Sutton asked all the right questions and made me work to provide often uneasy answers.

Elaine Ambrose, publisher and friend, shielded me from a media feeding frenzy while my son was in the hospital and provided countless moments of encouragement as I worked on this project. Ken Rodgers taught me to write without adverbs. My mother, Loralee Long, a career educator, took frequent Friday afternoon phone calls and shared frontline classroom insights. Steve Graci of the Idaho Federation of Families helped me to find my voice as a parent advocate.

I am particularly grateful to the individuals and families who shared their stories with me. The subject matter was painful, and I am humbled by the bravery of the mothers I spoke with. I was also inspired by the scientists, educators, law enforcement representatives, and clinicians who talked with me about real solutions.

I am grateful to my colleagues at Carrington College–Boise who covered classes for me so that I could attend conferences, conduct interviews, and research this book. I stand in awe of my son Michael's many health providers, caregivers, and teachers.

Finally, I am grateful to Ed Pack for filling the cracks of my life so seamlessly. And I am most grateful to my four children: we've had an interesting journey together so far, and I am looking forward to many more adventures.

# BIBLIOGRAPHY

Abelson, Reed. "Lacking rules, insurers balk at paying for intensive psychiatric care." *New York Times*, September 27, 2013.

Adams, Mark D., Susan E. Celniker, Robert A. Holt, Cheryl A. Evans, Jeannine D. Gocayne, Peter G. Amanatides, Steven E. Scherer, et al. "The genome sequence of Drosophila melanogaster." *Science* 287, no. 5461 (2000): 2185–95.

Aizer, Anna, and Joseph Doyle, Jr. "Juvenile incarceration, human capital and future crime: Evidence from randomly-assigned judges." National Bureau of Economic Research Working Paper No. 19102, June 2013.

Alexander, James, and Sexton, Thomas L. "Functional Family Therapy." *Juvenile Justice Bulletin*, December 2000. Retrieved from https://www.ncjrs.gov/pdf files1/ojjdp/184743.pdf.

Andrews, Jonathan, Asa Briggs, Roy Porter, Penny Tucker, and Keir Waddington. *The History of Bethlem*. London and New York: Routledge, 1997.

"Attitudes toward mental illness: 35 states, District of Columbia, and Puerto Rico, 2007." *Morbidity and Mortality Weekly Report* 59, no. 20 (2010), 619–25.

Auden, W. H. "Musée des Beaux Arts." In *Another Time*. London: Faber and Faber, 1940.

Avan, Bilal, Linda M. Richter, Paul G. Ramchandani, Shane A. Norris, and Alan Stein. "Maternal postnatal depression and children's growth and behaviour during the early years of life: Exploring the interaction between physical and mental health." *Archives of Disease in Childhood* 95, no. 9 (2010): 690–95.

Averill, Andrew. "Adam Lanza bullied as a student at Sandy Hook, his mother considered suing." *Christian Science Monitor*, April 17, 2013.

Awadalla, Philip, Julie Gauthier, Rachel A. Myers, Ferran Casals, Fadi F. Hamdan, Alexander R. Griffing, Mélanie Côté, et al. "Direct measure of the de novo mutation rate in autism and schizophrenia cohorts." *American Journal of Human Genetics* 87, no. 3 (2010): 316–24.

Ayoub, Catherine C., Robin M. Deutsch, and Andronicki Maraganore. "Emotional distress in children of high-conflict divorce." *Family Court Review* 37, no. 3 (1999): 297–315.

Baicker, Katherine, Sarah Taubman, Heidi Allen, Mira Bernstein, Jonathan Gruber, Joseph P. Newhouse, Eric Schneider, Bill Wright, Alan Zaslavsky, Amy Finkelstein, and the Oregon Health Study Group. "The Oregon experiment—Medicaid's effects on clinical outcomes." *New England Journal of Medicine* 368, no. 18 (May 2013).

Bailey, Martha J., and Susan M. Dynarski. "Gains and gaps: Changing inequality in U.S. college entry and completion." National Bureau of Economic Research Working Paper No. 17633, December 2011.

Bale, Tracy L., Tallie Z. Baram, Alan S. Brown, Jill M. Goldstein, Thomas R. Insel, Margaret M. McCarthy, Charles B. Nemeroff, et al. "Early life programming and neurodevelopmental disorders." *Biological Psychiatry* 68, no. 4 (2010): 314–19.

Barden, Louise S., Scott F. Dowell, Benjamin Schwartz, and Cheryl Lackey. "Current attitudes regarding use of antimicrobial agents: Results from physicians' and parents' focus group discussions." *Clinical Pediatrics* 37, no. 11 (1998): 665–71.

Bayer, Patrick, Randi Hjalmarsson, and David Pozen. "Building criminal capital behind bars: Peer effects in juvenile corrections." *Quarterly Journal of Economics* 124, no. 1 (2009): 105–47.

Behar, Lenore, Robert Friedman, Allison Pinto, Judith Katz-Leavy, and William G. Jones. "Protecting youth placed in unlicensed, unregulated residential 'treatment' facilities." *Family Court Review* 45, no. 3 (2007): 399–413.

Behrens, Donna, Julia Graham Lear, and Olga Acosta Price. "Improving access to children's mental health care: Lessons from a study of eleven states." Center for Health and Health Care in Schools, George Washington University (2013).

Bennett-Smith, Meredith. "Kathleen Taylor, neuroscientist, says religious fundamentalism could be treated as a mental illness." *Huffington Post*, May 31, 2013.

Ben-Sasson, A., A. S. Carter, and M. J. Briggs-Gowan. "Sensory over-responsivity in elementary school: Prevalence and social-emotional correlates." *Journal of Abnormal Child Psychology* 37, no. 5 (2009): 705–16.

Bernard Kuhn, Lisa. "Illegal ecstasy being studied to treat PTSD." *Cincinnati Enquirer*, April 22, 2013.

Beronio, Kirsten, Rosa Po, Laura Skopec, and Sherry Glied. "Affordable Care Act expands mental health and substance use disorder benefits and federal parity protections for 62 million Americans." ASPE Issue Brief, February 20, 2013.

Bertin, Mark. "ADHD goes to school." *Huffington Post*, May 15, 2012. Retrieved from http://www.huffingtonpost.com/mark-bertin-md/adhd_b_1517445.html.

Biasotti, Michael. "The impact of mental illness on law enforcement resources." Unpublished master's thesis, 2011.

Biederman, Joseph C., and Gabrielle A. Carlson. "Increased rates of bipolar disorder diagnoses among U.S. child, adolescent, and adult inpatients, 1996–2004." *Biological Psychiatry* 62, no. 2 (2007): 107–14.

Biswal, Bharat B., Maarten Mennes, Xi-Nian Zuo, Suril Gohel, Clare Kelly, Steve M. Smith, Christian F. Beckmann, et al. "Toward discovery science of human brain function." *Proceedings of the National Academy of Sciences* 107, no. 10 (2010): 4734–39.

Blader, Joseph C., and Gabrielle A. Carlson. "Increased rates of bipolar disorder diagnoses among US child, adolescent, and adult inpatients, 1996–2004."*Biological Psychiatry* 62, no. 2 (2007): 107–14.

Blumberg, Stephen J., Matthew D. Bramlett, Michael D. Kogan, Laura A. Schieve, Jessica R. Jones, and Michael C. Lu. "Changes in prevalence of parent-reported autism spectrum disorder in school-aged US children: 2007 to 2011–2012." *National Health Statistics Reports* 65 (2013): 1–11.

"Boy, 12, to be nation's youngest prison inmate." *New York Times*, January 30, 1996.

Bradstreet, James Jeffrey, Scott Smith, Matthew Baral, and Daniel A. Rossignol. "Biomarker-guided interventions of clinically relevant conditions associated with autism spectrum disorders and attention deficit hyperactivity disorder." *Alternative Medicine Review* 15, no. 1 (2010): 15–32.

Brady, Marion. "Eight problems with Common Core Standards." The Answer Sheet, *Washington Post*, August 21, 2012.

Brank, Eve M., and Josh Haby. "Why not blame the parents?" *APA Monitor* 42, no. 10 (November 2011).

Brennan, Patricia A., Sarnoff A. Mednick, and Sheilagh Hodgins. "Major mental disorders and criminal violence in a Danish birth cohort." *Archives of General Psychiatry* 57, no. 5 (2000): 494.

Bretherton, Inge. "The origins of attachment theory: John Bowlby and Mary Ainsworth." *Developmental Psychology* 28, no. 5 (1992): 759.

Bromley, Jo, Dougal Julian Hare, Kerry Davison, and Eric Emerson. "Mothers supporting children with autistic spectrum disorders: Social support, mental health status and satisfaction with services." *Autism* 8, no. 4 (2004): 409–23.

Cade, John F. J. "Lithium salts in the treatment of psychotic excitement." *Medical Journal of Australia* (1949).

Caetano, R., S. Ramisetty-Mikler, L. R. Floyd, and C. McGrath. "The epidemiology of drinking among women of child-bearing age." *Alcoholism: Clinical and Experimental Research* 30, no. 6 (2006): 1023–30.

Calabrese, Joseph R., Charles L. Bowden, Gary Sachs, Lakshmi N. Yatham, Kirsten Behnke, Olli-Pekka Mehtonen, Paul Montgomery, et al. "A placebo-controlled 18-month trial of lamotrigine and lithium maintenance treatment in recently depressed patients with bipolar I disorder." *Journal of Clinical Psychiatry* 64, no. 9 (2003): 1013–24.

Canuso, Carla M., and Gahan Pandina. "Gender and schizophrenia." *Psychopharmacology Bulletin* 40, no. 4 (2007): 178–90.

Cermak, Sharon A., Carol Curtin, and Linda G. Bandini. "Food selectivity and sensory sensitivity in children with autism spectrum disorders." *Journal of the American Dietetic Association* 110, no. 2 (2010): 238–46.

Chadwick, Bruce A., Brent L. Top, and Richard Jennings McClendon. *Shield of Faith: The Power of Religion in the Lives of LDS Youth and Young Adults.* Provo, UT: Religious Studies Center, Brigham Young University, 2010.

Champeau, Rachel. "Changing gut bacteria through diet affects brain function, UCLA study shows." *UCLA Newsroom*, May 28, 2013.

Chasson, Gregory S., Gerald E. Harris, and Wendy J. Neely. "Cost comparison of early intensive behavioral intervention and special education for children with autism." *Journal of Child and Family Studies* 16, no. 3 (2007): 401–13.

"Child and Adolescent Psychiatry Workforce Crisis: Solutions to Improve Early Intervention and Access to Care." American Academy of Child and Adolescent Psychiatrists, 2013.

"Child welfare and juvenile justice: Federal agencies could play a stronger role in helping states reduce the number of children placed solely to obtain mental health services." Government Accounting Office, April 2003.

Chua, Amy. *Battle Hymn of the Tiger Mom.* New York: Penguin, 2011.

Cidav, Zuleyha, Steven C. Marcus, and David S. Mandell. "Implications of childhood autism for parental employment and earnings." *Pediatrics* 129, no. 4 (2012): 617–23.

Cline, Foster, Jim Fay, and Tom Raabe. *Parenting with Love and Logic: Teaching Children Responsibility.* Colorado Springs, CO: Piñon Press, 1990.

Collins, F. S., E. S. Lander, J. Rogers, R. H. Waterston, and I. H. G. S. Conso. "Finishing the euchromatic sequence of the human genome." *Nature* 431, no. 7011 (2004): 931–45.

"Common Core State Standards." Washington, DC: National Governors Association Center for Best Practices and the Council of Chief State School Officers, 2010.

Compton, Michael T., Masuma Bahora, Amy C. Watson, and Janet R. Oliva. "A comprehensive review of extant research on Crisis Intervention Team (CIT) programs." *Journal of the American Academy of Psychiatry and the Law Online* 36, no. 1 (2008): 47–55.

Correll, Christoph U., Peter Manu, Vladimir Olshanskiy, Barbara Napolitano, John M. Kane, and Anil K. Malhotra. "Cardiometabolic risk of second-generation antipsychotic medications during first-time use in children and adolescents." *JAMA* 302, no. 16 (2009): 1765–73.

"Cost-benefit analysis of juvenile justice programs." Juvenile Justice Guide Book for Legislators. Denver, CO: National Conference of State Legislatures, no date.

Costello, E. Jane, Scott N. Compton, Gordon Keeler, and Adrian Angold. "Relationships between poverty and psychopathology." *JAMA* 290, no. 15 (2003): 2023–29.

Creffield, Claire. "Are parents morally responsible for their children?" *Salon.com,* June 23, 2013.

Croen, Lisa A., Judith K. Grether, Cathleen K. Yoshida, Roxana Odouli, and Victoria Hendrick. "Antidepressant use during pregnancy and childhood autism spectrum disorders." *Archives of General Psychiatry* 68, no. 11 (2011): 1104.

Cullen, Dave. *Columbine.* New York: Hachette Digital, 2009.

Dawson, Deborah A. "Family structure and children's health and well-being: Data from the 1988 National Health Interview Survey on Child Health." *Journal of Marriage and the Family* (1991): 573–84.

Degn, Laura. "Mormon women and depression: Are Latter-day Saint women becoming casualties of perfectionism?" *Sunstone,* May 1985, pp. 19–27.

Dein, Kalpana, Gill Livingston, and Christopher Bench. " 'Why did I become a psychiatrist?': Survey of consultant psychiatrists." *Psychiatric Bulletin* 31, no. 6 (2007): 227–30.

Derzon, James H., Ping Yu, Bruce Ellis, Sharon Xiong, Carmen Arroyo, Danyelle Mannix, Michael E. Wells, Gary Hill, and Julia Rollison. "A national evaluation of Safe Schools/Healthy Students: Outcomes and influences." *Evaluation and Program Planning* 35, no. 2 (2012): 293–302.

"Digest of education statistics, 2009." U.S. Department of Education, National Center for Education Statistics, 2010 (NCES 2010-013), chapter 2.

Diller, Lawrence H. *Running on Ritalin: A Physician Reflects on Children, Society, and Performance in a Pill.* New York: Random House Digital, 2009.

Dols, Michael W. "Galen and mental illness." In *Majnūn: The Madman in Medieval Islamic Society.* Oxford, England: Clarendon Press, 1992.

Doornbos, Mary Molewyk. "The strengths of families coping with serious mental illness." *Archives of Psychiatric Nursing* 10, no. 4 (1996): 214–20.

Doty, Kristine, Danna Lindemann, and Heather Hirsche. "In the culture but not of the culture: Experiences of LDS women with depression." Paper presented to the Utah Valley University 2013 Mental Health Symposium.

Drexler, Madeline. "Guns and suicide: The hidden toll." *Harvard School of Public Health News*, Spring 2013.

Dutton, Audrey. "Child psychiatrist accused of misconduct seeks license back." *Idaho Statesman*, July 19, 2013.

Earley, Pete. *Crazy: A Father's Search through America's Mental Health Madness.* New York: Berkley, 2007.

"Education on lockdown: The schoolhouse to jailhouse track." Advancement Project, March 2005, p. 15.

Evans, Katie, J. McGrath, and R. Milns. "Searching for schizophrenia in ancient Greek and Roman literature: A systematic review." *Acta Psychiatrica Scandinavica* 107, no. 5 (2003): 323–30.

"Extracts from the Report of the Committee Employed to Visit Houses and Hospitals for the Confinement of Insane Persons, with Remarks, by Philanthropus." *Medical and Physical Journal* 32 (August 1814): 122–28.

Eyberg, Sheila. "Parent-child interaction therapy: Integration of traditional and behavioral concerns." *Child and Family Behavior Therapy* 10, no. 1 (1988): 33–46.

Fabrega, Horacio, Jr. "Psychiatric stigma in non-Western societies." *Comprehensive Psychiatry* 32, no. 6 (1991): 534–51.

Fairchild, Graeme, Luca Passamonti, Georgina Hurford, Cindy C. Hagan, Elisabeth A. H. von dem Hagen, Stephanie H. M. van Goozen, Ian M. Goodyer, and Andrew J. Calder. "Brain structure abnormalities in early-onset and adolescent-onset conduct disorder." *American Journal of Psychiatry* 168, no. 6 (2011): 624–33.

Falk, Gerhard. *Stigma: How We Treat Outsiders*. Amherst, NY: Prometheus Books, 2001.

Fazel, Seena, Helen Doll, and Niklas Långström. "Mental disorders among adolescents in juvenile detention and correctional facilities: A systematic review and metaregression analysis of 25 surveys." *Journal of the American Academy of Child and Adolescent Psychiatry* 47, no. 9 (2008): 1010–19.

Feifel, David, Christine Yu Moutier, and Neal R. Swerdlow. "Attitudes toward psychiatry as a prospective career among students entering medical school." *American Journal of Psychiatry* 156, no. 9 (1999): 1397–1402.

Fensterwald, John. "California drops to 49th in school spending in annual Ed Week report." *EdSource*, January 14, 2013.

Fernandes, Gina Kaysen. "Saving troubled teens: A greedy industry?" Momlogic. com, December 2009.

Fernandez, Melanie. "Managing problem behavior at home: A guide to more confident, consistent and effective parenting." Child Mind Institute, February 10, 2012.

Fombonne, Eric. "The prevalence of autism." *JAMA* 289, no. 1 (2003): 87–89.

Fox, James A. "Nancy Lanza was a victim, too." *USA Today*, December 11, 2013. Retrieved from http://www.usatoday.com/story/opinion/2013/12/11/nancy-lanza-adam-newtown-sandy-hook-anniversary-column/3991237/.

Frances, Allen. *Saving Normal: An Insider's Revolt against Out-of-Control Psychiatric Diagnosis, DSM-5, Big Pharma, and the Medicalization of Ordinary Life*. New York: HarperCollins, 2013.

Frank, D. A., M. Augustyn, W. G. Knight, T. Pell, and B. Zuckerman. "Growth, development, and behavior in early childhood following prenatal cocaine exposure: A systematic review." *JAMA* 285 (2001): 1613–25.

Gardener, Hannah, Donna Spiegelman, and Stephen L. Buka. "Perinatal and neonatal risk factors for autism: A comprehensive meta-analysis." *Pediatrics* 128, no. 2 (2011): 344–55.

Garey, Juliann. "Conflicts over parenting: When parents don't agree on how to handle the kids, the kids are the losers." Child Mind Institute, September 3, 2013.

Geddes, John R., Sally Burgess, Keith Hawton, Kay Jamison, and Guy M. Goodwin. "Long-term lithium therapy for bipolar disorder: Systematic review and meta-analysis of randomized controlled trials." *American Journal of Psychiatry* 161, no. 2 (2004): 217–22.

Giangregorio, Michael. "A day in the life of a family coping with autism." Autism Speaks, no date.

Goines, Paula, and Judy Van de Water. "The immune system's role in the biology of autism." *Current Opinion in Neurology* 23, no. 2 (2010): 111.

Goldman, Lynn R., and Sudha Koduru. "Chemicals in the environment and developmental toxicity to children: A public health and policy perspective." *Environmental Health Perspectives* 108, suppl. 3 (2000): 443.

Gonzalez, Juan. "Success Academy school chain comes under fire as parents fight 'zero tolerance' disciplinary policy." *New York Daily News*, August 28, 2013.

Gorman, Jeff D. "City can't blame parents for children's crimes." *Courthouse News Service*, Friday, November 19, 2010.

Gottschall, Elaine. *Breaking the Vicious Cycle*. Kirkton Press 2007, 1994.

Gracious, Barbara L., Madalina C. Chirieac, Stefan Costescu, Teresa L. Finucane, Eric A. Youngstrom, and Joseph R. Hibbeln. "Randomized, placebo-controlled trial of flax oil in pediatric bipolar disorder." *Bipolar Disorders* 12, no. 2 (2010): 142–54.

Gregory, Simon G., Rebecca Anthopolos, Claire E. Osgood, Chad A. Grotegut, and Marie Lynn Miranda. "Association of autism with induced or augmented childbirth in North Carolina Birth Record (1990–1998) and Education Research (1997–2007) Databases." *JAMA Pediatrics* 167, no. 10 (2013).

Grohol, John M. "A disorder by any other name . . ." Psych Central, October 1996.

———. "The double standard of forced treatment." Psych Central, November 26, 2012.

Gureje, Oye, Benjamin Oladapo Olley, Ephraim-Oluwanuga Olusola, and Lola Kola. "Do beliefs about causation influence attitudes to mental illness?" *World Psychiatry* 5, no. 2 (2006): 104.

Hackman, Daniel A., Martha J. Farah, and Michael J. Meaney. "Socioeconomic status and the brain: Mechanistic insights from human and animal research." *Nature Reviews Neuroscience* 11, no. 9 (2010): 651–59.

Hall, Harriett. "Brain Balance." *Science-Based Medicine*, September 14, 2010.

Hallowell, Edward. *Delivered from Distraction: Getting the Most out of Life with Attention Deficit Disorder*. New York: Ballantine Books, 2005.

Harper, Matthew. "Johnson & Johnson is reinventing the party drug ketamine to treat depression." *Forbes*, May 23, 2013.

Harris, Judith Rich. *The Nurture Assumption: Why Children Turn Out the Way They Do*. New York: Free Press, 2009.

Hartley, Sigan L., Erin T. Barker, Marsha Mailick Seltzer, Frank Floyd, Jan Greenberg, Gael Orsmond, and Daniel Bolt. "The relative risk and timing of divorce in families of children with an autism spectrum disorder." *Journal of Family Psychology* 24, no. 4 (2010): 449.

Hastings, Richard P. "Brief report: Behavioral adjustment of siblings of children with autism." *Journal of Autism and Developmental Disorders* 33, no. 1 (2003): 99–104.

Hembree-Kigin, Toni L., and Cheryl Bodiford MacNeil. *Parent-Child Interaction Therapy*. New York: Springer, 1995.

Henrichson, Christian, and Delaney, Ruth. *The Price of Prisons: What Incarceration Costs Taxpayers*. New York: Vera Institute of Justice, 2012.

Hevesi, Dennis. "Katie Beckett, who inspired health reform, dies at 34." *New York Times*, May 22, 2012.

Ho, Beng-Choon, Nancy C. Andreasen, Steven Ziebell, Ronald Pierson, and Vincent Magnotta. "Long-term antipsychotic treatment and brain volumes: A longitudinal study of first-episode schizophrenia." *Archives of General Psychiatry* 68, no. 2 (2011): 128.

Holland, Jeffrey. "Like a broken vessel." *Ensign*, October 2013.

Howe, Jeff. "Paying for Finn: A special needs child." *Money*, May 2013.

Hultman, C. M., Sven Sandin, S. Z. Levine, Paul Lichtenstein, and A. Reichenberg. "Advancing paternal age and risk of autism: New evidence from a population-based study and a meta-analysis of epidemiological studies." *Molecular Psychiatry* 16, no. 12 (2010): 1203–12.

Insel, Thomas. "Transforming Diagnosis." Director's Blog. National Institute of Mental Health, April 29, 2013.

Iversen, Leslie L. *Speed, Ecstasy, Ritalin: The Science of Amphetamines*. New York: Oxford University Press, 2008.

Jaffe, D. J. "Book Review: Anatomy of an Epidemic by Robert Whitaker." *Huffington Post*, November 2, 2011.

Jamain, Stéphane, Hélène Quach, Catalina Betancur, Maria Råstam, Catherine Colineaux, I. Carina Gillberg, Henrik Soderstrom, et al. "Mutations of the X-linked genes encoding neuroligins NLGN3 and NLGN4 are associated with autism." *Nature Genetics* 34, no. 1 (2003): 27–29.

James, S. Jill, Paul Cutler, Stepan Melnyk, Stefanie Jernigan, Laurette Janak, David W. Gaylor, and James A. Neubrander. "Metabolic biomarkers of increased oxidative stress and impaired methylation capacity in children with autism." *American Journal of Clinical Nutrition* 80, no. 6 (2004): 1611–17.

Jones, Robert L., David M. Homa, Pamela A. Meyer, Debra J. Brody, Kathleen L. Caldwell, James L. Pirkle, and Mary Jean Brown. "Trends in blood lead levels and blood lead testing among US children aged 1 to 5 years, 1988–2004." *Pediatrics* 123, no. 3 (2009): e376–85.

Judd, Daniel K., ed. *Religion, Mental Health, and the Latter-day Saints.* Provo, UT: Religious Studies Center, Brigham Young University, 1999.

Kalkbrenner, Amy E., Julie L. Daniels, Jiu-Chiuan Chen, Charles Poole, Michael Emch, and Joseph Morrissey. "Perinatal exposure to hazardous air pollutants and autism spectrum disorders at age 8." *Epidemiology* 21, no. 5 (2010): 631.

Kanner, Leo. "Problems of nosology and psychodynamics of early infantile autism." *American Journal of Orthopsychiatry* 19, no. 3 (1949): 416–26.

Kaplan, Stuart L. "U.S. children misdiagnosed with bipolar disorder." *Newsweek,* June 19, 2011.

Karnik, Niranjan, Marie Soller, Allison Redlich, Melissa Silverman, Helena Kraemer, Rudy Haapanen, and Hans Steiner. "Prevalence of and gender differences in psychiatric disorders among juvenile delinquents incarcerated for nine months." *Psychiatric Services* 60, no. 6 (2009): 838–41.

Kataoka, Sheryl H., Lily Zhang, and Kenneth B. Wells. "Unmet need for mental health care among US children: Variation by ethnicity and insurance status." *American Journal of Psychiatry* 159, no. 9 (2002): 1548–55.

Kato, Takahiro A., Masaru Tateno, Wakako Umene-Nakano, Yatan P. S. Balhara, Alan R. Teo, Daisuke Fujisawa, Ryuji Sasaki, Tetsuya Ishida, and Shigenobu Kanba. "Impact of biopsychosocial factors on psychiatric training in Japan and overseas: Are psychiatrists oriented to mind, brain, or sociocultural issues?" *Psychiatry and Clinical Neurosciences* 64, no. 5 (2010): 520–30.

Kavilanz, Parija. "5 hot franchises." *CNNMoney,* February 2013.

Kazin, Alfred. "The cult of love." *Playboy* 20, no. 6 (June 1973).

Keefe, Patrick Raddon. "Could university officials have stopped a killer?" *New Yorker,* July 11, 2013.

Kelly, A. M., Lucina Q. Uddin, Bharat B. Biswal, F. Xavier Castellanos, and Michael P. Milham. "Competition between functional brain networks mediates behavioral variability." *Neuroimage* 39, no. 1 (2008): 527–37.

Kessler, Rodger, and Dale Stafford. "Primary care *is* the de facto mental health system." In *Collaborative Medicine Case Studies*. Edited by R. Kessler and D. Stafford. New York: Springer, 2008, pp. 9–21.

Kim, James H., and Anthony R. Scialli. "Thalidomide: The tragedy of birth defects and the effective treatment of disease." *Toxicological Sciences* 122, no. 1 (2011): 1–6.

King, Bryan H., Eric Hollander, Linmarie Sikich, James T. McCracken, Lawrence Scahill, Joel D. Bregman, Craig L. Donnelly, et al. "Lack of efficacy of citalopram in children with autism spectrum disorders and high levels of repetitive behavior: Citalopram ineffective in children with autism." *Archives of General Psychiatry* 66, no. 6 (2009): 583.

King, Logan, and Lisa Bonner. "Synthesis of a novel DAT inhibitor with structural similarities to bupropion (Wellbutrin)." Saint Anselm College, Department of Chemistry, no date.

Klauck, Sabine M. "Genetics of autism spectrum disorder." *European Journal of Human Genetics* 14, no. 6 (2006): 714–20.

Koenig, Harold G. "Religion and mental health: What should psychiatrists do?" *Psychiatric Bulletin* 32, no. 6 (2008): 201–3.

———, ed. *Handbook of Religion and Mental Health*. San Diego, CA: Elsevier, 1998.

Kolko, D. J., and C. C. Swenson. *Assessing and Treating Physically Abused Children and Their Families: A Cognitive Behavioral Approach*. Thousand Oaks, CA: Sage Publications, 2002.

Koplewicz, Harold. "Don't let your child's disorder destroy your marriage." Child Mind Institute, March 14, 2011.

Kozol, Jonathan. *Savage Inequalities: Children in America's Schools*. New York: Random House Digital, 2012.

Kroll, Jerome, and Bernard Bachrach. "Sin and mental illness in the Middle Ages." *Psychological Medicine* 14, no. 3 (1984): 507–14.

Kruesi, Markus J. P., Manuel F. Casanova, Glenn Mannheim, and Adrienne Johnson-Bilder. "Reduced temporal lobe volume in early onset conduct disorder." *Psychiatry Research: Neuroimaging* 132, no. 1 (2004): 1–11.

Labbe, Colleen. "Interventions show promise in treating depression among preschoolers." National Institute of Mental Health, November 17, 2011.

Ladson-Billings, Gloria. "Race *still* matters: Critical race theory in education." In *Routledge International Handbook of Critical Education*. Edited by M. W. Apple et al. New York: Routledge, 2009, pp. 110–22.

Lagnado, Lucette. "U.S. probes psych drug use on kids." *Wall Street Journal*, August 12, 2013, pp. A1–2.

Landa, Rebecca. "Social language use in Asperger syndrome and high-functioning autism." *Asperger Syndrome* (2000): 125–55.

Långström, Niklas, Martin Grann, Vladislav Ruchkin, Gabrielle Sjöstedt, and Seena Fazel. "Risk factors for violent offending in autism spectrum disorder: A national study of hospitalized individuals." *Journal of Interpersonal Violence* 24, no. 8 (2009): 1358–70.

Leboyer, Marion, Isabella Soreca, Jan Scott, Mark Frye, Chantal Henry, Ryad Tamouza, and David J. Kupfer. "Can bipolar disorder be viewed as a multi-system inflammatory disease?" *Journal of Affective Disorders* 141, no. 1 (2012): 1–10.

Lee, Val. "Common Core." *Idaho Statesman*, September 1, 2013.

Lefley, Harriet P. "Aging parents as caregivers of mentally ill adult children: An emerging social problem." *Hospital and Community Psychiatry* 38, no. 10 (1987): 1063.

Leisman, Gerry, Raed Zaki Mualem, and Calixto Machado. "The integration of the neurosciences, child public health, and education practice: Hemisphere-specific remediation strategies as a discipline partnered rehabilitation tool in ADD/ADHD." *Frontiers in Public Health* 1 (2013): 22.

Leisman, Gerry, Robert Melillo, Sharon Thum, Mark A. Ransom, Michael Orlando, Christopher Tice, and Frederick R. Carrick. "The effect of hemisphere specific remediation strategies on the academic performance outcome of children with ADD/ADHD." *International Journal of Adolescent Medicine and Health* 22, no. 2 (2010): 275–84.

Leucht, Stefan, Magdolna Tardy, Katja Komossa, Stephan Heres, Werner Kissling, Georgia Salanti, and John M. Davis. "Antipsychotic drugs versus placebo for relapse prevention in schizophrenia: A systematic review and meta-analysis." *Lancet* 379, no. 9831 (2012): 2063–71.

Leyfer, Ovsanna T., Susan E. Folstein, Susan Bacalman, Naomi O. Davis, Elena Dinh, Jubel Morgan, Helen Tager-Flusberg, and Janet E. Lainhart. "Comorbid psychiatric disorders in children with autism: Interview development and rates of disorders." *Journal of Autism and Developmental Disorders* 36, no. 7 (2006): 849–61.

Lichtenstein, Paul, Benjamin H. Yip, Camilla Björk, Yudi Pawitan, Tyrone D. Cannon, Patrick F. Sullivan, and Christina M. Hultman. "Common genetic determinants of schizophrenia and bipolar disorder in Swedish families: A population-based study." *Lancet* 373, no. 9659 (2009): 234–39.

Lilienfeld, Scott O. "Psychological treatments that cause harm." *Perspectives on Psychological Science* 2, no. 1 (2007): 53–70.

Liu, Dong, Josie Diorio, Beth Tannenbaum, Christian Caldji, Darlene Francis, Alison Freedman, Shakti Sharma, Deborah Pearson, Paul M. Plotsky, and Michael J. Meaney. "Maternal care, hippocampal glucocorticoid receptors, and hypothalamic-pituitary-adrenal responses to stress." *Science* 277, no. 5332 (1997): 1659–62.

Loe, Irene M., and Heidi M. Feldman. "Academic and educational outcomes of children with ADHD." *Journal of Pediatric Psychology* 32, no. 6 (2007): 643–54.

Losen, Daniel J. "Discipline policies, successful schools, and racial justice." National Education Policy Center, October 2011.

Lysiak, Matthew. *Newtown: An American Tragedy.* New York: Simon and Schuster, 2013.

Madsen, Kreesten M., Marlene B. Lauritsen, Carsten B. Pedersen, Poul Thorsen, Anne-Marie Plesner, Peter H. Andersen, and Preben B. Mortensen. "Thimerosal and the occurrence of autism: Negative ecological evidence from Danish population-based data." *Pediatrics* 112, no. 3 (2003): 604–6.

Makin, Simon. "Can brain scans diagnose mental illness?" *Scientific American*, July 21, 2013.

Mann, Cindy, and Hyde, Pamela. "Coverage of behavioral health services for children, youth, and young adults." Joint CMCS and SAMHSA Informational Bulletin, May 7, 2013.

Marsh, Diane T., Harriet P. Lefley, Debra Evans-Rhodes, Vanessa I. Ansell, Brenda M. Doerzbacher, Laura LaBarbera, and Joan E. Paluzzi. "The family experience of mental illness: Evidence for resilience." *Psychiatric Rehabilitation Journal* 20, no. 2 (1996): 3.

McCarthy, Jan, Anita Marshall, Julie Collins, Girlyn Arganza, Kathy Deserly, and Juanita Milon. "A family's guide to the child welfare system." Georgetown University Center for Child and Human Development, December 2003.

"Measles—United States, January 1–August 24, 2013." *Morbidity and Mortality Weekly Report* 62, no. 36 (2013).

Medina, John. *Brain Rules: 12 Principles for Surviving and Thriving at Work, Home, and School.* Seattle: Pear Press, 2010.

Melillo, Robert. *Disconnected Kids: The Groundbreaking Brain Balance Program for Children with Autism, ADHD, Dyslexia, and Other Neurological Disorders.* New York: Penguin, 2009.

"Mental health surveillance among children—United States, 2005–2011." *Morbidity and Mortality Weekly Report* 62, no. 2 (2013).

Merikangas, Kathleen Ries, Jian-ping He, Marcy Burstein, Sonja A. Swanson, Shelli Avenevoli, Lihong Cui, Corina Benjet, Katholiki Georgiades, and Joel Swendsen. "Lifetime prevalence of mental disorders in US adolescents: Results from the National Comorbidity Survey Replication—Adolescent Supplement (NCS-A)." *Journal of the American Academy of Child and Adolescent Psychiatry* 49, no. 10 (2010): 980–89.

Mieszkowski, Katharine. "Scientology's war on psychiatry." *Salon.com*, July 1, 2005.

Miller, Matthew, Catherine Barber, Richard A. White, and Deborah Azrael. "Firearms and suicide in the United States: Is risk independent of underlying suicidal behavior?" *American Journal of Epidemiology* 178, no. 6 (2013): 946–55.

Miller, Matthew, Deborah Azrael, and Catherine Barber. "Suicide mortality in the United States: The importance of attending to method in understanding population-level disparities in the burden of suicide." *Annual Review of Public Health* 33 (2012): 393–408.

Miller, Tracy. " 'It's the one medicine we have seen work': Oregon parents use medical marijuana to help severely autistic son." *New York Daily News*, January 25, 2013.

Mills, Carrie L., and Dana L. Cunningham. "Building bridges: The role of expanded school mental health in supporting students with emotional and behavioral difficulties in the least restrictive environment." In *Handbook of School Mental Health*. Edited by M. D. Weist et al. New York: Springer, 2014, pp. 87–98.

Miranda, M. L., et al. "The relationship between early childhood blood lead levels and performance on end-of-grade tests." *Environmental Health Perspectives* 115 (2007):1242–47.

Molloy, Cynthia A., Ardythe L. Morrow, Jareen Meinzen-Derr, Kathleen Schleifer, Krista Dienger, Patricia Manning-Courtney, Mekibib Altaye, and Marsha Wills-Karp. "Elevated cytokine levels in children with autism spectrum disorder." *Journal of Neuroimmunology* 172, no. 1 (2006): 198–205.

Montes, Guillermo, and Jill S. Halterman. "Psychological functioning and coping among mothers of children with autism: A population-based study." *Pediatrics* 119, no. 5 (2007): e1040–46.

Moore, Robin C., and Nilda G. Cosco. "What makes a park inclusive and universally designed?" In *Open Space: People Space*. Edited by C. W. Thompson and P. Travlou. New York: Taylor and Frances, 2007, pp. 85–110.

Moreno, Joel. "Mom: School used isolation room to punish special-needs child." *Komonews.com*, April 23, 2013.

Mountain Mama. "How I gave my son autism." *Thinking Moms' Revolution*, February 20, 2013.

Mukolo, Abraham, Craig Anne Heflinger, and Kenneth A. Wallston. "The stigma of childhood mental disorders: A conceptual framework." *Journal of the American Academy of Child and Adolescent Psychiatry* 49, no. 2 (2010): 92–103.

Mullenholz, Greg. "Why the Common Core is good for special education students." Op-ed. *Take Part*, June 26, 2013.

Munkholm, Klaus, Maj Vinberg, and Lars Devel Kessing. "Cytokines in bipolar disorder: A systematic review and meta-analysis." *Journal of Affective Disorders* 144 (2013).

Najman, Jake M., Mohammad R. Hayatbakhsh, Alexandra Clavarino, William Bor, Michael J. O'Callaghan, and Gail M. Williams. "Family poverty over the early life course and recurrent adolescent and young adult anxiety and depression: A longitudinal study." *American Journal of Public Health* 100, no. 9 (2010): 1719–23.

"Nation's jails struggle with mentally ill prisoners." National Public Radio, September 4, 2011.

Newcomer, John W. "Second-generation (atypical) antipsychotics and metabolic effects." *CNS Drugs* 19, no. 1 (2005): 1–93.

Newman, Katherine, and Cybelle Fox. "Repeat tragedy rampage shootings in American high school and college settings, 2002–2008." *American Behavioral Scientist* 52, no. 9 (2009): 1286–1308.

Newman, Katherine S. *Rampage: The Social Roots of School Shootings.* New York: Basic Books, 2007.

Ng, Chee Hong. "The stigma of mental illness in Asian cultures." *Australian and New Zealand Journal of Psychiatry* 31, no. 3 (1997): 382–90.

Norton, Maria C., Archana Singh, Ingmar Skoog, Christopher Corcoran, JoAnn T. Tschanz, Peter P. Zandi, John C. S. Breitner, Kathleen A. Welsh-Bohmer, and David C. Steffens. "Church attendance and new episodes of major depression in a community study of older adults: The Cache County Study." *Journals of Gerontology Series B: Psychological Sciences and Social Sciences* 63, no. 3 (2008): P129–37.

Norton, Maria C., Ingmar Skoog, Lynn M. Franklin, Christopher Corcoran, JoAnn T. Tschanz, Peter P. Zandi, John C. S. Breitner, Kathleen A. Welsh-Bohmer, and David C. Steffens. "Gender differences in the association between religious involvement and depression: The Cache County (Utah) Study." *Journals of Gerontology Series B: Psychological Sciences and Social Sciences* 61, no. 3 (2006): P129–36.

O'Brien, Miles. "Mind of a Rampage Killer." *Nova*, February 20, 2013.

Owens, J., A. Spirito, A. Marcotte, M. McGuinn, and L. Berkelhammer. "Neuropsychological and behavioral correlates of obstructive sleep apnea syndrome in children: A preliminary study." *Sleep and Breathing* 4, no. 2 (2000), 67–77.

Palmer, Raymond F., Steven Blanchard, Zachary Stein, David Mandell, and Claudia Miller. "Environmental mercury release, special education rates, and autism disorder: An ecological study of Texas." *Health and Place* 12, no. 2 (2006): 203–9.

Pardini, Dustin, and Paul J. Frick. "Multiple developmental pathways to conduct disorder: Current conceptualizations and clinical implications." *Journal of the Canadian Academy of Child and Adolescent Psychiatry* 22, no. 1 (2013): 20.

Patterson, Paul H. "Immune involvement in schizophrenia and autism: Etiology, pathology and animal models." *Behavioural Brain Research* 204, no. 2 (2009): 313–21.

Pearson, Catherine. "Bullying and mental health: Study links anxiety, hyperactivity in kids to bullying." *Huffington Post*, October 22, 2012.

Pia, Lorenzo, and Marco Tamietto. "Unawareness in schizophrenia: Neuropsychological and neuroanatomical findings." *Psychiatry and Clinical Neurosciences* 60, no. 5 (2006): 531–37.

Pilgrim, David. "The survival of psychiatric diagnosis." *Social Science and Medicine* 65, no. 3 (2007): 536–47.

Pipkin, Cameron. "Why your special ed teachers are specially equipped to become powerful leaders in Common Core implementation." *Common Core Blog*.

Plumer, Brad. "Throwing children in prison turns out to be a really bad idea." *Washington Post*, June 15, 2013.

Quinn, Mary M., Robert B. Rutherford, and Peter E. Leone. "Students with disabilities in correctional facilities." ERIC Clearinghouse on Disabilities and Gifted Education, 2001.

Quinn, Mary Magee, David M. Osher, Jeffrey M. Poirier, Robert B. Rutherford, and Peter E. Leone. "Youth with disabilities in juvenile corrections: A national survey." *Exceptional Children* 71, no. 3 (2005): 339–45.

Quinton, Sophie. "Even experts can't spot the next violent shooter." *National Journal*, December 18, 2012.

Raine, Adrian. "An amygdala structural abnormality common to two subtypes of conduct disorder: A neurodevelopmental conundrum." *American Journal of Psychiatry* 168, no. 6 (2011): 569–71.

Reddy, Aravind, and Charles L. Braun. "Lead and the Romans." *Journal of Chemical Education* 87, no. 10 (2010): 1052–55.

Reichenberg, Abraham, Raz Gross, Mark Weiser, Michealine Bresnahan, Jeremy Silverman, Susan Harlap, Jonathan Rabinowitz, et al. "Advancing paternal age and autism." *Archives of General Psychiatry* 63, no. 9 (2006): 1026.

Repetti, Rena L., Shelley E. Taylor, and Teresa E. Seeman. "Risky families: Family social environments and the mental and physical health of offspring." *Psychological Bulletin* 128, no. 2 (2002): 330.

Ripley, Amanda. "Ritalin: Mommy's little helper." *Time*, February 12, 2001.

Rogers, Anne, and David Pilgrim. *A Sociology of Mental Health and Illness.* Maidenhead, Berkshire, England: McGraw-Hill International, 2010.

Roke, Yvette, Jan K. Buitelaar, Annemieke M. Boot, Diederik Tenback, and Peter N. van Harten. "Risk of hyperprolactinemia and sexual side effects in males 10–20 years old diagnosed with autism spectrum disorders or disruptive behavior disorder and treated with risperidone." *Journal of Child and Adolescent Psychopharmacology* 22, no. 6 (2012): 432–39.

Rooks, Noliwe. "The myth of bootstrapping." *Time*, September 7, 2012.

Rosner, David, and Gerald Markowitz. "Why it took decades of blaming parents before we banned lead paint." *Atlantic Monthly*, April 22, 2013.

Russell, Betsy. "Increasingly complex problems reported among Idaho's juvenile offenders." *Spokesman-Review*, February 6, 2012.

Saeed, Sy Atezaz, John Diamond, and Richard M. Bloch. "Use of telepsychiatry to improve care for people with mental illness in rural North Carolina." *North Carolina Medical Journal* 72, no. 3 (2011): 219–22.

Sartorius, Norman, Wolfgang Gaebel, Helen-Rose Cleveland, Heather Stuart, Tsuyoshi Akiyama, Julio Arboleda-Florez, Anja E. Baumann, et al. "WPA guidance on how to combat stigmatization of psychiatry and psychiatrists." *World Psychiatry* 9, no. 3 (2010): 131–44.

Sassi, Roberto B., Mark Nicoletti, Paolo Brambilla, Alan G. Mallinger, Ellen Frank, David J. Kupfer, Matcheri S. Keshavan, and Jair C. Soares. "Increased gray matter volume in lithium-treated bipolar disorder patients." *Neuroscience Letters* 329, no. 2 (2002): 243–45.

Saunders, Jana C. "Families living with severe mental illness: A literature review." *Issues in Mental Health Nursing* 24, no. 2 (2003): 175–98.

Schaefer, G. Bradley, and Nancy J. Mendelsohn. "Clinical genetics evaluation in identifying the etiology of autism spectrum disorders: 2013 guideline revisions." *Genetics in Medicine* 15, no. 5 (2013).

Schmidt, Michael. "Gunman said electronic brain attacks drove him to violence, F.B.I. says." *New York Times*, September 25, 2013.

Schofield, Michael. *January First: A Child's Descent into Madness and Her Father's Struggle to Save Her.* New York: Crown, 2012.

Schweitzer, Lindsay. "He did it!" *Jubilant Motherhood: Finding Joy in the Journey* (blog), August 30, 2012.

Scott, Elizabeth S., and Laurence Steinberg. *Rethinking Juvenile Justice.* Cambridge, MA: Harvard University Press, 2009.

Sedensky, Stephen J. "Report of the State's Attorney for the Judicial District of Danbury on the Shootings at Sandy Hook Elementary School and 36 Yogananda Street, Newtown, Connecticut on December 14, 2012." Office of the State's Attorney Judicial District of Danbury, November 25, 2013. Retrieved from http://www.ct.gov/csao/lib/csao/Sandy_Hook_Final_Report.pdf.

Seltzer, Marsha Mailick, Jan S. Greenberg, Jinkuk Hong, Leann E. Smith, David M. Almeida, Christopher Coe, and Robert S. Stawski. "Maternal cortisol levels and behavior problems in adolescents and adults with ASD." *Journal of Autism and Developmental Disorders* 40, no. 4 (2010): 457–69.

Severance, Emily G., Didier Dupont, Faith B. Dickerson, Cassie R. Stallings, Andrea E. Origoni, Bogdana Krivogorsky, Shuojia Yang, Willem Haasnoot, and Robert H. Yolken. "Immune activation by casein dietary antigens in bipolar disorder." *Bipolar Disorders* 12, no. 8 (2010): 834–42.

Sexton, Thomas L., and James F. Alexander. "Functional family therapy." OJJDP Juvenile Justice Bulletin, 2000.

Shanker, Stuart. "Emotion regulation through the ages." In *Moving Ourselves, Moving Others.* Edited by A. Foolen et al. Philadelphia: John Benjamins, 2012, pp. 105–38.

Sharpe, Donald, and Lucille Rossiter. "Siblings of children with a chronic illness: A meta-analysis." *Journal of Pediatric Psychology* 27, no. 8 (2002): 699–710.

Shaw, Amir. "Judge to serve 28 years after making $2 million for sending black children to jail." *Rolling Out*, July 30, 2013.

Shifrer, Dara. "Stigma of a label: Educational expectations for high school students labeled with learning disabilities." *Journal of Health and Social Behavior* 54, no. 4 (2013): 462–80.

Simon, Bennett. "Shame, stigma, and mental illness in ancient Greece." In *Stigma and Mental Illness.* Edited by P. J. Fink and A. Tasman. Washington, DC: American Psychiatric Press, 1992, pp. 29–39.

Simpson, Connor. "This woman helped prevent a tragic school shooting in Georgia." *Atlantic Wire,* August 21, 2013.

Slotkin, Theodore A., and Frederic J. Seidler. "Terbutaline impairs the development of peripheral noradrenergic projections: Potential implications for autism spectrum disorders and pharmacotherapy of preterm labor." *Neurotoxicology and Teratology* 36 (2012).

Smith, Leann E., Jinkuk Hong, Marsha Mailick Seltzer, Jan S. Greenberg, David M. Almeida, and Somer L. Bishop. "Daily experiences among mothers of adolescents and adults with autism spectrum disorder." *Journal of Autism and Developmental Disorders* 40, no. 2 (2010): 167–78.

Solomon, Andrew. *Far from the Tree: Parents, Children, and the Search for Identity.* New York: Scribner, 2012.

Stagliano, Kim. *All I Can Handle: A Life Raising Three Daughters with Autism.* New York: Skyhorse, 2010.

"Staying together: Preventing custody relinquishment for children's access to mental health services." Bazelon Center for Mental Health Law and the Federation of Families for Children's Mental Health, November 1999 (updated 2010).

Stein, Rob. "Staying healthy may mean learning to love our microbiomes." *Shots: Health News from NPR,* July 22, 2013.

Steinberg, Laurence. "Keeping adolescents out of prison." *Age* 15, no. 17 (2008): 18–20.

Stevens, Jane. "Lincoln High School in Walla Walla, WA, tries new approach to school discipline—suspensions drop 85%." *ACESTooHigh.com,* April 23, 2012.

Stiffman, Arlene Rubin, Wayne Stelk, Sarah McCue Horwitz, Mary E. Evans, Freida Hopkins Outlaw, and Marc Atkins. "A public health approach to children's mental health services: Possible solutions to current service inadequacies." *Administration and Policy in Mental Health and Mental Health Services Research* 37, no. 1 (2010): 120–24.

Strauss, Valerie. "Poll: Most Americans sick of high-stakes standardized tests." *Washington Post,* August 21, 2013.

Stutzman, Jessica, and Mendes, Elizabeth. "In U.S., single-parent households struggle more to buy food." *Gallup Well-Being,* July 17, 2013.

Swanson, J. W., C. E. Holzer III, V. K. Ganju, and R. T. Jano. "Violence and psychiatric disorder in the community: Evidence from the Epidemiologic Catchment Area surveys." *Hospital and Community Psychiatry* 41, no. 7 (1990): 761–70.

Swartz, Marvin S., Jeffrey W. Swanson, Henry J. Steadman, Pamela Clark Robbins, and John Monahan. "New York State assisted outpatient treatment program evaluation." Duke University School of Medicine, 2009.

Syse, Astri, Jon H. Loge, and Torkild H. Lyngstad. "Does childhood cancer affect parental divorce rates? A population-based study." *Journal of Clinical Oncology* 28, no. 5 (2010): 872–77.

Szasz, Thomas S. *The Myth of Mental Illness: Foundations of a Theory of Personal Conduct.* New York: HarperCollins, 2011.

Taylor, Mac. "The 2012–2013 budget: Completing juvenile justice realignment." California Legislative Analyst's Office, February 15, 2012.

Teplin, Linda A., Karen M. Abram, Gary M. McClelland, Mina K. Dulcan, and Amy A. Mericle. "Psychiatric disorders in youth in juvenile detention." *Archives of General Psychiatry* 59, no. 12 (2002): 1133.

"The condition of education, 2009." U.S. Department of Education, National Center for Education Statistics, 2009 (NCES 2009-081).

"The school to prison pipeline." *New York Times*, May 29, 2013.

Thomas, Christopher R., and Charles E. Holzer. "The continuing shortage of child and adolescent psychiatrists." *Journal of the American Academy of Child and Adolescent Psychiatry* 45, no. 9 (2006): 1023–31.

Thomas, Christopher R., and Joseph V. Penn. "Juvenile justice mental health services." *Child and Adolescent Psychiatric Clinics of North America* 11, no. 4 (2002): 731–48.

Torrey, E. Fuller. "Jails and prisons—America's new mental hospitals." *American Journal of Public Health* 85, no. 12 (1995): 1611–13.

"Trends with benefits." *This American Life* 490, March 22, 2013.

Trude, Sally, and Jeffrey J. Stoddard. "Referral gridlock." *Journal of General Internal Medicine* 18, no. 6 (2003): 442–49.

Tulman, Joseph B., and Douglas M. Weck. "Shutting off the school-to-prison pipeline for status offenders with education-related disabilities." *New York Law School Law Review* 54 (2009): 875.

Turnbaugh, Peter J., Ruth E. Ley, Micah Hamady, Claire M. Fraser-Liggett, Rob Knight, and Jeffrey I. Gordon. "The human microbiome project." *Nature* 449, no. 7164 (2007): 804–10.

Tyler, Jasmine L., Jason Ziedenberg, and Eric Lotke. "Cost-effective youth corrections: Rationalizing the fiscal architecture of juvenile justice systems." Washington, DC: Justice Policy Institute, 2006.

Villa, Richard A., and Jacqueline S. Thousand. "Making inclusive education work." In *Kaleidoscope: Contemporary and Classic Readings in Education*. Edited by K. Ryan and J. M. Cooper. Belmont, CA: Wadsworth, 2009, pp. 336–41.

Vitanza, Stephanie, Robert Cohen, Laura Lee Hall, Hollis Wechsler, Jessye Cohen, Angela Rothrock, and Adriana Montalvo. "Families on the brink: The impact of ignoring children with serious mental illness." National Alliance for the Mentally Ill, 1999.

Vozella, Laura. "Creigh Deeds released from hospital as son's friends reflect on his mental illness." *Washington Post*, November 22, 2013.

Wahl, O. F. *Media Madness: Public Images of Mental Illness*. New Brunswick, NJ: Rutgers University Press, 1995.

Wall, Barry W., Brandon H. Krupp, and Thomas Guilmette. "Restoration of competency to stand trial: A training program for persons with mental retardation." *Journal of the American Academy of Psychiatry and the Law Online* 31, no. 2 (2003): 189–201.

Wallace, Cameron, Paul E. Mullen, and Philip Burgess. "Criminal offending in schizophrenia over a 25-year period marked by deinstitutionalization and increasing prevalence of comorbid substance use disorders." *American Journal of Psychiatry* 161, no. 4 (2004): 716–27.

Wallace, Cameron, Paul Mullen, Philip Burgess, Simon Palmer, David Ruschena, and Chris Browne. "Serious criminal offending and mental disorder: Case linkage study." *British Journal of Psychiatry* 172, no. 6 (1998): 477–84.

Wallerstein, Judith S., and Joan B. Kelly. *Surviving the Breakup: How Children and Parents Cope with Divorce*. New York: Basic Books, 2008.

Walsh, Elizabeth, Alec Buchanan, and Thomas Fahy. "Violence and schizophrenia: Examining the evidence." *British Journal of Psychiatry* 180, no. 6 (2002): 490–95.

Wang, Philip S., Michael Lane, Mark Olfson, Harold A. Pincus, Kenneth B. Wells, and Ronald C. Kessler. "Twelve-month use of mental health services in the United States: Results from the National Comorbidity Survey Replication." *Archives of General Psychiatry* 62, no. 6 (2005): 629–40.

Webster-Stratton, Carolyn, and M. Jamila Reid. "The Incredible Years parents, teachers, and children training series: A multifaceted treatment approach for young children with conduct disorders." In *Evidence-Based Psychotherapies for Children and Adolescents*. Edited by J. R. Weisz and A. E. Kazdin. New York: Guilford Press, 2010, 194–210.

Whitaker, Robert. *Anatomy of an Epidemic: Magic Bullets, Psychiatric Drugs, and the Astonishing Rise of Mental Illness in America.* New York: Random House Digital, 2011.

Willingham, Emily. "Brain balance centers: A critique." A *Life Less Ordinary*, August 13, 2010.

Winter, Michael. "Hate mail urges autistic Canadian boy be 'euthanized.'" *USA Today*, August 21, 2013.

Yeargin-Allsopp, Marshalyn, Catherine Rice, Tanya Karapurkar, Nancy Doernberg, Coleen Boyle, and Catherine Murphy. "Prevalence of autism in a US metropolitan area." *JAMA* 289, no. 1 (2003): 49–55.

Yoshikawa, Hirokazu, J. Lawrence Aber, and William R. Beardslee. "The effects of poverty on the mental, emotional, and behavioral health of children and youth: Implications for prevention." *American Psychologist* 67, no. 4 (2012): 272.

Yu, Xi. "Three professors face sanctions following Harvard Medical School inquiry." *Harvard Crimson*, July 2, 2011.

Zeanah, Charles H., Anna T. Smyke, Sebastian F. Koga, and Elizabeth Carlson. "Attachment in institutionalized and community children in Romania." *Child Development* 76, no. 5 (2005): 1015–28.

Zirkel, Perry A., and Gina Scala. "Due process hearing systems under the IDEA: A state-by-state survey." *Journal of Disability Policy Studies* 21, no. 1 (2010): 3–8.

Zito, Julie Magno, Mehmet Burcu, Aloysius Ibe, Daniel J. Safer, and Laurence S. Magder. "Antipsychotic use by Medicaid-insured youths: Impact of eligibility and psychiatric diagnosis across a decade." *Psychiatric Services* 64, no. 3 (2013): 223–29.

# NOTES

## Introduction

xv **Journalists from Anderson Cooper to Miles O'Brien:** Michael and I participated in a PBS *Nova* documentary made by Miles O'Brien in February 2013. "Mind of a Rampage Killer" was a sensational attempt to bring viewers into a documentary about brain science. You can hear Michael talk about his mental illness in that documentary, linked here: http://www.pbs .org/wgbh/nova/body/mind-rampage-killer.html. The source: O'Brien, Miles. "Mind of a Rampage Killer." *Nova*, February 20, 2013.

xvi **similar to what soldiers in combat experience:** Seltzer, Marsha Mailick, Jan S. Greenberg, Jinkuk Hong, Leann E. Smith, David M. Almeida, Christopher Coe, and Robert S. Stawski. "Maternal cortisol levels and behavior problems in adolescents and adults with ASD." *Journal of Autism and Developmental Disorders* 40, no. 4 (2010): 457–69.

xvii **mental health advocate and author Pete Earley details:** Earley, Pete. *Crazy: A Father's Search through America's Mental Health Madness.* New York: Berkley, 2007.

xviii **a 2013 study conducted by the George Washington University Center for Health and Health Care in Schools:** Behrens, Donna, Julia Graham Lear, and Olga Acosta Price. "Improving access to children's mental health care: Lessons from a study of eleven states." Center for Health and Health Care in Schools, George Washington University (2013).

## Chapter One: A Day in My Life

3   **On the surface, my life may look like yours:** The statistics I cite here and elsewhere concerning prevalence of mental illness and mental disorders in children are from the National Institute of Mental Health website: http://www.nimh.nih.gov/statistics/1anydis_child.shtml.

7   **one insurance company refused to pay for hospitalization:** Abelson, Reed. "Lacking rules, insurers balk at paying for intensive psychiatric care." *New York Times*, September 27, 2013. Retrieved from http://mobile.nytimes.com/2013/09/29/business/lacking-rules-insurers-balk-at-paying-for-intensive-psychiatric-care.html?from=health.

9   **The juvenile magistrate will order a slew of social services:** Idaho Code, Section 20-511A reads in part: "The court may convene a screening team consisting of representatives from the department of health and welfare, county probation, local school officials, teen early intervention specialists as provided for under section 16-2404A, Idaho Code, the department of juvenile corrections and/or other agencies or persons designated by the court to review the plan of treatment and provide written recommendations to the court. Parents and guardians of the juvenile, if available, shall be included in the screening team and consulted with regard to the plan of treatment." Retrieved from http://www.idjc.idaho.gov/LinkClick.aspx?fileticket=BdWLLPlYgmY%3D&tabid=87.

12   **a 2001 survey found that incarcerated children:** Quinn, Mary M., Robert B. Rutherford, and Peter E. Leone. "Students with disabilities in correctional facilities." ERIC Clearinghouse on Disabilities and Gifted Education, 2001. See also Thomas, Christopher R., and Joseph V. Penn. "Juvenile justice mental health services." *Child and Adolescent Psychiatric Clinics of North America* 11, no. 4 (2002): 731–48.

13   **according to a state government budget analysis:** Taylor, Mac. "The 2012–2013 budget: Completing juvenile justice realignment." California Legislative Analyst's Office, February 15, 2012. Retrieved from http://www.lao.ca.gov/analysis/2012/crim_justice/juvenile-justice-021512.pdf.

13   **California public schools spent just over $9,000 per pupil:** This number was taken from U.S. Census Bureau data and can be retrieved at http://www2.census.gov/govs/school/11f33pub.pdf.

13   **death because the younger child refused to steal candy:** "Boy, 12, to be nation's youngest prison inmate." *New York Times*, January 30, 1996. Re-

trieved from http://www.nytimes.com/1996/01/30/us/boy-12-to-be-nation-s-youngest-prison-inmate.html.

13   **children and young teens simply do not have adult brains:** Scott, Elizabeth S., and Laurence Steinberg. *Rethinking Juvenile Justice.* Cambridge, MA: Harvard University Press, 2009.

14   **compared to the stress that soldiers experience under fire:** Smith, Leann E., Jinkuk Hong, Marsha Mailick Seltzer, Jan S. Greenberg, David M. Almeida, and Somer L. Bishop. "Daily experiences among mothers of adolescents and adults with autism spectrum disorder." *Journal of Autism and Developmental Disorders* 40, no. 2 (2010): 167–78. See also Bromley, Jo, Dougal Julian Hare, Kerry Davison, and Eric Emerson. "Mothers supporting children with autistic spectrum disorders: Social support, mental health status and satisfaction with services." *Autism* 8, no. 4 (2004): 409–23.

15   **Michael had been on a Section 504 plan for several years to accommodate his dysgraphia:** For more information about dysgraphia and other learning disabilities, see the National Center for Learning Disabilities website at http://www.ncld.org/types-learning-disabilities/dysgraphia/what-is-dysgraphia.

15   **a label that may actually limit educational opportunities for students with learning disabilities:** Shifrer, Dara. "Stigma of a label: Educational expectations for high school students labeled with learning disabilities." *Journal of Health and Social Behavior* 54, no. 4 (2013): 462–80.

16   **Later studies have not confirmed:** Owens, J., A. Spirito, A. Marcotte, M. McGuinn, and L. Berkelhammer. "Neuropsychological and behavioral correlates of obstructive sleep apnea syndrome in children: A preliminary study." *Sleep and Breathing* 4, no. 2 (2000), 67–77.

16   **The role of sleep disruption in children:** Soffer-Dudek, Nirit, Avi Sadeh, Ronald E. Dahl, and Shiran Rosenblat-Stein. "Poor sleep quality predicts deficient emotion information processing over time in early adolescence." *Sleep* 34, no. 11 (2011): 1499.

18   **where up to 75 percent of the population:** Teplin, Linda A., Karen M. Abram, Gary M. McClelland, Mina K. Dulcan, and Amy A. Mericle. "Psychiatric disorders in youth in juvenile detention." *Archives of General Psychiatry* 59, no. 12 (2002): 1133.

18   **disproportionately affects poor children and their families:** See inter alia Ladson-Billings, Gloria. "Race *still* matters: Critical race theory in education." In *Routledge International Handbook of Critical Education.* Edited by M. W. Apple et al. New York: Routledge, 2009, pp. 110–22.

24 **experts tell us there's no way to predict:** Newman, Katherine S. *Rampage: The Social Roots of School Shootings.* New York: Basic Books, 2007. See also Quinton, Sophie. "Even experts can't spot the next violent shooter." *National Journal,* December 18, 2012. Retrieved from http://www.nationaljournal.com/domesticpolicy/even-experts-can-t-spot-the-next-violent-shooter-20121218. See also Newman, Katherine, and Cybelle Fox. "Repeat tragedy rampage shootings in American high school and college settings, 2002–2008." *American Behavioral Scientist* 52, no. 9 (2009): 1286–1308.

24 **According to the final report on the Sandy Hook shootings:** Sedensky, Stephen J. "Report of the State's Attorney for the Judicial District of Danbury on the Shootings at Sandy Hook Elementary School and 36 Yogananda Street, Newtown, Connecticut on December 14, 2012." Office of the State's Attorney Judicial District of Danbury, November 25, 2013. Retrieved from http://www.ct.gov/csao/lib/csao/Sandy_Hook_Final_Report.pdf.

24 **Suicide is a common factor in mass shootings and is the third most common cause of death:** These statistics are from 2010 and were taken from the U.S. Centers for Disease Control "Ten Leading Causes of Death by Age Group" report, retrieved from http://www.cdc.gov/injury/wisqars/pdf/10L-CID_All_Deaths_By_Age_Group_2010-a.pdf.

25 **a 2009 study of sensory processing problems in elementary school children reported a prevalence of 16.5 percent of the total population:** Ben-Sasson, A., A. S. Carter, and M. J. Briggs-Gowan. "Sensory over-responsivity in elementary school: Prevalence and social-emotional correlates." *Journal of Abnormal Child Psychology* 37, no. 5 (2009): 705–16.

25 **The cause of this increase in sensory processing problems is not completely understood:** Ibid.

25 **Psychologist Stuart Shanker, who has explored self-regulation:** Shanker, Stuart. "Emotion regulation through the ages." In *Moving Ourselves, Moving Others.* Edited by A. Foolen et al. Philadelphia: John Benjamins, 2012, 105–38.

27 **a perfect moment that belies the storms that would rage through their loves and lives:** The Kennedy family had their own experiences with mental illness, most notably Rosemary Kennedy, who was lobotomized at the age of twenty-three to calm her violent mood swings. See El-Hai, Jack. *The Lobotomist: A Maverick Medical Genius and His Tragic Quest to Rid the World of Mental Illness.* Hoboken, NJ: Wiley, 2004.

30 **one of my favorite poets, Robert Frost:** Frost, Robert. "Two Tramps in Mud Time." 1936, st. 9.

30  **I think of Nelba Marquez-Greene's words at the Sandy Hook parents'
first news conference:** Siemaszko, Corky. "Parents of slain Sandy Hook victims call for national dialogue on gun madness one month after the school
massacre." *The New York Daily News*, January 14, 2013. Retrieved from
http://www.nydailynews.com/news/national/parents-slain-sandy-hook-kids-
call-national-dialogue-gun-madness-article-1.1239915. Ana Grace's parents
started a foundation called "Love Wins" to honor their daughter.

## Chapter Two: Stigma

31  **She felt as if there were no other options:** You can read more about Pam's
successes at the advocacy website One in Four, http://www.oneinfour.info/
pam-kazmaier.html. Her essay "Losing My Mind, Bit by Bit," which chronicles the events that led to her suicide pact with her son, was originally
posted on August 13, 2005, and can be read here: http://www.salamander
society.com/blacksheep/pam_kazmaier.html.

32  **the Greeks viewed mental illness with a sense of shame:** Simon, Bennett.
"Shame, stigma, and mental illness in ancient Greece." In *Stigma and Men-
tal Illness*. Edited by P. J. Fink and A. Tasman. Washington, DC: American
Psychiatric Press, 1992, pp. 29–39.

33  **This by no means exhaustive list contains examples:** Wahl, O. F. *Media
Madness: Public Images of Mental Illness*. New Brunswick, NJ: Rutgers University Press, 1995.

33  **Harold Koplewicz summed up the problem:** I took this quote directly from
Dr. Koplewicz's testimony to the U.S. House of Representatives Energy and
Commerce Committee Forum, "After Newtown: A National Conversation
on Violence and Severe Mental Illness." March 5, 2013, retrieved from
http://energycommerce.house.gov/event/after-newtown-national-
conversation-violence-and-severe-mental-illness. I also testified in this forum.

33  **a Toronto grandmother of a boy with autism:** Winter, Michael. "Hate mail
urges autistic Canadian boy be 'euthanized.'" *USA Today*, August 21, 2013.
Retrieved from http://www.usatoday.com/story/news/world/2013/08/19/
canada-autistic-boy-hate-mail/2674331/.

34  **while 57 percent of healthy adults believe:** "Attitudes toward mental illness: 35 states, District of Columbia, and Puerto Rico, 2007." *Morbidity and
Mortality Weekly Report* 59, no. 20 (2010), 619–25. Retrieved from http://
www.cdc.gov/mmwr/preview/mmwrhtml/mm5920a3.htm.

36 **Susan Klebold, mother of Dylan Klebold:** This entire interview is well worth reading, as is the entire book. Solomon, Andrew. *Far from the Tree: Parents, Children, and the Search for Identity.* New York: Scribner, 2012.

37 **NAMI tried to rebrand mental disorders as neurobiological disorders:** Grohol, John M. "A disorder by any other name . . ." Psych Central, October 1996. Retrieved from http://psychcentral.com/archives/naming.htm.

38 **many children with autism also have other comorbid psychiatric disorders:** Leyfer, Ovsanna T., Susan E. Folstein, Susan Bacalman, Naomi O. Davis, Elena Dinh, Jubel Morgan, Helen Tager-Flusberg, and Janet E. Lainhart. "Comorbid psychiatric disorders in children with autism: Interview development and rates of disorders." *Journal of Autism and Developmental Disorders* 36, no. 7 (2006): 849–61.

38 **One Swedish study found that 7 percent:** Långström, Niklas, Martin Grann, Vladislav Ruchkin, Gabrielle Sjöstedt, and Seena Fazel. "Risk factors for violent offending in autism spectrum disorder: A national study of hospitalized individuals." *Journal of Interpersonal Violence* 24, no. 8 (2009): 1358–70.

38 **But more than 90 percent of people who complete suicide:** I took this grim statistic from NAMI's suicide fact sheet, which can be retrieved here: http://www.nami.org/factsheets/suicide_factsheet.pdf.

38 **three out of four people who survived a suicide attempt:** Drexler, Madeline. "Guns and suicide: The hidden toll." *Harvard School of Public Health News,* Spring 2013. Retrieved from http://www.hsph.harvard.edu/news/magazine/guns-suicide-the-hidden-toll/. Also Miller, Matthew, Deborah Azrael, and Catherine Barber. "Suicide mortality in the United States: The importance of attending to method in understanding population-level disparities in the burden of suicide." *Annual Review of Public Health* 33 (2012): 393–408.

39 **first incidence and diagnosis of schizophrenia occur between the ages of twenty and thirty:** All of this information can be found on the Centers for Disease Control website at www.cdc.gov.

39 **adult children with serious mental illness continue to reside with their parents:** Lefley, Harriet P. "Aging parents as caregivers of mentally ill adult children: An emerging social problem." *Hospital and Community Psychiatry* 38, no. 10 (1987): 1063.

39 **author Michael Schofield's daughter, Jani:** Schofield, Michael. *January First: A Child's Descent into Madness and Her Father's Struggle to Save Her.* New York: Crown, 2012.

39   **risk of suicide that is two to five times higher:** Miller, Matthew, Catherine
     Barber, Richard A. White, and Deborah Azrael. "Firearms and suicide in
     the United States: Is risk independent of underlying suicidal behavior?"
     *American Journal of Epidemiology* 178, no. 6 (2013): 946–55.

39   **The oft-quoted assertion attributed to rocker and National Rifle Associ-
     ation board member Ted Nugent:** You can hear more of Nugent's views on
     the Second Amendment in a KLRU interview with Evan Smith, editor of
     *Texas Monthly*, retrieved from http://www.liveleak.com/view?i=088_13300
     92628&comments=1.

40   **For the one in five children with a diagnosable mental illness:** See this
     February 2013 response to the Sandy Hook shootings: "Improving lives,
     avoiding tragedy," a joint statement from the American Academy of Child
     and Adolescent Psychiatry (AACAP), the National Alliance on Mental
     Illness (NAMI), and other organizations here: http://www.aacap.org/App_
     Themes/AACAP/docs/Advocacy/policy_resources/Children's_Mental_
     Health_Fact_Sheet_FINAL.pdf.

40   **a survey of fifty-seven primary source descriptions of mental illness:**
     Kroll, Jerome, and Bernard Bachrach. "Sin and mental illness in the Middle
     Ages." *Psychological Medicine* 14, no. 3 (1984): 507–14.

41   **This quicksand beneath our cherished idea of the American Dream:** For
     more on the "bootstrap myth" and the American Dream, see Rooks, No-
     liwe. "The myth of bootstrapping." *Time*, September 7, 2012. Retrieved
     from http://ideas.time.com/2012/09/07/the-myth-of-bootstrapping/.

41   **Yet eighteenth- and nineteenth-century mental hospitals focused on Bi-
     ble reading:** Falk, Gerhard. *Stigma: How We Treat Outsiders.* Amherst, NY:
     Prometheus Books, 2001, pp. 53–54.

42   **Oxford neuroscientist Kathleen Taylor made news:** Bennett-Smith, Mer-
     edith. "Kathleen Taylor, neuroscientist, says religious fundamentalism could
     be treated as a mental illness." *Huffington Post*, May 31, 2013. Retrieved
     from http://www.huffingtonpost.com/2013/05/31/kathleen-taylor-religious-
     fundamentalism-mental-illness_n_3365896.html).

42   **"Religion is an important psychological and social factor":** Koenig, Har-
     old G. "Religion and mental health: What should psychiatrists do?" *Psychi-
     atric Bulletin* 32, no. 6 (2008): 201–3.

42   **Harold Koenig, MD, the director of Duke University's Center:** Koenig,
     Harold G., ed. *Handbook of Religion and Mental Health.* San Diego, CA: El-
     sevier, 1998.

42 **Take this statement from one fundamentalist Christian website:** I wish these sentiments were the exception rather than the rule in the Christian community. Google "mental illness sin" and you'll find a plethora of similar statements, which only serve to perpetuate stigma and shame and keep people from getting help. I took this quote from http://www.bible.ca/psychiatry/psychiatry-mental-illness-bible-sin-guilt-conscience-cognitive-dissonance.htm.

43 **mental illness is stigmatized by religions and cultures around the world:** Fabrega, Horacio, Jr. "Psychiatric stigma in non-Western societies." *Comprehensive Psychiatry* 32, no. 6 (1991): 534–51. See also Ng, Chee Hong. "The stigma of mental illness in Asian cultures." *Australian and New Zealand Journal of Psychiatry* 31, no. 3 (1997): 382–90.

43 **Japan's high suicide rates suggest:** Kato, Takahiro A., Masaru Tateno, Wakako Umene-Nakano, Yatan P. S. Balhara, Alan R. Teo, Daisuke Fujisawa, Ryuji Sasaki, Tetsuya Ishida, and Shigenobu Kanba. "Impact of biopsychosocial factors on psychiatric training in Japan and overseas: Are psychiatrists oriented to mind, brain, or sociocultural issues?" *Psychiatry and Clinical Neurosciences* 64, no. 5 (2010): 520–30.

43 **In one study of Nigerian attitudes:** Gureje, Oye, Benjamin Oladapo Olley, Ephraim-Oluwanuga Olusola, and Lola Kola. "Do beliefs about causation influence attitudes to mental illness?" *World Psychiatry* 5, no. 2 (2006): 104.

43 **Mormon and evangelical Christian women seem especially vulnerable:** Degn, Laura. "Mormon women and depression: Are Latter-day Saint women becoming casualties of perfectionism?" *Sunstone*, May 1985, pp. 19–27. Retrieved from https://www.sunstonemagazine.com/pdf/049-19-27.pdf.

44 **A 2008 study showed higher rates of depression:** This study focused on older Latter-day Saint adults. Norton, Maria C., Archana Singh, Ingmar Skoog, Christopher Corcoran, JoAnn T. Tschanz, Peter P. Zandi, John C. S. Breitner, Kathleen A. Welsh-Bohmer, and David C. Steffens. "Church attendance and new episodes of major depression in a community study of older adults: The Cache County Study." *Journals of Gerontology Series B: Psychological Sciences and Social Sciences* 63, no. 3 (2008): P129–37.

44 **higher rates suggest that Utah's non–Latter-day Saint population is more depressed:** Judd, Daniel K., ed. *Religion, Mental Health, and the Latter-day Saints.* Provo, UT: Religious Studies Center, Brigham Young University, 1999. See also Chadwick, Bruce A., Brent L. Top, and Richard Jennings

McClendon. *Shield of Faith: The Power of Religion in the Lives of LDS Youth and Young Adults*. Provo, UT: Religious Studies Center, Brigham Young University, 2010.

44 **"In the LDS church it's like, 'I feel depressed'":** Doty, Kristine, Danna Lindemann, and Heather Hirsche. "In the culture but not of the culture: Experiences of LDS women with depression." Paper presented to the Utah Valley University 2013 Mental Health Symposium. See also Norton, Maria C., Ingmar Skoog, Lynn M. Franklin, Christopher Corcoran, JoAnn T. Tschanz, Peter P. Zandi, John C. S. Breitner, Kathleen A. Welsh-Bohmer, and David C. Steffens. "Gender differences in the association between religious involvement and depression: The Cache County (Utah) Study." *Journals of Gerontology Series B: Psychological Sciences and Social Sciences* 61, no. 3 (2006): P129–36.

45 **In 1979, Jan Barker, a mother of four and a devout Mormon:** Degn, Louise. "Mormon women and depression: Are Latter-day Saint women becoming casualties of crippling perfectionism?" *Sunstone*, May 1985, pp. 19–27. Retrieved from https://www.sunstonemagazine.com/pdf/049-19-27 .pdf.

46 **Elder Jeffrey R. Holland, a Mormon apostle, declared:** Holland, Jeffrey. "Like a broken vessel." *Ensign*, October 2013. Retrieved from http://www .lds.org/general-conference/2013/10/like-a-broken-vessel.

47 **The literary critic Alfred Kazin wrote:** Kazin, Alfred. "The cult of love." *Playboy* 20, no. 6 (June 1973).

47 **a population-based survey of mothers of autistic children:** Montes, Guillermo, and Jill S. Halterman. "Psychological functioning and coping among mothers of children with autism: A population-based study." *Pediatrics* 119, no. 5 (2007): e1040–46.

48 **Leo Kanner, who first identified autism as a discrete disorder in 1949:** Kanner, Leo. "Problems of nosology and psychodynamics of early infantile autism." *American Journal of Orthopsychiatry* 19, no. 3 (1949): 416–26.

48 **While the "Refrigerator Mother" hypothesis has long been discredited:** Bretherton, Inge. "The origins of attachment theory: John Bowlby and Mary Ainsworth." *Developmental Psychology* 28, no. 5 (1992): 759.

49 **"the family is responsible for the mental illness of the patient":** Falk, Gerhard. *Stigma: How We Treat Outsiders*. Amherst, NY: Prometheus Books, 2001, pp. 53–54.

50 **won a 2000 Peabody Award with Idaho Public Television producer Mar-**

cia Franklin: The Peabody Award information can be found here: http://
peabodyawards.com/past-winners/award/?pbaward=1262&pb_
search=1&pb_title=&pb_year=&pb_porg=&pb_query=HEARTS%20
AND%20MINDS. The NAMI press release can be found here: http://www.
nami.org/Template.cfm?Section=-1'&template=/ContentManagement/
ContentDisplay.cfm&ContentID=89786.

52 **Ann was also recognized with a NAMI Voice Award for her community
leadership: :** The NAMI press release can be found here: http://www.nami.
org/Template.cfm?Section=-1'&template=/ContentManagement/Content-
Display.cfm&ContentID=89786. See also the SAMSHA website http://
www.samhsa.gov/VoiceAwards/2009winners.asp#ConsumerLeadership
2009.

52 **This one-day training seminar also received national recognition:** NAMI
has a write-up of this program on its website: "NAMI Idaho's Better Todays
(formerly Red Flags) Program Alerts Gatekeepers and Caregivers for Early
Warning Signs of Mental Illness in Children." Retrieved from http://www
.nami.org/Template.cfm?Section=State_and_Local_Programs&Template=/
ContentManagement/ContentDisplay.cfm&ContentID=10624.

55 **This is the kind of "there's a pill for that" mentality:** Frances, Allen.
*Saving Normal: An Insider's Revolt against Out-of-Control Psychiatric Diagno-
sis, DSM-5, Big Pharma, and the Medicalization of Ordinary Life.* New York:
HarperCollins, 2013.

56 **I asked Michael the same question in my June 2013 StoryCorps interview with him:** To listen to an excerpt of this interview, visit http://story
corps.org/listen/liza-long-and-her-son/. The transcript can be found here:
http://www.npr.org/templates/transcript/transcript.php?storyId=207865719.

57 **before him Thomas Szasz, who denied the existence of mental illness
altogether:** Szasz, Thomas S. *The Myth of Mental Illness: Foundations of a
Theory of Personal Conduct.* New York: HarperCollins, 2011.

### Chapter Three: Science

60 **conduct disorder is the perfect storm:** Pardini, Dustin, and Paul J. Frick.
"Multiple developmental pathways to conduct disorder: Current conceptu-
alizations and clinical implications." *Journal of the Canadian Academy of
Child and Adolescent Psychiatry* 22, no. 1 (2013): 20.

60 **Poverty is also a risk factor:** Webster-Stratton, Carolyn, and M. Jamila

Reid. "The Incredible Years parents, teachers, and children training series: A multifaceted treatment approach for young children with conduct disorders." In *Evidence-Based Psychotherapies for Children and Adolescents*. Edited by J. R. Weisz and A. E. Kazdin. New York: Guilford Press, 2010, pp. 194–210.

60   **In a 2004 study, brain scans of children diagnosed with CD:** Kruesi, Markus J. P., Manuel F. Casanova, Glenn Mannheim, and Adrienne Johnson-Bilder. "Reduced temporal lobe volume in early onset conduct disorder." *Psychiatry Research: Neuroimaging* 132, no. 1 (2004): 1–11.

60   **The amygdalae (named for their almond shape):** Raine, Adrian. "An amygdala structural abnormality common to two subtypes of conduct disorder: A neurodevelopmental conundrum." *American Journal of Psychiatry* 168, no. 6 (2011): 569–71.

60   **Since the amygdala plays a role in the "fight-or-flight" response:** Fairchild, Graeme, Luca Passamonti, Georgina Hurford, Cindy C. Hagan, Elisabeth A. H. von dem Hagen, Stephanie H. M. van Goozen, Ian M. Goodyer, and Andrew J. Calder. "Brain structure abnormalities in early-onset and adolescent-onset conduct disorder." *American Journal of Psychiatry* 168, no. 6 (2011): 624–33.

63   **"I induced labor with all three of my boys":** Gregory, Simon G., Rebecca Anthopolos, Claire E. Osgood, Chad A. Grotegut, and Marie Lynn Miranda. "Association of autism with induced or augmented childbirth in North Carolina Birth Record (1990–1998) and Education Research (1997–2007) Databases." *JAMA Pediatrics* 167, no. 10 (2013).

63   **what causes schizophrenia or bipolar disorder or depression:** Evans, Katie, J. McGrath, and R. Milns. "Searching for schizophrenia in ancient Greek and Roman literature: A systematic review." *Acta Psychiatrica Scandinavica* 107, no. 5 (2003): 323–30.

63   **Bringing the humors back into balance:** Simon, Bennett. "Shame, stigma, and mental illness in ancient Greece." In *Stigma and Mental Illness*. Edited by P. J. Fink and A. Tasman. Washington, DC: American Psychiatric Press, 1992, pp. 29–39.

63   **emotion can play a role in mental conditions:** This quote from Galen was taken from Dols, Michael W. "Galen and mental illness." In *Majnūn: The Madman in Medieval Islamic Society*. Oxford, England: Clarendon Press, 1992. Retrieved July 16, 2013, from http://www.oxfordscholarship.com/view/10.1093/acprof:oso/9780198202219.001.0001/acprof-9780198202219-chapter-2.

63 **Both Galen and Hippocrates influenced medical thinking about mental illness:** Pilgrim, David. "The survival of psychiatric diagnosis." *Social Science and Medicine* 65, no. 3 (2007): 536–47.

64 **most people are familiar with the "chemical imbalance" model:** According to NAMI, "Just as diabetes is a disorder of the pancreas, mental illnesses are medical conditions that often result in a diminished capacity for coping with the ordinary demands of life." Retrieved from http://www.nami.org/Template.cfm?Section=By_Illness.

64 **NIMH director Thomas Insel wrote:** Insel, Thomas. "Transforming Diagnosis." Director's Blog. National Institute of Mental Health, April 29, 2013. Retrieved from http://www.nimh.nih.gov/about/director/2013/transforming -diagnosis.shtml.

65 **the *Scientific American* study may actually reveal the inadequacies of our current diagnostic system:** Makin, Simon. "Can brain scans diagnose mental illness?" *Scientific American*, July 21, 2013. Retrieved from http://www.scientific american.com/article.cfm?id=can-brain-scans-diagnose-mental-illness.

65 **Dr. Michael Milham works on the furthest edges of neuroimaging to identify mental disorders:** Recent papers include: Kelly, A. M., Lucina Q. Uddin, Bharat B. Biswal, F. Xavier Castellanos, and Michael P. Milham. "Competition between functional brain networks mediates behavioral variability." *Neuroimage* 39, no. 1 (2008): 527–37. Biswal, Bharat B., Maarten Mennes, Xi-Nian Zuo, Suril Gohel, Clare Kelly, Steve M. Smith, Christian F. Beckmann, et al. "Toward discovery science of human brain function." *Proceedings of the National Academy of Sciences* 107, no. 10 (2010): 4734–39.

67 **Often the medications and therapies the experts prescribe do not work:** King, Bryan H., Eric Hollander, Linmarie Sikich, James T. McCracken, Lawrence Scahill, Joel D. Bregman, Craig L. Donnelly, et al. "Lack of efficacy of citalopram in children with autism spectrum disorders and high levels of repetitive behavior: Citalopram ineffective in children with autism." *Archives of General Psychiatry* 66, no. 6 (2009): 583.

68 **In their book on the sociology of mental illness:** Rogers, Anne, and David Pilgrim. *A Sociology of Mental Health and Illness.* Maidenhead, Berkshire, England: McGraw-Hill International, 2010, p. 3.

68 **More than half of all identical twins share autism:** Klauck, Sabine M. "Genetics of autism spectrum disorder." *European Journal of Human Genetics* 14, no. 6 (2006): 714–20.

68 **"Heritability for schizophrenia and bipolar disorder was 64% and 59%,**

respectively": Lichtenstein, Paul, Benjamin H. Yip, Camilla Björk, Yudi Pawitan, Tyrone D. Cannon, Patrick F. Sullivan, and Christina M. Hultman. "Common genetic determinants of schizophrenia and bipolar disorder in Swedish families: A population-based study." *Lancet* 373, no. 9659 (2009): 234–39.

69  males affected at four times the rate of females: Yeargin-Allsopp, Marshalyn, Catherine Rice, Tanya Karapurkar, Nancy Doernberg, Coleen Boyle, and Catherine Murphy. "Prevalence of autism in a US metropolitan area." *JAMA* 289, no. 1 (2003): 49–55.

69  imprinted X-linked genes, which are only expressed on the X chromosome inherited from the father: Jamain, Stéphane, Hélène Quach, Catalina Betancur, Maria Råstam, Catherine Colineaux, I. Carina Gillberg, Henrik Soderstrom, et al. "Mutations of the X-linked genes encoding neuroligins NLGN3 and NLGN4 are associated with autism." *Nature Genetics* 34, no. 1 (2003): 27–29.

69  a much-publicized 2010 study reported in *Nature* linking older fathers to higher rates of autism: Hultman, C. M., Sven Sandin, S. Z. Levine, Paul Lichtenstein, and A. Reichenberg. "Advancing paternal age and risk of autism: New evidence from a population-based study and a meta-analysis of epidemiological studies." *Molecular Psychiatry* 16, no. 12 (2010): 1203–12. See also Reichenberg, Abraham, Raz Gross, Mark Weiser, Michealine Bresnahan, Jeremy Silverman, Susan Harlap, Jonathan Rabinowitz, et al. "Advancing paternal age and autism." *Archives of General Psychiatry* 63, no. 9 (2006): 1026.

69  "an autism mom has more badges than an Eagle Scout": Stagliano, Kim. *All I Can Handle: A Life Raising Three Daughters with Autism*. New York: Skyhorse, 2010.

70  An entire chromosome may also be to blame: Schaefer, G. Bradley, and Nancy J. Mendelsohn. "Clinical genetics evaluation in identifying the etiology of autism spectrum disorders: 2013 guideline revisions." *Genetics in Medicine* 15, no. 5 (2013).

70  seems slightly more prevalent in women, though with later onset of first symptoms: Canuso, Carla M., and Gahan Pandina. "Gender and schizophrenia." *Psychopharmacology Bulletin* 40, no. 4 (2007): 178–90.

70  a possible biomarker for disorders like autism: James, S. Jill, Paul Cutler, Stepan Melnyk, Stefanie Jernigan, Laurette Janak, David W. Gaylor, and James A. Neubrander. "Metabolic biomarkers of increased oxidative stress

and impaired methylation capacity in children with autism." *American Journal of Clinical Nutrition* 80, no. 6 (2004): 1611–17. See also Bradstreet, James Jeffrey, Scott Smith, Matthew Baral, and Daniel A. Rossignol. "Biomarker-guided interventions of clinically relevant conditions associated with autism spectrum disorders and attention deficit hyperactivity disorder." *Alternative Medicine Review* 15, no. 1 (2010): 15–32.

70 **including the prenatal environment in the mother's womb:** Bale, Tracy L., Tallie Z. Baram, Alan S. Brown, Jill M. Goldstein, Thomas R. Insel, Margaret M. McCarthy, Charles B. Nemeroff, et al. "Early life programming and neurodevelopmental disorders." *Biological Psychiatry* 68, no. 4 (2010): 314–19.

70 **"may be collectively responsible for a substantial portion of mental illness":** Awadalla, Philip, Julie Gauthier, Rachel A. Myers, Ferran Casals, Fadi F. Hamdan, Alexander R. Griffing, Mélanie Côté, et al. "Direct measure of the de novo mutation rate in autism and schizophrenia cohorts." *American Journal of Human Genetics* 87, no. 3 (2010): 316–24.

70 **the genetic problem may also be new and unique to the child:** Ibid.

71 **Daniel Tammet, whose synesthesia enables him:** His new book, *Thinking in Numbers*, is a collection of essays that provide insight into the mind of a savant who was profiled by CBS in a segment aptly entitled "Brain Man."

71 **though the link between autism and vaccinations has not been substantiated by further studies:** Autism rates actually started to increase after thimerosal was discontinued. Madsen, Kreesten M., Marlene B. Lauritsen, Carsten B. Pedersen, Poul Thorsen, Anne-Marie Plesner, Peter H. Andersen, and Preben B. Mortensen. "Thimerosal and the occurrence of autism: Negative ecological evidence from Danish population-based data." *Pediatrics* 112, no. 3 (2003): 604–6.

72 **Chemicals in foods and household products:** Goldman, Lynn R., and Sudha Koduru. "Chemicals in the environment and developmental toxicity to children: A public health and policy perspective." *Environmental Health Perspectives* 108, suppl. 3 (2000): 443.

72 **one in eighty-eight children was diagnosed with an autism spectrum disorder:** This number is taken from the U.S. Centers for Disease Control Website, retrieved from http://www.cdc.gov/ncbddd/autism/data.html.

72 **As of this writing, it's closer to one in fifty:** Blumberg, Stephen J., Matthew D. Bramlett, Michael D. Kogan, Laura A. Schieve, Jessica R. Jones, and Michael C. Lu. "Changes in prevalence of parent-reported autism spec-

trum disorder in school-aged US children: 2007 to 2011–2012." *National Health Statistics Reports* 65 (2013): 1–11. Retrieved from http://www.cdc .gov/nchs/data/nhsr/nhsr065.pdf.

72  **speech delays and mental retardation were often the markers used to track prevalence:** Fombonne, Eric. "The prevalence of autism." *JAMA* 289, no. 1 (2003): 87–89.

72  **a 43 percent increase in special education student rates for each one thousand pounds of mercury-tainted emissions:** Palmer, Raymond F., Steven Blanchard, Zachary Stein, David Mandell, and Claudia Miller. "Environmental mercury release, special education rates, and autism disorder: An ecological study of Texas." *Health and Place* 12, no. 2 (2006): 203–9.

72  **methylene chloride, a ubiquitous clear liquid used in industrial manufacturing:** Kalkbrenner, Amy E., Julie L. Daniels, Jiu-Chiuan Chen, Charles Poole, Michael Emch, and Joseph Morrissey. "Perinatal exposure to hazardous air pollutants and autism spectrum disorders at age 8." *Epidemiology* 21, no. 5 (2010): 631.

72  **Some scholars have posited that lead used in water pipes:** Reddy, Aravind, and Charles L. Braun. "Lead and the Romans." *Journal of Chemical Education* 87, no. 10 (2010): 1052–55.

72  **associated with neurological disorders that disproportionately affect children in low-income homes:** You can learn more about lead paint and safety concerns with renovation at the EPA's website, http://www2.epa.gov/lead. For more about the relationship between poverty and lead poisoning in children, see Jones, Robert L., David M. Homa, Pamela A. Meyer, Debra J. Brody, Kathleen L. Caldwell, James L. Pirkle, and Mary Jean Brown. "Trends in blood lead levels and blood lead testing among US children aged 1 to 5 years, 1988–2004." *Pediatrics* 123, no. 3 (2009): e376–85.

72  **For years the paint industry actually tried to blame uneducated parents for the health problems:** Rosner, David, and Gerald Markowitz. "Why it took decades of blaming parents before we banned lead paint." *Atlantic Monthly*, April 22, 2013. Retrieved from http://www.theatlantic.com/ health/archive/2013/04/why-it-took-decades-of-blaming-parents-before-we-banned-lead-paint/275169/.

72  **neurological underpinnings in high blood lead levels for lower-income students:** Miranda, M. L., et al. "The relationship between early childhood blood lead levels and performance on end-of-grade tests." *Environmental Health Perspectives* 115 (2007):1242–47.

73   **fetal or neonatal hypoxia (lack of oxygen) seemed to be a risk factor:** Gardener, Hannah, Donna Spiegelman, and Stephen L. Buka. "Perinatal and neonatal risk factors for autism: A comprehensive meta-analysis." *Pediatrics* 128, no. 2 (2011): 344–55.

73   **Maternal drug and alcohol use during pregnancy is irrefutably linked:** Caetano, R., S. Ramisetty-Mikler, L. R. Floyd, and C. McGrath. "The epidemiology of drinking among women of child-bearing age." *Alcoholism: Clinical and Experimental Research* 30, no. 6 (2006): 1023–30. For cocaine, see Frank, D. A., M. Augustyn, W. G. Knight, T. Pell, and B. Zuckerman. "Growth, development, and behavior in early childhood following prenatal cocaine exposure: A systematic review." *JAMA* 285 (2001): 1613–25.

73   **Prenatal exposure to selective serotonin reuptake inhibitors (SSRIs), such as Zoloft, used to treat maternal depression:** Croen, Lisa A., Judith K. Grether, Cathleen K. Yoshida, Roxana Odouli, and Victoria Hendrick. "Antidepressant use during pregnancy and childhood autism spectrum disorders." *Archives of General Psychiatry* 68, no. 11 (2011): 1104.

73   **inducing labor may increase a woman's risk:** Gregory, Simon G., Rebecca Anthopolos, Claire E. Osgood, Chad A. Grotegut, and Marie Lynn Miranda. "Association of autism with induced or augmented childbirth in North Carolina Birth Record (1990–1998) and Education Research (1997–2007) Databases." *JAMA Pediatrics* 167, no. 10 (2013).

73   **terbutaline (Brethine), an asthma medication used off-label:** Slotkin, Theodore A., and Frederic J. Seidler. "Terbutaline impairs the development of peripheral noradrenergic projections: Potential implications for autism spectrum disorders and pharmacotherapy of preterm labor." *Neurotoxicology and Teratology* 36 (2012).

74   **another potentially deadly childhood disease that we thought we had eradicated:** "Measles—United States, January 1–August 24, 2013." *Morbidity and Mortality Weekly Report* 62, no. 36 (2013). Retrieved from http://www.cdc.gov/mmwr/preview/mmwrhtml/mm6236a2.htm.

75   **"Terbutaline should not be used to stop or prevent premature labor in pregnant women":** http://www.nlm.nih.gov/medlineplus/druginfo/meds/a682144.html.

75   **comparisons with thalidomide, the infamous 1960s drug prescribed off-label for morning sickness:** Kim, James H., and Anthony R. Scialli. "Thalidomide: The tragedy of birth defects and the effective treatment of disease." *Toxicological Sciences* 122, no. 1 (2011): 1–6.

76 **Morrow is attractive, poised, and confident, a successful small business owner and mother:** Morrow has written two books about her med-free method, one for adults, and one for children. You can learn more at http://www.medfreemethod.com/.

77 **Gotttschall claimed she had cured her own child using diet alone:** Gottschall, Elaine. *Breaking the Vicious Cycle: Intestinal Health Through Diet.* Kirkton Press, 2007.

77 **kids who are already finicky about the foods they eat:** Children diagnosed with autism spectrum disorders often prefer bland, processed foods to healthier alternatives. Mealtimes can inadvertently become battlegrounds. For information on food sensitivity, see Cermak, Sharon A., Carol Curtin, and Linda G. Bandini. "Food selectivity and sensory sensitivity in children with autism spectrum disorders." *Journal of the American Dietetic Association* 110, no. 2 (2010): 238–46.

78 **A 2013 viral blog post in which a mother "confessed":** Mountain Mama. "How I gave my son autism." *The Thinking Moms' Revolution*, February 20, 2013. Retrieved from http://thinkingmomsrevolution.com/how-i-gave-my-son-autism/#sthash.I7nhJwrP.dpuf.

78 **patients with bipolar disorder often have elevated levels of antibodies to casein:** Severance, Emily G., Didier Dupont, Faith B. Dickerson, Cassie R. Stallings, Andrea E. Origoni, Bogdana Krivogorsky, Shuojia Yang, Willem Haasnoot, and Robert H. Yolken. "Immune activation by casein dietary antigens in bipolar disorder." *Bipolar Disorders* 12, no. 8 (2010): 834–42.

79 **some studies suggest that omega-3 fatty acids found in fish oil:** Gracious, Barbara L., Madalina C. Chirieac, Stefan Costescu, Teresa L. Finucane, Eric A. Youngstrom, and Joseph R. Hibbeln. "Randomized, placebo-controlled trial of flax oil in pediatric bipolar disorder." *Bipolar Disorders* 12, no. 2 (2010): 142–54.

79 **A recent UCLA study suggests that "gut feelings" may be exactly that:** Champeau, Rachel. "Changing gut bacteria through diet affects brain function, UCLA study shows." *UCLA Newsroom*, May 28, 2013. Retrieved from http://newsroom.ucla.edu/portal/ucla/changing-gut-bacteria-through-245617.aspx.

80 **Mental illness may actually be a manifestation of a nervous system under attack:** Goines, Paula, and Judy Van de Water. "The immune system's role in the biology of autism." *Current Opinion in Neurology* 23, no. 2 (2010): 111.

80    **may begin while the fetus is developing in the mother's womb:** Molloy, Cynthia A., Ardythe L. Morrow, Jareen Meinzen-Derr, Kathleen Schleifer, Krista Dienger, Patricia Manning-Courtney, Mekibib Altaye, and Marsha Wills-Karp. "Elevated cytokine levels in children with autism spectrum disorder." *Journal of Neuroimmunology* 172, no. 1 (2006): 198–205.

80    **Cytokines also appear to play a role in bipolar disorder and schizophrenia:** Munkholm, Klaus, Maj Vinberg, and Lars Devel Kessing. "Cytokines in bipolar disorder: A systematic review and meta-analysis." *Journal of Affective Disorders* 144 (2013). See also Patterson, Paul H. "Immune involvement in schizophrenia and autism: Etiology, pathology and animal models." *Behavioural Brain Research* 204, no. 2 (2009): 313–21.

80    **"Comorbid medical illnesses in bipolar disorder might be viewed":** Leboyer, Marion, Isabella Soreca, Jan Scott, Mark Frye, Chantal Henry, Ryad Tamouza, and David J. Kupfer. "Can bipolar disorder be viewed as a multisystem inflammatory disease?" *Journal of Affective Disorders* 141, no. 1 (2012): 1–10. Retrieved from http://www.ncbi.nlm.nih.gov/pmc/articles/PMC3498820/.

80    **The National Institute of Mental Health is actively pursuing research:** Retrieved from http://www.nimh.nih.gov/health/publications/pandas/index.shtml.

81    **One of the most promising areas of research for physical health:** Turnbaugh, Peter J., Ruth E. Ley, Micah Hamady, Claire M. Fraser-Liggett, Rob Knight, and Jeffrey I. Gordon. "The human microbiome project." *Nature* 449, no. 7164 (2007): 804–10.

81    **To their surprise, the actual number was only twenty thousand or so:** Collins, F. S., E. S. Lander, J. Rogers, R. H. Waterston, and I. H. G. S. Conso. "Finishing the euchromatic sequence of the human genome." *Nature* 431, no. 7011 (2004): 931–45. Retrieved from http://www.ncbi.nlm.nih.gov/pubmed/15496913.

81    **humans share 60 percent of their genes with fruit flies:** Adams, Mark D., Susan E. Celniker, Robert A. Holt, Cheryl A. Evans, Jeannine D. Gocayne, Peter G. Amanatides, Steven E. Scherer, et al. "The genome sequence of Drosophila melanogaster." *Science* 287, no. 5461 (2000): 2185–95.

81    **In fact, there are ten times as many microbial cells as human cells:** For more information on the Human Microbiome Project, visit http://commonfund.nih.gov/hmp/overview.aspx.

81    **"You have your lungs, you have your heart":** Stein, Rob. "Staying healthy

may mean learning to love our microbiomes." *Shots: Health News from NPR*, July 22, 2013. Retrieved from http://www.npr.org/blogs/health/2013/07/22/203659797/staying-healthy-may-mean-learning-to-love-our-microbiomes.

81 **broad-spectrum antibiotics often kill good gut bacteria along with bad ones:** Barden, Louise S., Scott F. Dowell, Benjamin Schwartz, and Cheryl Lackey. "Current attitudes regarding use of antimicrobial agents: Results from physicians' and parents' focus group discussions." *Clinical Pediatrics* 37, no. 11 (1998): 665–71.

82 **they actually *cause* the mental illness they are supposed to cure:** Whitaker, Robert. *Anatomy of an Epidemic: Magic Bullets, Psychiatric Drugs, and the Astonishing Rise of Mental Illness in America*. New York: Random House Digital, 2011.

82 **"sleepiness, headache, vomiting, extrapyramidal disorder":** These side effects are taken directly from the manufacturer's website at http://www.abilify.com/.

82 **Zyprexa (olanzapine) is prescribed for adolescents with schizophrenia:** God, I hate this drug! It made my son gain thirty pounds and turned him into a little zombie. Information on side effects is taken from the manufacturer's website: http://pi.lilly.com/us/zyprexa-pi.pdf.

83 **Risperdal (risperidone) is used to treat children aged five to sixteen:** Side effects retrieved from http://www.nlm.nih.gov/medlineplus/druginfo/meds/a694015.html.

83 **In boys, this drug can cause a condition called gynecomastia:** Roke, Yvette, Jan K. Buitelaar, Annemieke M. Boot, Diederik Tenback, and Peter N. van Harten. "Risk of hyperprolactinemia and sexual side effects in males 10–20 years old diagnosed with autism spectrum disorders or disruptive behavior disorder and treated with risperidone." *Journal of Child and Adolescent Psychopharmacology* 22, no. 6 (2012): 432–39.

83 **Clonidine is a medication used to treat high blood pressure:** Information retrieved from MedlinePlus: http://www.nlm.nih.gov/medlineplus/druginfo/meds/a682243.html.

83 **In 2007, the FDA requested that all SSRIs include the increased risk of suicidality for young people in a black box warning:** http://www.fda.gov/Drugs/DrugSafety/InformationbyDrugClass/ucm096273.htm.

83 **In addition to increased suicidal thoughts, other side effects include:** Side effects retrieved from MedlinePlus: http://www.nlm.nih.gov/medlineplus/druginfo/meds/a699001.html.

84    **in his book on Ritalin as a reflection of our modern culture, physician Lawrence Diller notes:** Diller, Lawrence H. *Running on Ritalin: A Physician Reflects on Children, Society, and Performance in a Pill.* New York: Random House Digital, 2009.

84    **the joke may actually have some truth to it:** Ripley, Amanda. "Ritalin: Mommy's little helper." *Time*, February 12, 2001. Retrieved from http://www.time.com/time/magazine/article/0,9171,999209,00.html.

84    **may all be signs of something seriously wrong:** Side effects retrieved from http://www.nlm.nih.gov/medlineplus/druginfo/meds/a681038.html.

84    **Intuniv (guanfacine) is used to treat high blood pressure:** Michael takes a slow-release version that costs significantly more than the generic. Information on this drug and its side effects was retrieved from MedlinePlus: http://www.nlm.nih.gov/medlineplus/druginfo/meds/a601059.html.

84    **Trileptal (oxcarbazepine) is an anticonvulsant antiseizure medication:** Information on this drug and its side effects retrieved from MedlinePlus: http://www.nlm.nih.gov/medlineplus/druginfo/meds/a601245.html.

85    **Drowsiness, uncontrollable shaking, nausea, and excessive sweating are more benign side effects:** http://www.nlm.nih.gov/medlineplus/druginfo/meds/a695033.html.

85    **has become the gold standard by which all other bipolar medications are judged:** In 1949, an Australian researcher reported on the use of lithium salts in treatment of manic episode: Cade, John F. J. "Lithium salts in the treatment of psychotic excitement." *Medical Journal of Australia* (1949). See for example, Calabrese, Joseph R., Charles L. Bowden, Gary Sachs, Lakshmi N. Yatham, Kirsten Behnke, Olli-Pekka Mehtonen, Paul Montgomery, et al. "A placebo-controlled 18-month trial of lamotrigine and lithium maintenance treatment in recently depressed patients with bipolar I disorder." *Journal of Clinical Psychiatry* 64, no. 9 (2003): 1013–24.

85    **The drug has been in use for more than fifty years now:** Geddes, John R., Sally Burgess, Keith Hawton, Kay Jamison, and Guy M. Goodwin. "Long-term lithium therapy for bipolar disorder: Systematic review and meta-analysis of randomized controlled trials." *American Journal of Psychiatry* 161, no. 2 (2004): 217–22.

85    **Recent MRI scan studies have shown that lithium:** Sassi, Roberto B., Mark Nicoletti, Paolo Brambilla, Alan G. Mallinger, Ellen Frank, David J. Kupfer, Matcheri S. Keshavan, and Jair C. Soares. "Increased gray matter volume in lithium-treated bipolar disorder patients." *Neuroscience Letters* 329, no. 2 (2002): 243–45.

85 **"the benefits of second-generation antipsychotic medications must be balanced":** Correll, Christoph U., Peter Manu, Vladimir Olshanskiy, Barbara Napolitano, John M. Kane, and Anil K. Malhotra. "Cardiometabolic risk of second-generation antipsychotic medications during first-time use in children and adolescents." *JAMA* 302, no. 16 (2009): 1765–73.

86 **"may even aggravate progressive brain tissue volume reductions":** Leucht, Stefan, Magdolna Tardy, Katja Komossa, Stephan Heres, Werner Kissling, Georgia Salanti, and John M. Davis. "Antipsychotic drugs versus placebo for relapse prevention in schizophrenia: A systematic review and meta-analysis." *Lancet* 379, no. 9831 (2012): 2063–71. Quote from Ho, Beng-Choon, Nancy C. Andreasen, Steven Ziebell, Ronald Pierson, and Vincent Magnotta. "Long-term antipsychotic treatment and brain volumes: A longitudinal study of first-episode schizophrenia." *Archives of General Psychiatry* 68, no. 2 (2011): 128.

87 **"After the casino opened, the mean level of behavioral symptoms":** Costello, E. Jane, Scott N. Compton, Gordon Keeler, and Adrian Angold. "Relationships between poverty and psychopathology." *JAMA* 290, no. 15 (2003): 2023–29.

87 **childhood poverty is correlated with an increased risk of mental illness:** Najman, Jake M., Mohammad R. Hayatbakhsh, Alexandra Clavarino, William Bor, Michael J. O'Callaghan, and Gail M. Williams. "Family poverty over the early life course and recurrent adolescent and young adult anxiety and depression: A longitudinal study." *American Journal of Public Health* 100, no. 9 (2010): 1719–23.

87 **may help therapists to design more effective and earlier interventions:** Yoshikawa, Hirokazu, J. Lawrence Aber, and William R. Beardslee. "The effects of poverty on the mental, emotional, and behavioral health of children and youth: Implications for prevention." *American Psychologist* 67, no. 4 (2012): 272.

88 **Some of these children are as young as two years old:** Lagnado, Lucette. "U.S. probes psych drug use on kids." *Wall Street Journal*, August 12, 2013, pp. A1–2.

88 **"reflects increased medication use for behavioral problems":** Zito, Julie Magno, Mehmet Burcu, Aloysius Ibe, Daniel J. Safer, and Laurence S. Magder. "Antipsychotic use by Medicaid-insured youths: Impact of eligibility and psychiatric diagnosis across a decade." *Psychiatric Services* 64, no. 3 (2013): 223–29.

88 **The good news is that at least some of these negative effects are revers-**

**ible:** Hackman, Daniel A., Martha J. Farah, and Michael J. Meaney. "Socioeconomic status and the brain: Mechanistic insights from human and animal research." *Nature Reviews Neuroscience* 11, no. 9 (2010): 651–59. Retrieved from http://www.ncbi.nlm.nih.gov/pmc/articles/PMC2950073/.

88   **Small changes in family income:** Costello, E. Jane, Scott N. Compton, Gordon Keeler, and Adrian Angold. "Relationships between poverty and psychopathology." *JAMA* 290, no. 15 (2003): 2023–29.

89   **"a product of our culture—a cherished cultural myth":** Harris, Judith Rich. *The Nurture Assumption: Why Children Turn Out the Way They Do.* New York: Free Press, 2009.

89   **philosopher Claire Creffield notes that "a host of chance events":** Creffield, Claire. "Are parents morally responsible for their children?" *Salon.com*, June 23, 2013.

89   **negative impact on a child's emotional and behavioral development:** Repetti, Rena L., Shelley E. Taylor, and Teresa E. Seeman. "Risky families: Family social environments and the mental and physical health of offspring." *Psychological Bulletin* 128, no. 2 (2002): 330.

89   **In rats, increased maternal licking of pups:** Maternal care during infancy regulates the development of neural systems mediating the expression of fearfulness in the rat. Liu, Dong, Josie Diorio, Beth Tannenbaum, Christian Caldji, Darlene Francis, Alison Freedman, Shakti Sharma, Deborah Pearson, Paul M. Plotsky, and Michael J. Meaney. "Maternal care, hippocampal glucocorticoid receptors, and hypothalamic-pituitary-adrenal responses to stress." *Science* 277, no. 5332 (1997): 1659–62.

89   **A single gene in a depressed mother could predict:** Avan, Bilal, Linda M. Richter, Paul G. Ramchandani, Shane A. Norris, and Alan Stein. "Maternal postnatal depression and children's growth and behaviour during the early years of life: Exploring the interaction between physical and mental health." *Archives of Disease in Childhood* 95, no. 9 (2010): 690–95.

## Chapter Four: Mental Health Care

93   **that's one in five children in any given year:** These statistics are taken from the National Institute of Mental Health website: http://www.nimh.nih .gov/statistics/1anydis_child.shtml.

93   **Mental Health Parity and Addiction Equity Act of 2008 failed:** Beronio, Kirsten, Rosa Po, Laura Skopec, and Sherry Glied. "Affordable Care Act

expands mental health and substance use disorder benefits and federal parity protections for 62 million Americans." ASPE Issue Brief, February 20, 2013. Retrieved from http://aspe.hhs.gov/health/reports/2013/mental/rb_mental.cfm.

93  **"It's not that we don't know how to treat mental illness":** NAMI director Michael Fitzpatrick testified to a U.S. House of Representatives Energy and Commerce Committee forum entitled "After Newtown" on March 5, 2013. You can watch the entire forum here: http://energycommerce.house.gov/event/after-newtown-national-conversation-violence-and-severe-mental-illness.

93  **around $225,000 for a student starting in 2013:**At least students at Harvard are often eligible for financial aid. This cost estimate was taken from Harvard University's admissions website: http://www.admissions.college .harvard.edu/financial_aid/cost.html.

98  **between 43 and 60 percent of all mental illness is treated solely by patients' primary care providers:** Kessler, Rodger, and Dale Stafford. "Primary care is the de facto mental health system." In *Collaborative Medicine Case Studies.* Edited by R. Kessler and D. Stafford. New York: Springer, 2008, pp. 9–21.

98  **nearly 23 percent were treated by a general practitioner:** Wang, Philip S., Michael Lane, Mark Olfson, Harold A. Pincus, Kenneth B. Wells, and Ronald C. Kessler. "Twelve-month use of mental health services in the United States: Results from the National Comorbidity Survey Replication." *Archives of General Psychiatry* 62, no. 6 (2005): 629–40.

98  **pediatricians lack the level of education about mental illness to be able to diagnose those symptoms:** Trude, Sally, and Jeffrey J. Stoddard. "Referral gridlock." *Journal of General Internal Medicine* 18, no. 6 (2003): 442–49.

99  **According to the American Academy of Child and Adolescent Psychiatry, in 2012, there were just 8,300 practicing child and adolescent psychiatrists in the entire United States:** "Child and Adolescent Psychiatry Workforce Crisis: Solutions to Improve Early Intervention and Access to Care." The American Academy of Child and Adolescent Psychiatrists, 2013. Retrieved from http://www.aacap.org/App_Themes/AACAP/docs/resources_for_primary_care/workforce_issues/workforce_brochure_2013 .pdf.

99  **In 2001, there were only seventeen child psychiatrists in the entire state of Idaho:** Thomas, Christopher R., and Charles E. Holzer. "The continuing

shortage of child and adolescent psychiatrists." *Journal of the American Academy of Child and Adolescent Psychiatry* 45, no. 9 (2006): 1023–31.

99 **psychiatry is not highly regarded as a career choice by future doctors:** Feifel, David, Christine Yu Moutier, and Neal R. Swerdlow. "Attitudes toward psychiatry as a prospective career among students entering medical school." *American Journal of Psychiatry* 156, no. 9 (1999): 1397–1402.

99 **psychiatry is somehow seen as a lesser science:** Sartorius, Norman, Wolfgang Gaebel, Helen-Rose Cleveland, Heather Stuart, Tsuyoshi Akiyama, Julio Arboleda-Florez, Anja E. Baumann, et al. "WPA guidance on how to combat stigmatization of psychiatry and psychiatrists." *World Psychiatry* 9, no. 3 (2010): 131–44.

99 **"negative attitudes toward a career in psychiatry compared with other specialties":** Feifel, David, Christine Yu Moutier, and Neal R. Swerdlow. "Attitudes toward psychiatry as a prospective career among students entering medical school." *American Journal of Psychiatry* 156, no. 9 (1999): 1397–1402.

100 **In a 2007 survey of British doctors who chose to specialize in psychiatry:** Dein, Kalpana, Gill Livingston, and Christopher Bench. " 'Why did I become a psychiatrist?': Survey of consultant psychiatrists." *Psychiatric Bulletin* 31, no. 6 (2007): 227–30.

100 **After three and a half years and 185 telepsychiatry consultations:** Saeed, Sy Atezaz, John Diamond, and Richard M. Bloch. "Use of telepsychiatry to improve care for people with mental illness in rural North Carolina." *North Carolina Medical Journal* 72, no. 3 (2011): 219–22.

100 **The investigation alleged improper sexual conduct with underage boys:** Dutton, Audrey. "Child psychiatrist accused of misconduct seeks license back." *Idaho Statesman*, July 19, 2013. Retrieved from http://www.idaho statesman.com/2013/07/19/2661916/child-psychiatrist-accused-of.html.

101 **other child psychiatrists have also been implicated in improper relationships:** For example, Charles Henry Fischer in Texas, who was accused of abuse over a twenty-year period (Ron Zimmerman, "Child psychiatrist faces multiple allegations of sexual abuse," *Medscape Medical News*, December 1, 2011; retrieved from http://www.medscape.com/viewarticle/754557). William Ayres of San Mateo County, California, was sentenced to eight years for child sex abuse (Mike Aldax, "Ex-psychiatrist William Ayres gets 8 years in prison for child molestations," *San Francisco Examiner*, August 27, 2013; retrieved from http://www.sfexaminer.com/sanfrancisco/ex-psychiatrist-william

-ayres-gets-8-years-in-prison-for-child-molestations/Content?oid=2560400). David F. Wilson, a child psychiatrist in Ogden, Utah, lost his medical license after it was found that he'd accessed child pornography through his work computer (Michael Mcfall, "Ogden child psychiatrist investigated for child pornography," *Salt Lake Tribune*, September 9, 2013; retrieved from http://www.sltrib.com/sltrib/news/56847538-78/wilson-computer-child pornography.html.csp).

101 **the tremendous stigma that attaches to labeling a child with a serious mental illness:** For a systematic review of the literature on stigma and children's mental illness, see Mukolo, Abraham, Craig Anne Heflinger, and Kenneth A. Wallston. "The stigma of childhood mental disorders: A conceptual framework." *Journal of the American Academy of Child and Adolescent Psychiatry* 49, no. 2 (2010): 92–103.

101 **clear violation of the school's conflict-of-interest policies:** Yu, Xi. "Three professors face sanctions following Harvard Medical School inquiry." *Harvard Crimson*, July 2, 2011. Retrieved from http://www.thecrimson.com/article/2011/7/2/school-medical-harvard-investigation/.

101 **The dramatic increase in children discharged from the hospital with bipolar diagnoses:** Blader, Joseph C., and Gabrielle A. Carlson. "Increased rates of bipolar disorder diagnoses among US child, adolescent, and adult inpatients, 1996–2004."*Biological Psychiatry* 62, no. 2 (2007): 107–14.

101 **In an article for *Newsweek* castigating the diagnosis of bipolar disorder:** Kaplan, Stuart L. "U.S. children misdiagnosed with bipolar disorder." *Newsweek*, June 19, 2011. Retrieved from http://www.newsweek.com/us-children-misdiagnosed-bipolar-disorder-67871.

102 **new controversial diagnosis in the DSM-5:** The exact criteria for this diagnosis can be found here: http://www.dsm5.org/Documents/Disruptive%20 Mood%20Dysregulation%20Disorder%20Fact%20Sheet.pdf.

103 **one Oregon couple has treated their son's severe autism with medical marijuana:** Miller, Tracy. " 'It's the one medicine we have seen work': Oregon parents use medical marijuana to help severely autistic son." *New York Daily News*, January 25, 2013. Retrieved from http://www.nydailynews.com/life-style/health/oregon-family-medical-marijuana-treat-son-autistic-rage-article-1.1247745.

104 **Wellbutrin is cocaine without the high:** King, Logan, and Lisa Bonner. "Synthesis of a novel DAT inhibitor with structural similarities to bupropion (Wellbutrin)." Saint Anselm College, Department of Chemistry, no

date. Retrieved from http://www.anselm.edu/Documents/Academics/Depart ments/Chemistry/King%20SOAR%20poster.pdf.

104    **Ritalin is closely related to speed:** Iversen, Leslie L. *Speed, Ecstasy, Ritalin: The Science of Amphetamines.* New York: Oxford University Press, 2008.

104    **19,045 children under the age of five were given these medications under Medicaid:** Lagnado, Lucette. "U.S. probes psych drug use on kids." *Wall Street Journal*, August 12, 2013, pp. A1–2.

104    **the long-term metabolic changes they cause may adversely affect both quality and quantity of life:** Newcomer, John W. "Second-generation (atypical) antipsychotics and metabolic effects." *CNS Drugs* 19, no. 1 (2005): 1–93.

104    **Lithium, for example, has been used for more than fifty years:** For more information on lithium and its history, see http://health.nytimes.com/ health/guides/disease/bipolar-disorder/medications.html.

104    **ecstasy, which has shown promise in treating post-traumatic stress disorder:** Bernard Kuhn, Lisa. "Illegal ecstasy being studied to treat PTSD." *Cincinnati Enquirer*, April 22, 2013. Retrieved from http://www.usatoday.com/ story/news/nation/2013/04/22/ecstasy-drug-post-traumatic-stress/2102983/.

104    **ketamine, which has been shown to stop suicidal ideation in its tracks:** Harper, Matthew. "Johnson & Johnson is reinventing the party drug ketamine to treat depression." *Forbes*, May 23, 2013. Retrieved from http:// www.forbes.com/sites/matthewherper/2013/05/23/johnson-johnson-is-reinventing-the-party-drug-ketamine-to-treat-depression/.

104    **classified as Schedule III controlled substances:** For a description of the DEA's controlled substances, see "Drug Scheduling" at http://www.justice .gov/dea/druginfo/ds.shtml.

105    **approved for a treatment course of four doses:** For more information on the NIMH clinical trial "Intranasal Ketamine in the Treatment of Pediatric Bipolar Disorder (IKBP)," which is recruiting study subjects, visit http://www .clinicaltrials.gov/ct2/show/NCT01504659?term=ketamine+bipolar+disorder&rank=1. For more information on Dr. Papolos, visit www.jbrf.org.

106    **their reality does not correspond to everyone else's:** Pia, Lorenzo, and Marco Tamietto. "Unawareness in schizophrenia: Neuropsychological and neuroanatomical findings." *Psychiatry and Clinical Neurosciences* 60, no. 5 (2006): 531–37.

108    **Attention Exercise, developed from Edward Hallowell's book on managing ADHD:** Hallowell, Edward. *Delivered from Distraction: Getting the Most out of Life with Attention Deficit Disorder.* New York: Ballantine Books, 2005.

109 **One of the earliest psychiatric hospitals in the West was Bedlam:** Andrews, Jonathan, Asa Briggs, Roy Porter, Penny Tucker, and Keir Waddington. *The History of Bethlem*. London and New York: Routledge; 1997.

109 **Edward Wakefield described a visit in 1814 as follows:** "Extracts from the Report of the Committee Employed to Visit Houses and Hospitals for the Confinement of Insane Persons, with Remarks, by Philanthropus." *Medical and Physical Journal* 32 (August 1814): 122–28.

110 **Gina Fernandes, who told Diana and Brendan's story on Momlogic.com:** Fernandes, Gina Kaysen. "Saving troubled teens: A greedy industry?" Momlogic.com, December 2009. Retrieved from http://www.momlogic.com/2009 /12/saving_troubled_teens_a_greedy_industry.php#ixzz2daDRopgt.

110 **The organization Teen Advocates USA monitors abuses of the system:** This advocacy group's information can be found here: http://teenadvocate-susa.homestead.com/FrontPage.html. The Coalition Against Institutionalized Child Abuse, or CAICA, also monitors residential treatment programs. You can learn more here: http://www.caica.org.

110 **The program was profiled in an Idaho Public Television *Outdoor Idaho* documentary:** You can read more about the show here: http://idahoptv.org/ outdoors/shows/dtherapy/about.cfm.

111 **"Your child will experience the highest standards of safety and therapy":** Read about Aspen's residential treatment schools and wilderness survival camps at http://aspeneducation.crchealth.com/.

111 **Experts agree that the very worst option for a teen with a mental disorder:** Lilienfeld, Scott O. "Psychological treatments that cause harm." *Perspectives on Psychological Science* 2, no. 1 (2007): 53–70.

111 **"a significant number of children are being mistreated in such programs":** Behar, Lenore, Robert Friedman, Allison Pinto, Judith Katz-Leavy, and William G. Jones. "Protecting youth placed in unlicensed, unregulated residential 'treatment' facilities." *Family Court Review* 45, no. 3 (2007): 399–413.

111 **Even the National Association of Therapeutic Schools and Programs, an industry group:** You can visit www.NATSAP.org for more information about the therapeutic school industry.

112 **The Centers for Disease Control estimates the annual aggregate cost of children's mental health care:** "Mental health surveillance among children—United States, 2005–2011." *Morbidity and Mortality Weekly Report* 62, no. 2 (2013).

112   **Families who have a child with autism spend an average of $60,000:** This statistic comes from Autism Speaks, a national advocacy group for children and families. Retrieved from http://www.autismspeaks.org/what-autism/facts-about-autism.

112   **mothers of children with autism earn 56 percent less on average:** Cidav, Zuleyha, Steven C. Marcus, and David S. Mandell. "Implications of childhood autism for parental employment and earnings." *Pediatrics* 129, no. 4 (2012): 617–23.

112   **Jeff Howe was castigated for his honest assessment of the costs:** Howe, Jeff. "Paying for Finn: A special needs child." *Money*, May 2013. Retrieved from http://money.cnn.com/2013/05/01/pf/autism-costs.moneymag/index.html.

112   **the estimated lifetime cost of raising a single child with autism at $3.2 million:** Giangregorio, Michael. "A day in the life of a family coping with autism." Autism Speaks, no date. Retrieved September 27, 2013, from http://www.autismspeaks.org/news/news-item/%5Btitle-raw%5D-29.

113   **depression rates were reduced by 30 percent for those who were able to obtain services through Medicaid:** Katherine Baicker, Sarah Taubman, Heidi Allen, Mira Bernstein, Jonathan Gruber, Joseph P. Newhouse, Eric Schneider, Bill Wright, Alan Zaslavsky, Amy Finkelstein, and the Oregon Health Study Group. "The Oregon experiment—Medicaid's effects on clinical outcomes." *New England Journal of Medicine* 368, no. 18 (May 2013).

113   **Do your best to read this entire quote:** Mann, Cindy, and Hyde, Pamela. "Coverage of behavioral health services for children, youth, and young adults." Joint CMCS and SAMHSA Informational Bulletin, May 7, 2013. Retrieved from http://medicaid.gov/Federal-Policy-Guidance/Downloads/CIB-05-07-2013.pdf.

114   **"Latinos and the uninsured have especially high rates of unmet need relative to other children":** Kataoka, Sheryl H., Lily Zhang, and Kenneth B. Wells. "Unmet need for mental health care among US children: Variation by ethnicity and insurance status." *American Journal of Psychiatry* 159, no. 9 (2002): 1548–55.

115   **Aaron Alexis sought treatment at two Veterans Affairs hospitals:** Schmidt, Michael. "Gunman said electronic brain attacks drove him to violence, F.B.I. says." *New York Times*, September 25, 2013. Retrieved from http://www.nytimes.com/2013/09/26/us/shooter-believed-mind-was-under-attack-official-says.html?_r=0.

117   **As Virginia senator Creigh Deeds tweeted after his son Gus wounded his**

**father:** Vozella, Laura. "Creigh Deeds released from hospital as son's friends reflect on his mental illness." *The Washington Post*, November 22, 2013. Retrieved from http://www.washingtonpost.com/local/virginia-politics/ creigh-deeds-released-from-hospital/2013/11/22/45ced676-52e4-11e3-9e2c-e1d01116fd98_story.html.

117   **"psychiatric drug industry that is based on marketing and not science":** The slick, Scientology-funded Citizens Commission on Human Rights (CCHR) website can be viewed at http://www.cchrint.org/about-us/.

118   **The for-profit organization's treatment philosophy is based on the book:** Melillo, Robert. *Disconnected Kids: The Groundbreaking Brain Balance Program for Children with Autism, ADHD, Dyslexia, and Other Neurological Disorders*. New York: Penguin, 2009.

118   **"No one was looking at the other problems these children had":** Ibid., p. ix.

118   **A 2010 preliminary study of 122 children with ADHD:** It should be noted that this research was undertaken by the Carrick Institute, a chiropractic training center with which Dr. Melillo is affiliated. Leisman, Gerry, Robert Melillo, Sharon Thum, Mark A. Ransom, Michael Orlando, Christopher Tice, and Frederick R. Carrick. "The effect of hemisphere specific remediation strategies on the academic performance outcome of children with ADD/ADHD." *International Journal of Adolescent Medicine and Health* 22, no. 2 (2010): 275–84.

118   **The Brain Balance website home page trumpets:** Leisman, Gerry, Raed Zaki Mualem, and Calixto Machado. "The integration of the neurosciences, child public health, and education practice: Hemisphere-specific remediation strategies as a discipline partnered rehabilitation tool in ADD/ADHD." *Frontiers in Public Health* 1 (2013): 22.

119   **CNNMoney profiled Brain Balance:** Kavilanz, Parija. "5 hot franchises." *CNNMoney*, February 2013. Retrieved from http://money.cnn.com/gallery/ smallbusiness/2013/02/12/hot-franchises/index.html.

119   **Even cancer has its Cancer Treatment Centers of America:** Information can be found here: www.cancercenter.com.

119   **the Church of Scientology's well-publicized abhorrence of psychiatry:** Mieszkowski, Katharine. "Scientology's war on psychiatry." *Salon.com*, July 1, 2005. Retrieved from http://www.salon.com/2005/07/01/sci_psy/.

119   **"When I walked out of that presentation":** Schweitzer, Lindsay. "He did it!" *Jubilant Motherhood: Finding Joy in the Journey* (blog), August 30, 2012. Retrieved from http://jubilantmotherhood.com/category/brain-balance/.

120  **Some prominent science bloggers, including Emily Willingham:** Willing-
     ham, Emily. "Brain Balance Centers: A critique." *A Life Less Ordinary*, August
     13, 2010. Retrieved from http://daisymayfattypants.blogspot.co.uk/2010/08/
     brain-balance-centers-critique.html; Hall, Harriett. "Brain Balance." *Science-
     Based Medicine*, September 14, 2010. Retrieved from http://www.sciencebased
     medicine.org/brain-balance/; "Brain Balance Centers: Total and Utter Neuro-
     bollocks." *NeuroBollocks*, March 5, 2013. Retrieved from http://neurobollocks
     .wordpress.com/2013/03/05/brain-balance-centers-total-and-utter
     -neurobollocks/.

122  **one popular example is the 1990 book:** Cline, Foster, Jim Fay, and Tom
     Raabe. *Parenting with Love and Logic: Teaching Children Responsibility*. Colo-
     rado Springs, CO: Piñon Press, 1990.


## Chapter Five: Education

124  **a common experience for children who have developmental or mental
     disorders:** Averill, Andrew. "Adam Lanza bullied as a student at Sandy
     Hook, his mother considered suing." *Christian Science Monitor*, April 17,
     2013. Retrieved from http://www.csmonitor.com/The-Culture/Family/
     Modern-Parenthood/2013/0417/Adam-Lanza-bullied-as-student-at-Sandy-
     Hook-his-mother-considered-suing. This premise was also explored by *New
     York Daily News* reporter Matthew Lysiak in his book *Newtown: An Ameri-
     can Tragedy*. New York: Simon and Schuster, 2013.

125  **in 2012, the price tag for one year of juvenile detention for a child in
     California was $179,400:** This figure was retrieved from the California
     legislative analyst office: http://www.lao.ca.gov/analysis/2012/crim_justice/
     juvenile-justice-021512.aspx.

125  **yet the state was forty-ninth in the nation on per pupil public school
     spending:** Fensterwald, John. "California drops to 49th in school spending
     in annual Ed Week report." *EdSource*, January 14, 2013. Retrieved from
     http://www.edsource.org/today/2013/california-drops-to-49th-in-school-
     spending-in-annual-ed-week-report/25379#.UiTERbusim4.

126  **"A child facing status offense charges is likely to be":** Tulman, Joseph B.,
     and Douglas M. Weck. "Shutting off the school-to-prison pipeline for status
     offenders with education-related disabilities." *New York Law School Law
     Review* 54 (2009): 875.

126  **but they are also likely to be the bully, especially if they have oppositional
     defiant disorder:** Pearson, Catherine. "Bullying and mental health: Study

links anxiety, hyperactivity in kids to bullying." *Huffington Post*, October 22, 2012. Retrieved from http://www.huffingtonpost.com/2012/10/22/bullying-mental-health-problems_n_2001583.html.

126 **A 2011 report from the National Education Policy Center, entitled "Discipline Policies, Successful Schools, and Racial Justice":** Losen, Daniel J. "Discipline policies, successful schools, and racial justice." National Education Policy Center, October 2011. Retrieved from http://nepc.colorado.edu/files/NEPC-SchoolDiscipline.pdf.

128 **The phenomenon of the Asian Tiger Mothers:** I'm fascinated by the Tiger Mom controversy because I saw Tiger Moms in action: many of my high school friends are second-generation Asian Americans. Their mothers would never have allowed them to major in Classics. Chua, Amy. *Battle Hymn of the Tiger Mom.* New York: Penguin, 2011. See also Chua's *Wall Street Journal* article, "Why Chinese mothers are superior," January 8, 2011. Retrieved from http://online.wsj.com/article/SB10001424052748704111150 4576059713528698754.html.

128 **in 2012 the states were only reimbursed an average of 16 percent of their excess costs:** "Individuals with Disabilities Education Act—funding distribution." Federal Education Budget Project, November 8, 2013. Retrieved from http://febp.newamerica.net/background-analysis/individuals-disabilities-education-act-funding-distribution.

129 **The school's suspension rate in 2010–11 was 22 percent of the total student population:** Gonzalez, Juan. "Success Academy school chain comes under fire as parents fight 'zero tolerance' disciplinary policy." *New York Daily News*, August 28, 2013. Retrieved from http://www.nydailynews.com/new-york/education/success-academy-fire-parents-fight-disciplinary-policy-article-1.1438753.

129 **"Many schools find it easier to let children drop out":** Stiffman, Arlene Rubin, Wayne Stelk, Sarah McCue Horwitz, Mary E. Evans, Freida Hopkins Outlaw, and Marc Atkins. "A public health approach to children's mental health services: Possible solutions to current service inadequacies." *Administration and Policy in Mental Health and Mental Health Services Research* 37, no. 1 (2010): 120–24. Retrieved from http://www.ncbi.nlm.nih.gov/pmc/articles/PMC2874610/.

129 **Lincoln High School principal Jim Sporleder changed his school's entire approach to discipline:** Medina, John. *Brain Rules: 12 Principles for Surviving and Thriving at Work, Home, and School.* Seattle: Pear Press, 2010.

129 **students admitted to challenges in their lives, then actually apologized for**

**their behavior and changed it:** Stevens, Jane. "Lincoln High School in Walla Walla, WA, tries new approach to school discipline—suspensions drop 85%." *ACESTooHigh.com*, April 23, 2012. Retrieved from http://aces-toohigh.com/2012/04/23/lincoln-high-school-in-walla-walla-wa-tries-new-approach-to-school-discipline-expulsions-drop-85/.

130  **In an article pointing out the functional difficulties children with ADHD face in navigating a regular classroom:** Bertin, Mark. "ADHD goes to school." May 15, 2012. Retrieved from http://www.huffingtonpost.com/mark-bertin-md/adhd_b_1517445.html.

130  **Special-needs children are also disproportionately affected:** "The school to prison pipeline." *New York Times*, May 29, 2013. Retrieved from http://www.nytimes.com/2013/05/30/opinion/new-york-citys-school-to-prison-pipeline.html?_r=0.

131  **A 2011 study of the SS/HS initiative found that grant recipients were better able to address the mental health needs:** Derzon, James H., Ping Yu, Bruce Ellis, Sharon Xiong, Carmen Arroyo, Danyelle Mannix, Michael E. Wells, Gary Hill, and Julia Rollison. "A national evaluation of Safe Schools/Healthy Students: Outcomes and influences." *Evaluation and Program Planning* 35, no. 2 (2012): 293–302.

131  **Americans supported increased access to mental health services in schools:** Strauss, Valerie. "Poll: Most Americans sick of high-stakes standardized tests." *Washington Post*, August 21, 2013. Retrieved from http://www.washingtonpost.com/blogs/answer-sheet/wp/2013/08/21/poll-most-americans-sick-of-high-stakes-standardized-tests/.

131  **including Section 504 of the Rehabilitation Act of 1973:** A fact sheet summarizing Section 504 can be found at http://www.hhs.gov/ocr/civilrights/resources/factsheets/504.pdf. "Under this law, individuals with disabilities are defined as persons with a physical or mental impairment which substantially limits one or more major life activities. People who have a history of, or who are regarded as having a physical or mental impairment that substantially limits one or more major life activities, are also covered."

131  **Title II of the Americans with Disabilities Act:** "Title II applies to State and local government entities, and, in subtitle A, protects qualified individuals with disabilities from discrimination on the basis of disability in services, programs, and activities provided by State and local government entities." Retrieved from www.ada.gov.

131  **the Individuals with Disabilities Education Act of 2004:** http://idea.ed.gov/.

132   **1.5 million in 2007, an increase from 850,000 in 1999 and 1.1 million in 2003:** "The condition of education, 2009." U.S. Department of Education, National Center for Education Statistics, 2009 (NCES 2009-081).

133   **a behavior some children with autism have, where they recite words:** Landa, Rebecca. "Social language use in Asperger syndrome and high-functioning autism." *Asperger Syndrome* (2000): 125–55.

135   **Parents who are not satisfied with the outcome can appeal to federal court:** Some areas have disproportionately high levels of due process rulings, including New York and the District of Columbia. See Zirkel, Perry A., and Gina Scala. "Due process hearing systems under the IDEA: A state-by-state survey." *Journal of Disability Policy Studies* 21, no. 1 (2010): 3–8.

137   **the category commonly used for children diagnosed with ADHD:** Loe, Irene M., and Heidi M. Feldman. "Academic and educational outcomes of children with ADHD." *Journal of Pediatric Psychology* 32, no. 6 (2007): 643–54.

137   **The "emotional disturbance" category is used more than any other:** Mills, Carrie L., and Dana L. Cunningham. "Building bridges: The role of expanded school mental health in supporting students with emotional and behavioral difficulties in the least restrictive environment." In *Handbook of School Mental Health*. Edited by M. D. Weist et al. New York: Springer, 2014, pp. 87–98.

138   **The school district claims that this program "makes learning and socializing possible":** The very brief information on this program is here: http://special-education.school.boiseschools.org/modules/groups/group_pages.phtml?gid=3711834&nid=361315&sessionid=7398f5de3d4b0cf12ec6a47a2f9fc923&sessionid=7398f5de3d4b0cf12ec6a47a2f9fc923#ASCENT.

139   **one angry mother in Washington claimed:** Moreno, Joel. "Mom: School used isolation room to punish special-needs child." *Komonews.com*, April 23, 2013. Retrieved from http://www.komonews.com/news/local/Mom-School-used-isolation-room-to-punish-special-needs-child-204384941.html.

140   **the latest example being the 2013 national debate about bipartisan-backed Common Core State Standards:** See the *Washington Post*'s editorial on Common Core: http://www.washingtonpost.com/blogs/answer-sheet/wp/2013/05/31/why-extreme-common-core-rhetoric-is-a-problem/.

140   **"Our nation's schools are failing our children":** Retrieved from http://

prisonjusticeproject.org/capturedwords/?p=27. See also Kozol, Jonathan. *Savage Inequalities: Children in America's Schools*. New York: Random House Digital, 2012.

141  **The Common Core State Standards Initiative was developed jointly:** "Common Core State Standards." Washington, DC: National Governors Association Center for Best Practices and the Council of Chief State School Officers, 2010. Retrieved from www.corestandards.org.

141  **In 2007–08, IDEA reported the following IEP percentages for children and young people aged three through twenty-one:** "Digest of education statistics, 2009." U.S. Department of Education, National Center for Education Statistics, 2010 (NCES 2010-013), chapter 2.

141  **Blogger Cameron Pipkin noted that special education teachers:** Pipkin, Cameron. "Why your special ed teachers are specially equipped to become powerful leaders in Common Core implementation." *Common Core Blog*, no date. Retrieved from http://www.schoolimprovement.com/common-core-360/blog/common-core-implementation-udl/.

142  **"We also saw increases in academic achievement, student engagement, and overall self-confidence":** Mullenholz, Greg. "Why the Common Core is good for special education students." Op-ed. *Take Part*, June 26, 2013. Retrieved from http://www.takepart.com/article/2013/06/26/op-ed-inclusion-common-core-good-students-special-education. For more information on inclusion, see also Villa, Richard A., and Jacqueline S. Thousand. "Making inclusive education work." In *Kaleidoscope: Contemporary and Classic Readings in Education*. Edited by K. Ryan and J. M Cooper. Belmont, CA: Wadsworth, 2009, pp. 336–41.

142  **"The issues involving psychological testing and privacy are issues":** This letter was published on the conservative activist–backed Truth in American Education website: http://truthinamericaneducation.com/common-core-state-standards/a-mental-health-professionals-perspective-on-the-common-core/.

142  **"various brainwashing techniques will turn your David or Sarah into a little Obama":** The letters to the editor are without a doubt the most entertaining part of the *Idaho Statesman*. Lee, Val. "Common Core." *Idaho Statesman*, September 1, 2013. Retrieved from http://www.idahostatesman.com/2013/09/01/2737417/letters-to-the-editor.html.

142  **as long-time teacher and administrator Marion Brady:** Brady, Marion. "Eight problems with Common Core Standards." The Answer Sheet, *Wash-*

*ington Post*, August 21, 2012. Retrieved from http://www.washingtonpost .com/blogs/answer-sheet/post/eight-problems-with-common-core-standards/2012/08/21/821b300a-e4e7-11e1-8f62-58260e3940a0_blog.html.

143 **only 9 percent of children born into low-income households during that period were college completers:** Bailey, Martha J., and Susan M. Dynarski. "Gains and gaps: Changing inequality in U.S. college entry and completion." National Bureau of Economic Research Working Paper No. 17633, December 2011.

143 **18 percent of Harvard's graduating senior class applied to Teach for America:** This statistic was taken directly from Teach for America's website: http://www.teachforamerica.org/why-teach-for-america.

146 **one possible public health–based solution to this problem:** Stiffman, Arlene Rubin, Wayne Stelk, Sarah McCue Horwitz, Mary E. Evans, Freida Hopkins Outlaw, and Marc Atkins. "A public health approach to children's mental health services: Possible solutions to current service inadequacies." *Administration and Policy in Mental Health and Mental Health Services Research* 37, no. 1 (2010): 120–24. Retrieved from http://www.ncbi.nlm.nih .gov/pmc/articles/PMC2874610/.

## Chapter Six: Crime and Punishment

149 **court-ordered competency restoration classes:** For more information on competency restoration and mental retardation, see Wall, Barry W., Brandon H. Krupp, and Thomas Guilmette. "Restoration of competency to stand trial: A training program for persons with mental retardation." *Journal of the American Academy of Psychiatry and the Law Online* 31, no. 2 (2003): 189–201.

150 **much more likely to go to prison as adults:** Aizer, Anna, and Joseph Doyle, Jr. "Juvenile incarceration, human capital and future crime: Evidence from randomly-assigned judges." National Bureau of Economic Research Working Paper No. 19102, June 2013. Retrieved from http://nber.org/papers/ w19102.

150 **But the U.S. prison industry is booming:** Plumer, Brad. "Throwing children in prison turns out to be a really bad idea." *Washington Post*, June 15, 2013. Retrieved from http://www.washingtonpost.com/blogs/wonkblog/ wp/2013/06/15/throwing-children-in-prison-turns-out-to-be-a-really-bad-idea.

150   **over half of all youth also have substance abuse problems:** Teplin, Linda
      A., Karen M. Abram, Gary M. McClelland, Mina K. Dulcan, and Amy A.
      Mericle. "Psychiatric disorders in youth in juvenile detention." *Archives of
      General Psychiatry* 59, no. 12 (2002): 1133.

150   **88 percent of boys and 92 percent of girls in the California juvenile de-
      tention system had at least one psychiatric disorder:** Karnik, Niranjan,
      Marie Soller, Allison Redlich, Melissa Silverman, Helena Kraemer, Rudy
      Haapanen, and Hans Steiner. "Prevalence of and gender differences in psy-
      chiatric disorders among juvenile delinquents incarcerated for nine
      months." *Psychiatric Services* 60, no. 6 (2009): 838–41.

150   **Rikers Island, the Los Angeles County Jail, and Cook County Jail in Illi-
      nois:** "Nation's jails struggle with mentally ill prisoners." National Public
      Radio, September 4, 2011. Retrieved from http://www.npr.org/2011/09/04/
      140167676/nations-jails-struggle-with-mentally-ill-prisoners.

150   **proof of U.S. Representative Tim Murphy's assertion in a March 2013
      congressional forum on mental health:** Quote taken from Representative
      Murphy's opening remarks at the U.S. House of Representatives Energy and
      Commerce Committee Forum, "After Newtown: A National Conversation
      on Violence and Severe Mental Illness." March 5, 2013, retrieved from
      http://energycommerce.house.gov/event/after-newtown-national-
      conversation-violence-and-severe-mental-illness.

154   **Jayden's story is a textbook example:** "Education on lockdown: The
      schoolhouse to jailhouse track." Advancement Project, March 2005, p. 15.

154   **number of children with learning disabilities in prison was more than 30
      percent:** Quinn, Mary Magee, David M. Osher, Jeffrey M. Poirier, Robert
      B. Rutherford, and Peter E. Leone. "Youth with disabilities in juvenile cor-
      rections: A national survey." *Exceptional Children* 71, no. 3 (2005): 339–45.

154   **three hundred people with mental illness were jailed for an average of five
      days:** Torrey, E. Fuller. "Jails and prisons—America's new mental hospitals."
      *American Journal of Public Health* 85, no. 12 (1995): 1611–13.

154   **Teplin et al. looked at the rates of psychiatric disorders:** Teplin, Linda A.,
      Karen M. Abram, Gary M. McClelland, Mina K. Dulcan, and Amy A.
      Mericle. "Psychiatric disorders in youth in juvenile detention." *Archives of
      General Psychiatry* 59, no. 12 (2002): 1133.

155   **A 2008 meta-analysis of twenty-five studies revealed that youth in juve-
      nile detention:** Fazel, Seena, Helen Doll, and Niklas Långström. "Mental
      disorders among adolescents in juvenile detention and correctional facili-

ties: A systematic review and metaregression analysis of 25 surveys." *Journal of the American Academy of Child and Adolescent Psychiatry* 47, no. 9 (2008): 1010–19.

155   **Harrigfeld noted in a 2012 Idaho legislature budget session:** Russell, Betsey. "Increasingly complex problems reported among Idaho's juvenile offenders." *The Spokesoman-Review*, February 6, 2012. Retrieved from http://www.spokesman.com/blogs/boise/2012/feb/06/increasingly-complex-problems-reported-among-idahos-juvenile-offenders/.

155   **"permitted juvenile-on-juvenile sexual liaisons in the facility":** Idaho Case 1:12-cv-00326-BLW, filed June 25, 2012. Retrieved from http://m.idaho press.com/juvenile-corrections-lawsuit/pdf_4e4e7a3c-bfeb-11e1-8412-001 a4bcf887a.html?mode=jqm.

155   **One of the most egregious cases involved Michael Conahan and Mark A. Ciavarella:** Frank, Thomas. "Thomas Frank Says 'Kids for Cash' Incentivizes the Prison Industry." *Wall Street Journal*, April 1, 2009. Retrieved from http://online.wsj.com/news/articles/SB123854010220075533. See also Ecenbarger, William. *Kids for Cash: Two Judges, Thousands of Children, and a $2.6 Million Kickback Scheme.* New York: The New Press, 2012.

156   **Pennsylvania Supreme Court overturned some four thousand convictions from Ciavarella's courtroom:** Shaw, Amir. "Judge to serve 28 years after making $2 million for sending black children to jail." *Rolling Out*, July 30, 2013. Retrieved from http://rollingout.com/criminal-behavior/judge-must-serve-28-years-after-making-2-million-for-sending-children-to-jail/.

156   **"12.5 percent of the juveniles committed to us are diagnosed with a developmental disability":** Russell, Betsy. "Increasingly complex problems reported among Idaho's juvenile offenders." *Spokesman-Review*, February 6, 2012. Retrieved from http://www.spokesman.com/blogs/boise/2012/feb/06/increasingly-complex-problems-reported-among-idahos-juvenile-offenders/.

156   **the Vera Institute of Justice partnered with the Pew Center on the States to find out just how much prisons were costing taxpayers:** Henrichson, Christian, and Ruth Delaney. *The Price of Prisons: What Incarceration Costs Taxpayers.* New York: Vera Institute of Justice, 2012.

156   **if they were providing care within the community:** Tyler, Jasmine L., Jason Ziedenberg, and Eric Lotke. "Cost-effective youth corrections: Rationalizing the fiscal architecture of juvenile justice systems." Washington, DC: Justice Policy Institute, 2006. Retrieved from http://www.justicepolicy.org/uploads/justicepolicy/documents/06-03_rep_costeffective_jj.pdf.

157 **an average of 44 percent and saving the state $3.55 million:** "Cost-benefit analysis of juvenile justice programs." Juvenile Justice Guide Book for Legislators. Denver, CO: National Conference of State Legislatures, no date. Retrieved from http://www.ncsl.org/documents/cj/jjguidebook-costbenefit.pdf.

158 **"so much good for children and society with such minimal net expenditures":** Steinberg, Laurence. "Keeping adolescents out of prison." *Age* 15, no. 17 (2008): 18–20. Retrieved from http://futureofchildren.org/futureofchildren /publications/docs/18_02_PolicyBrief.pdf.

158 **parents can be held liable if their children are out past curfew:** Brank, Eve M., and Josh Haby. "Why not blame the parents?" *APA Monitor* 42, no. 10 (November 2011). Retrieved from http://www.apa.org/monitor/2011/11/ jn.aspx.

158 **"we do not know if punishing the parents would have the intended effect":** Ibid.

158 **The case in question was brought by a single mother:** Gorman, Jeff D. "City can't blame parents for children's crimes." *Courthouse News Service*, Friday, November 19, 2010. Retrieved from http://www.courthousenews .com/2010/11/19/31997.htm.

159 **both Dylan Klebold's and Eric Harris's parents were actively engaged:** Cullen, Dave. *Columbine*. New York: Hachette Digital, 2009.

159 **Claire Creffield posits that "bad luck" is the deciding factor:** Creffield, Claire. "Are parents morally responsible for their children?" *Salon.com*, June 23, 2013.

159 **A 2007 study of eight thousand young people in Florida:** Bayer, Patrick, Randi Hjalmarsson, and David Pozen. "Building criminal capital behind bars: Peer effects in juvenile corrections." *Quarterly Journal of Economics* 124, no. 1 (2009): 105–47.

159 **Raney oversees the largest local law enforcement agency in Idaho:** Taken from the Ada County sheriff's website September 9, 2013: http://www.ada sheriff.org/AboutUs.aspx.

162 **there are now more than four hundred CIT programs in the United States:** Compton, Michael T., Masuma Bahora, Amy C. Watson, and Janet R. Oliva. "A comprehensive review of extant research on Crisis Intervention Team (CIT) programs." *Journal of the American Academy of Psychiatry and the Law Online* 36, no. 1 (2008): 47–55.

162 **One study of a CIT program in Georgia showed marked positive changes:** Ibid.

162 **Other studies noted lower arrest rates:** Ibid.

164 **"Something has got to change":** This quote is from a January 2013 e-mail I received from "Karl's" sister-in-law. Because the case is still ongoing, and Karl continues to lash out at family members, she requested that I not use her name and change identifying details.

164 **especially if they are also substance abusers:** Wallace, Cameron, Paul E. Mullen, and Philip Burgess. "Criminal offending in schizophrenia over a 25-year period marked by deinstitutionalization and increasing prevalence of comorbid substance use disorders." *American Journal of Psychiatry* 161, no. 4 (2004): 716–27.

164 **and the chances that someone with schizophrenia will commit murder are even smaller:** Wallace, Cameron, Paul Mullen, Philip Burgess, Simon Palmer, David Ruschena, and Chris Browne. "Serious criminal offending and mental disorder: Case linkage study." *British Journal of Psychiatry* 172, no. 6 (1998): 477–84.

165 **"Less focus on the relative risk and more on the absolute risk of violence":** Walsh, Elizabeth, Alec Buchanan, and Thomas Fahy. "Violence and schizophrenia: Examining the evidence." *British Journal of Psychiatry* 180, no. 6 (2002): 490–95.

165 **you're much more likely to suffer violence:** The National Institute of Mental Health provides a quick synopsis of this information and more on its website: http://www.nimh.nih.gov/health/publications/schizophrenia/index.shtml.

165 **comorbid substance abuse was usually associated with criminal behavior:** Swanson, J. W., C. E. Holzer III, V. K. Ganju, and R. T. Jano. "Violence and psychiatric disorder in the community: Evidence from the Epidemiologic Catchment Area surveys." *Hospital and Community Psychiatry* 41, no. 7 (1990): 761–70.

165 **a Danish study of a birth cohort ruled out comorbid substance abuse and socioeconomic factors:** Brennan, Patricia A., Sarnoff A. Mednick, and Sheilagh Hodgins. "Major mental disorders and criminal violence in a Danish birth cohort." *Archives of General Psychiatry* 57, no. 5 (2000): 494.

166 **they did not protect the faculty members who were killed and wounded:** Keefe, Patrick Raddon. "Could university officials have stopped a killer?" *New Yorker*, July 11, 2013. Retrieved from http://www.newyorker.com/online/blogs/newsdesk/2013/07/did-university-officials-know-amy-bishop-was-dangerous.html.

166   "the overwhelming evidence is that the person that I am reading about is me": Ibid.

166   **Michael Biasotti, 2012 president of the New York State Association of Chiefs of Police:** Biasotti, Michael. "The impact of mental illness on law enforcement resources." Unpublished master's thesis, 2011. Retrieved from http://treatmentadvocacycenter.org/storage/documents/The_Impact_of_Mental_Illness_on_Law_Enforcement_Resources__TAC.pdf.

167   **found to be effective in reducing hospitalization rates:** Swartz, Marvin S., Jeffrey W. Swanson, Henry J. Steadman, Pamela Clark Robbins, and John Monahan. "New York State assisted outpatient treatment program evaluation." Duke University School of Medicine. 2009. Retrieved from http://www.omh.ny.gov/omhweb/resources/publications/aot_program_evaluation/.

167   **Psychiatrist John Grohol argues against the laws:** Grohol, John M. "The double standard of forced treatment." Psych Central, November 26, 2012. Retrieved from http://psychcentral.com/blog/archives/2012/11/26/the-double-standard-of-forced-treatment/.

168   **As D. J. Jaffe, executive director of advocacy organization Mental Illness Policy Org.:** Jaffe, D. J. "Book Review: Anatomy of an Epidemic by Robert Whitaker." *Huffington Post*, November 2, 2011. Retrieved from http://www.huffingtonpost.com/dj-jaffe/book-review-anatomy-of-an_b_1071163.html.

171   **Hill surrendered to police and asked Tuff to apologize to the schoolchildren:** Simpson, Connor. "This woman helped prevent a tragic school shooting in Georgia." *Atlantic Wire*, August 21, 2013. Retrieved from http://www.theatlanticwire.com/national/2013/08/woman-helped-prevent-tragic-school-shooting-georgia/68593/.

171   **$208,500 per child over the course of eighteen years of public education:** Chasson, Gregory S., Gerald E. Harris, and Wendy J. Neely. "Cost comparison of early intensive behavioral intervention and special education for children with autism." *Journal of Child and Family Studies* 16, no. 3 (2007): 401–13.

## Chapter Seven: Family

174   **"We cannot, as a nation, permit this tragedy to persist":** Vitanza, Stephanie, Robert Cohen, Laura Lee Hall, Hollis Wechsler, Jessye Cohen, An-

gela Rothrock, and Adriana Montalvo. "Families on the brink: The impact of ignoring children with serious mental illness." National Alliance for the Mentally Ill, 1999.

174 **Dr. Thomas Insel, the NIMH director:** Quote taken from Dr. Insel's testimony at the U.S. House of Representatives Energy and Commerce Committee Forum, "After Newtown: A National Conversation on Violence and Severe Mental Illness." March 5, 2013, retrieved from http://energycommerce .house.gov/event/after-newtown-national-conversation-violence-and-severe-mental-illness.

176 **"The sibling relationship is paradoxical, incorporating both conflict and companionship":** Sharpe, Donald, and Lucille Rossiter. "Siblings of children with a chronic illness: A meta-analysis." *Journal of Pediatric Psychology* 27, no. 8 (2002): 699–710.

176 **siblings of children with autism may be more at risk for behavioral problems than other children:** Hastings, Richard P. "Brief report: Behavioral adjustment of siblings of children with autism." *Journal of Autism and Developmental Disorders* 33, no. 1 (2003): 99–104.

176 **There are several sibling support networks online and within communities:** For more information, visit http://www.siblingsupport.org/.

180 **"It was our fault":** Vitanza, Stephanie, Robert Cohen, Laura Lee Hall, Hollis Wechsler, Jessye Cohen, Angela Rothrock, and Adriana Montalvo. "Families on the brink: The impact of ignoring children with serious mental illness." National Alliance for the Mentally Ill, 1999.

180 **Rett syndrome, a rare genetic mutation that affects brain function:** Information taken from http://www.rettsyndrome.org/.

181 **reactive attachment disorder is a common diagnosis for children who were raised in institutions and adopted from foreign countries:** Romania, where the Lindigs adopted their daughter, has been especially well studied. See Zeanah, Charles H., Anna T. Smyke, Sebastian F. Koga, and Elizabeth Carlson. "Attachment in institutionalized and community children in Romania." *Child Development* 76, no. 5 (2005): 1015–28.

183 **helped to develop the early stages portion of Idaho's Department of Health and Welfare child website:** See http://www.healthandwelfare.idaho .gov/?TabId=80.

183 **she read about universally accessible playgrounds:** For more about the features of universally accessible playgrounds, see Moore, Robin C., and Nilda G. Cosco. "What makes a park inclusive and universally designed?"

In *Open Space: People Space*. Edited by C. W. Thompson and P. Travlou. New York: Taylor and Frances, 2007, pp. 85–110.

186  **SSI benefits their children receive for mental health issues:** "Trends with benefits." *This American Life* 490, March 22, 2013. Retrieved from http:// www.thisamericanlife.org/radio-archives/episode/490/trends-with-benefits.

186  **Caregivers also have protected status under federal law:** The U.S. Equal Employment Opportunity (EEOC) website gives guidance for caregivers and employers: http://www.eeoc.gov/policy/docs/caregiver-best-practices .html.

186  **Medicaid is the most common form of funding for mental health services for children and adults:** Information retrieved from NAMI's website: http://www.nami.org/Template.cfm?Section=Issues_Spotlights&Template =/ContentManagement/ContentDisplay.cfm&ContentID=21571.

187  **the mother of a child named John shares her poignant story:** McCarthy, Jan, Anita Marshall, Julie Collins, Girlyn Arganza, Kathy Deserly, and Juanita Milon. "A family's guide to the child welfare system." Georgetown University Center for Child and Human Development, December 2003. Retrieved from http://www.cwla.org/childwelfare/familyguide.htm.

187  **at least 12,700 children were placed in the child welfare system or juvenile justice system to receive mental health care:** "Child welfare and juvenile justice: Federal agencies could play a stronger role in helping states reduce the number of children placed solely to obtain mental health services." Government Accounting Office, April 2003. Retrieved from http:// www.gao.gov/new.items/d03397.pdf.

187  **named for a girl who inspired changes to the rules for parents and children with disabilities:** Hevesi, Dennis. "Katie Beckett, who inspired health reform, dies at 34." *New York Times*, May 22, 2012. Retrieved from http:// www.nytimes.com/2012/05/23/us/katie-beckett-who-inspired-health-reform-dies-at-34.html.

188  **"Parents forced to make this devastating choice are victims":** For more information on the Bazelon Center, visit www.bazelon.org.

188  **"many families are forced to give up custody to the child welfare system to get help":** "Staying together: Preventing custody relinquishment for children's access to mental health services." Bazelon Center for Mental Health Law and the Federation of Families for Children's Mental Health, November 1999 (updated 2010). Retrieved from http://www.bazelon.org/ LinkClick.aspx?fileticket=yyGp4r_Em-U%3d&tabid=104.

189  **"But when children have psychiatric disorders, the effect is often, sadly, different":** Koplewicz, Harold. "Don't let your child's disorder destroy your marriage." Child Mind Institute, March 14, 2011. Retrieved from http://www.childmind.org/en/posts/articles/2011-3-14-dont-let-childs-disorder-destroy-your-marriage.

189  **a greater risk of divorce for parents of a child with an autism spectrum disorder:** Hartley, Sigan L., Erin T. Barker, Marsha Mailick Seltzer, Frank Floyd, Jan Greenberg, Gael Orsmond, and Daniel Bolt. "The relative risk and timing of divorce in families of children with an autism spectrum disorder." *Journal of Family Psychology* 24, no. 4 (2010): 449.

189  **childhood cancer does not result in higher divorce rates:** Syse, Astri, Jon H. Loge, and Torkild H. Lyngstad. "Does childhood cancer affect parental divorce rates? A population-based study." *Journal of Clinical Oncology* 28, no. 5 (2010): 872–77.

189  **only 10 percent of noncustodial fathers earn less than poverty-level incomes:** These statistics about divorce are taken from the U.S. Census Bureau website: http://www.census.gov/newsroom/releases/archives/marital_status_living_arrangements/cb11-144.html.

189  **A 2013 Gallup Poll revealed that 31 percent of single parents had struggled to buy food:** Stutzman, Jessica, and Mendes, Elizabeth. "In U.S., single-parent households struggle more to buy food." *Gallup Well-Being*, July 17, 2013. Retrieved from http://www.gallup.com/poll/163544/single-parent-households-struggle-buy-food.aspx.

189  **In 2008, 21.7 percent of all households with children:** U.S. Census Bureau, retrieved from http://www.census.gov/compendia/statab/2012/tables/12s1337.pdf.

189  **women who are employed at the time of divorce do not suffer nearly as badly as their unemployed counterparts:** For an excellent discussion of all the issues that surround children and divorce, see Wallerstein, Judith S., and Joan B. Kelly. *Surviving the Breakup: How Children and Parents Cope with Divorce.* New York: Basic Books, 2008.

190  **But the correlation exists:** Merikangas, Kathleen Ries, Jian-ping He, Marcy Burstein, Sonja A. Swanson, Shelli Avenevoli, Lihong Cui, Corina Benjet, Katholiki Georgiades, and Joel Swendsen. "Lifetime prevalence of mental disorders in US adolescents: Results from the National Comorbidity Survey Replication—Adolescent Supplement (NCS-A)." *Journal of the American Academy of Child and Adolescent Psychiatry* 49, no. 10 (2010):

980–89. Retrieved from http://www.ncbi.nlm.nih.gov/pmc/articles/PMC 2946114/.

190   **High-conflict divorces like mine are especially toxic:** Ayoub, Catherine C., Robin M. Deutsch, and Andronicki Maraganore. "Emotional distress in children of high-conflict divorce." *Family Court Review* 37, no. 3 (1999): 297–315.

190   **children living with single mothers were more likely to have been treated:** Dawson, Deborah A. "Family structure and children's health and well-being: Data from the 1988 National Health Interview Survey on Child Health." *Journal of Marriage and the Family* (1991): 573–84.

190   **"substance use disorders and behavior disorders were higher for respondents whose parents were divorced":** Merikangas, Kathleen Ries, Jianping He, Marcy Burstein, Sonja A. Swanson, Shelli Avenevoli, Lihong Cui, Corina Benjet, Katholiki Georgiades, and Joel Swendsen. "Lifetime prevalence of mental disorders in US adolescents: Results from the National Comorbidity Survey Replication—Adolescent Supplement (NCS-A)." *Journal of the American Academy of Child and Adolescent Psychiatry* 49, no. 10 (2010): 980–89. Retrieved from http://www.ncbi.nlm.nih.gov/pmc/articles/ PMC2946114/.

190   **"the child always suffers because the child never gets the treatment that he needs":** Garey, Juliann. "Conflicts over parenting: When parents don't agree on how to handle the kids, the kids are the losers." Child Mind Institute, September 3, 2013. Retrieved from http://www.childmind.org/en/ posts/articles/2013-9-3-conflicts-over-parenting-styles-disruptive-kids.

191   **developed in the 1970s as a means to ameliorate family conditions for juvenile offenders:** Sexton, Thomas L., and James F. Alexander. "Functional family therapy." *OJJDP Juvenile Justice Bulletin*, 2000. Retrieved from https://www.ncjrs.gov/pdffiles1/ojjdp/184743.pdf.

191   **Often, participation is court-ordered:** Ibid.

191   **The goal of Functional Family Therapy is to keep children out of juvenile detention:** Ibid.

192   **reduce problem behaviors and improve the quality of parent-child relationships:** Taken from the Partnerships for Families website at http://www .partnershipsforfamilies.org/about/project-objectives.php.

192   **"partners in the community who deal with these issues every day":** Quote taken from the Partnerships for Families website, http://www.partnershipsfor families.org/documents/BetterToolsforDiscipline.pdf.

192 **AF-CBT is rated a 3, which is a "promising practice":** Kolko, D. J., and C. C. Swenson. *Assessing and Treating Physically Abused Children and Their Families: A Cognitive Behavioral Approach.* Thousand Oaks, CA: Sage Publications, 2002.

192 **Parent-Child Interaction Therapy (PCIT) is another evidence-based treatment:** Hembree-Kigin, Toni L., and Cheryl Bodiford MacNeil. *Parent-Child Interaction Therapy.* New York: Springer, 1995.

192 **PCIT has also been shown to alleviate symptoms of depression:** Labbe, Colleen. "Interventions show promise in treating depression among preschoolers." National Institute of Mental Health, November 17, 2011. Retrieved from http://www.nimh.nih.gov/news/science-news/2011/interventions-show-promise-in-treating-depression-among-preschoolers.shtml.

193 **Eyberg incorporated hands-on techniques, including positive play:** Eyberg, Sheila. "Parent-child interaction therapy: Integration of traditional and behavioral concerns." *Child and Family Behavior Therapy* 10, no. 1 (1988): 33–46.

193 **Fernandez encourages parents to be very specific about identifying problem behaviors:** Fernandez, Melanie. "Managing problem behavior at home: A guide to more confident, consistent and effective parenting." Child Mind Institute, February 10, 2012. Retrieved from http://www.childmind.org/en/posts/articles/2012-2-10-parents-guide-managing-problem-behavior.

195 **In his book *January First,* he wrote words that felt familiar to my experience:** Schofield, Michael. *January First: A Child's Descent into Madness and Her Father's Struggle to Save Her.* New York: Crown, 2013.

195 **some families develop resilience as a result of living with a child who has mental illness:** Marsh, Diane T., Harriet P. Lefley, Debra Evans-Rhodes, Vanessa I. Ansell, Brenda M. Doerzbacher, Laura LaBarbera, and Joan E. Paluzzi. "The family experience of mental illness: Evidence for resilience." *Psychiatric Rehabilitation Journal* 20, no. 2 (1996): 3.

195 **families also have clear strengths related to family coping, adaptability, and conflict management:** Doornbos, Mary Molewyk. "The strengths of families coping with serious mental illness." *Archives of Psychiatric Nursing* 10, no. 4 (1996): 214–20.

195 **support groups like Federation of Families helped to reduce the sense of social isolation:** Saunders, Jana C. "Families living with severe mental illness: A literature review." *Issues in Mental Health Nursing* 24, no. 2 (2003): 175–98.

## Epilogue

199   **Vice President Joe Biden, whose initial response to the tragedy was to push for tighter gun control:** See the Department of Health and Human Services press release here: http://www.hhs.gov/news/press/2013pres/12/20131210a.html.

199   **The official report about the school shooting at Sandy Hook Elementary School:** Sedensky, Stephen J. "Report of the State's Attorney for the Judicial District of Danbury on the Shootings at Sandy Hook Elementary School and 36 Yogananda Street, Newtown, Connecticut on December 14, 2012." Office of the State's Attorney Judicial District of Danbury, November 25, 2013. Retrieved from http://www.ct.gov/csao/lib/csao/Sandy_Hook_Final_Report.pdf.

199   **Some have speculated that perhaps guns were a way for Nancy Lanza to connect with her son:** See, for example, Fox, James A. "Nancy Lanza was a victim, too." *USA Today*, December 11, 2013. Retrieved from http://www.usatoday.com/story/opinion/2013/12/11/nancy-lanza-adam-newtown-sandy-hook-anniversary-column/3991237/.

203   **Martin Drell, MD, president of the American Academy of Child and Adolescent Psychiatry:** Drell, Martin. 2012 AACAP Annual Report, 2013. Retrieved from http://www.aacap.org/App_Themes/AACAP/docs/about_us/annual_report/AACAP_2012_Annual_Report.pdf.

# INDEX